A Pocket Guide to Twentieth Century Drama

Stephen Unwin is Artistic Director of English Touring
Theatre and has directed more than fifty professional theatre
and opera productions. He is the joint author, with Kenneth
McLeish, of *A Pocket Guide to Shakespeare's Plays*.

Carole Woddis is a freelance theatre journalist and writer.
For the past ten years she has been *The Herald's* London
drama critic. She has co-edited two editions of the *Bloomsbury
Theatre Guide* (with Trevor R. Griffiths) and published a
collection of interviews with actresses, *Sheer Bloody Magic*
(Virago). She is a Visiting Tutor in Journalism at Goldsmiths
College, University of London.

in the same series

A POCKET GUIDE TO SHAKESPEARE'S PLAYS
by Kenneth McLeish and Stephen Unwin

A POCKET GUIDE TO
Twentieth Century Drama

Stephen Unwin
with Carole Woddis

faber and faber

First published in 2001
by Faber and Faber Limited
3 Queen Square London WC1N 3AU

Published in the United States by Faber and Faber Inc.
an affiliate of Farrar, Straus and Giroux LLC, New York

Typeset by Faber and Faber
Printed in England by Mackays of Chatham

A CIP record for this book is available from the British Library

ISBN 0-571-20014-1

10 9 8 7 6 5 4 3 2 1

Contents

Introduction

If great drama flourishes in a changing world, the twentieth century may prove itself the most dramatically fruitful ever. The briefest historical sketch shows a century of quite extraordinary upheaval. The great achievement of its drama was that it managed to reflect those changes with courage, vision and artistry.

A Dramatic Century

The twentieth century started remarkably peacefully. Britain got a bloody nose in its war against the Boers, and Imperial Russia was shocked to be defeated by Japan, but 'the long Edwardian summer' completed forty years of peace and prosperity in Europe. August 1914, however, brought the First World War (1914–18) and mechanized slaughter, triggering a long struggle for dominance in Europe which was only resolved by the fall of the Berlin Wall in 1989. It also brought a questioning of the social order which led to both the Russian Revolution of 1917 and the widespread nationalist, pacifist and socialist ideals which had such a decisive influence on the course of the century.

The energy of Germany's Weimar Republic sprang from the chaos of war, as did the great advances made by women in the 1920s. While American industrial might marched onwards, in Europe the struggle between labour and capital was brought home to Britain in the General Strike of 1926. Meanwhile, the new Soviet Union was consumed by the practical consequences of its revolution and in Stalin found a leader whose purges and persecutions took terror to unprecedented heights. The Great Crash of 1929, and the Depression which followed, unleashed Fascism in Germany, Italy and Spain, as well as timidity in the West, which initially failed to challenge this new barbarism. The impact of the Second

World War (1939–45) was even more massive than the First. The world plumbed new depths in man's inhumanity to man, whether in the Nazi Holocaust or on the Russian front, and with the development and use of nuclear weapons the human race became for the first time capable of destroying itself. The Second World War also brought profound changes in industrial production and social structure, and the scepticism, pessimism and democratic questioning which was the hallmark of the second half of the century.

However, 1945 was a time of new beginnings, with the establishment of the Welfare State in Britain, the launching of the Marshall Plan for the reconstruction of Europe and a determination, expressed in the 1948 Declaration of Human Rights, that the disasters of the Second World War should never be repeated. However, in Communist China and the Soviet Bloc, repression and mass murder reached levels comparable to the excesses of European Fascism. With the coming of the Cold War, the world found itself dangerously divided into two nuclear-armed blocs, which fought each other directly in Korea and by proxy on innumerable third-world battlefields, and came close to catastrophe over Cuba in 1962. The United States became the unquestioned economic superpower, while the old European empires finally crumbled, and Africa, Asia and Latin America assumed a role of their own in international affairs.

The revolutionary moment of 1968 in Europe and North America emerged on the back of new technology and an economic boom, and brought significant cultural and social change. 'Peace and love' may have been only a phrase, but the culture which demanded America's eventual withdrawal from Vietnam in 1975, and claimed for youth a central role in social affairs, led to a significant change in the role of women in society. The optimism of this time was cut short by the oil crisis of 1973, the recession that followed it and the rise of the New Right. Under Margaret Thatcher and Ronald Reagan, the 1980s saw a United States and Britain in a new confrontational mode, with denunciations of the Soviet 'evil empire', reduction of trade-union power and the pursuit of monetarist economic policies. In Britain, there was an attempt to return to 'Victorian values' in moral and family matters, while the 1982 Falklands War saw a brief revival of jingoism. The fall of the Berlin Wall and the end of Soviet Communism in 1989 faced the world with new challenges, and North–South tensions came to replace East–West ones. Extraordinary breakthroughs, whether in the Soviet Union (1989) or in South Africa (1994), heralded the possibility of a new, more positive, political culture, while the barbaric 'ethnic cleansing' unleashed in former Yugoslavia and the mass genocide in Rwanda (1994) made the world pause for thought, as did Iraq's invasion of Kuwait (1990). In the 1990s, Europe and America saw the emergence of centre-left governments, which tried to negotiate a 'third way' between the command economies of old-style socialism and the excesses of the unrestrained free market. And at the end of the century the major industrial powers were at peace with each other, if not always with others.

Such headline-making changes were accompanied by fundamental shifts in attitude and belief, particularly in Europe and the United States. These were caused by technological development, political struggle, experience and catastrophe. The family changed from being the narrowly defined basic unit of society into the multi-formed, diverse thing it is today. The liberation movements of the 1960s legitimized different kinds of personal expression, especially in sexuality. Religion lost its privileged position, although in some places the last quarter of the century saw a growth in religious fundamentalism. The guiding principles of race relations changed utterly, from the casual bigotry of empire to the complex linguistics of political correctness (even if it took racial genocide in the middle of the century to help bring that about). Women's position in society was transformed, partly because of changes in employment, but also because of contraception (particularly the Pill) and the demands of feminism. Psychoanalysis changed for many the way human beings think about themselves. Modern physics turned traditional science on its head. The concept of class, even in Britain, was eroded and the notion of empire vanished from the language of international relations. Both forced and voluntary migration occurred on an unprecedented scale and undermined notions of home and community. International capitalism – albeit sometimes regulated by social democracy – went through many contortions, but emerged as the guiding principle under which most western societies came to be governed.

These deep-rooted changes in thought found appropriate expression in art, and in novelists such as Marcel Proust, James Joyce, D. H. Lawrence and Franz Kafka the twentieth century found figures to set alongside the giants of the nineteenth. Great political art, sometimes naturalistic in form, sometimes modernist, came out of the Depression and the rise of Fascism. After the Second World War, a new and often surreal internationalism emerged, with great writers coming from Latin America, India, China and Africa, as well as Western Europe and the United States. Photography encouraged painters to move beyond Impressionism, and artists such as Pablo Picasso, Vasilly Kandinsky, Mark Rothko and Jackson Pollock all took painting into territory unrecognizable to the late Victorian sensibility. In the last twenty years of the century the ironic stance of postmodernism became widespread. Architects created new notions of how people could live together, and it took only twenty or thirty years for the cinema to become the most wide-reaching and popular art form of the century. The atonal music of the Second Viennese School seemed at the time like a new musical universe, and in jazz, Black Americans found their finest artistic expression. And finally, as everyone knows, rock'n'roll changed the world.

The material conditions of everyday life, particularly in the rich West, changed with extraordinary speed and to an unprecedented degree. With the invention and mass production of the motor car, mobility was radically altered. Radio linked up people from all over the world and became an important medium for news and current affairs as well as drama and music. The boom in jet travel made the world seem like a village. Neil Armstrong walked on the moon in 1969. Communications connected parts of the world with a speed unthinkable a hundred years before. Information technology and robotic engineering changed the nature of work, and in Western Europe at least the century witnessed the almost total disappearance of the peasantry. The rise of television and cinema fundamentally altered leisure patterns (and presented a radical challenge to older art forms). Great advances in medicine and pharmaceuticals transformed life expectancy and levels of health. Weapons became more terrible than ever, but target bombing replaced carpet bombing, and anxiety about television images of collateral damage minimized the chance of a second Dresden. The possibilities of genetic engineering posed new moral challenges. But while the West faced up to food scares, in the developing nations population growth and migration were accompanied by both natural and man-made disasters and famines.

At the end of the century, new problems came to the fore. The disintegration of the Soviet Union threatened hardship on a scale not seen in the developed world since the 1930s. The spectre of mass unemployment briefly returned to haunt the industrialized West. The Asian economic crisis spread, and relations with the Muslim world became increasingly complex. Some developing countries grew out of poverty, while others, crippled by corruption, climate, overpopulation or debt, seemed condemned to pauperism. AIDS threatened to decimate the population of sub-Saharan Africa. The demands of global capitalism took the place of imperial power. Environmental disaster threatened the whole globe, and vulnerable developing countries in particular. While most of the world grew richer, or at least less poor, a significant part of the world's population still lived in abject poverty.

At the end of the century the world did not arrive at 'the end of history' – as one American thinker put it – and the great challenge of the future may well be the clash between the rich northern hemisphere and the poor southern one. Yet the dramatic struggles of the twentieth century produced an odd kind of consensus of values and opinions which dominate the rich North as it enters the third millennium.

A Century of Drama

The twentieth century witnessed an extraordinary profusion of dramatists, as many of its literary greats chose drama as their favoured medium. There were a handful of giants, but literally hundreds of others, from all kinds of backgrounds, working in many different ways, with wildly diverse notions of what the theatre could be. A huge variety of forms were explored with restless energy and inventiveness. What united it all was the attempt to use this most ancient of arts to reflect and embrace in a contemporary way the unique realities of the twentieth century.

Great dramatists are understandably wary of being pigeon-holed into genres and schools, and it is important to see them as individuals, making their own unique contribution, working within their own particular circumstances and pursuing their own preoccupations. Yet it is also possible to glimpse certain stylistic connections and formal innovations running through the drama of the century. Probably the most significant of these is what can very loosely be called 'naturalism'. Its greatest proponents were Henrik Ibsen and Anton Chekhov, whose plays drew on the novels of Zola, Tolstoy, Balzac and Dickens, and the philosophical and scientific understanding that character is defined by circumstance and environment. Naturalism was committed to representing the day-to-day realities of ordinary life, free from the influence of either the Shakespearean epic or eighteenth-century artificiality. It provided the twentieth century with its dominant form, and wherever you look it is naturalism which is continually drawn on and referred to. At times, writers rebelled against its hegemony, and in the development of symbolism, expressionism and poetic drama attempted to find ways of

touching on more profound psychological insights than naturalism seemed capable of yielding. In attempting to grapple
with an increasingly complex social and political world,
dramatists explored new techniques of montage, agitprop and
epic structures. In the post-war period, avant-garde movements in painting and literature contributed to a theatre style
more at home with surrealism, Dadaism and modernism. A
new internationalism allowed for greater stylistic eclecticism,
with naturalism being challenged by non-European theatrical forms. But it is a strange irony that at the end of a century of ceaseless formal experimentation it is still naturalism,
albeit often of a fragmented kind, which is the dominant form
in new writing for the theatre throughout Europe and
America.

Dramatists need theatres and managements to stage their
plays, and from the outset one of the key developments was
the emergence of directors committed to presenting contemporary work. These men and women of vision set up companies and opened theatres, each with its own distinct ethos. By
1900, Konstantin Stanislavski's Moscow Art Theatre had
been established and was extraordinarily influential. The
Barker–Vedrenne management's seasons at the Royal Court
Theatre in London – which started in 1904 – provided an
ideal home for George Bernard Shaw and Harley Granville
Barker himself. Elsewhere, visionary figures like Miss
Hornimann and Barry Jackson advanced the cause of the
English Repertory Movement, while in Dublin W. B. Yeats
and Lady Gregory founded the Abbey Theatre, which was to
be the centre for the great flowering of Irish drama. August
Strindberg established his 161-seat Intimate Theatre in
Stockholm in 1907. During the 1920s, Vsevelod Meyerhold
pursued his extraordinary work in the complex environment
of the new Soviet Union, while London's West End in the
1930s and 1940s flourished under the commercial management of men like C. B. Cochran and Hugh 'Binkie' Beaumont.
In the United States, the Group Theatre was set up in 1931
to produce work of a distinctly social kind.

In 1949, Bertolt Brecht set up the Berliner Ensemble in the ruins of defeated Germany; while in London, in 1953, Joan Littlewood's Theatre Workshop took up its residency at Stratford East. In the 1950s, Lee Strasberg developed his Method School in New York, while Elia Kazan directed influential productions of new plays by Tennessee Williams, Arthur Miller and others. In 1956, George Devine founded the Royal Court, which to this day is one of the most significant centres for new drama in the world. The 1960s and 1970s saw the flourishing of alternative theatres such as the Traverse in Edinburgh, the Open Space in London, the Market in Johannesburg and the Tarragon in Toronto. It also saw the arrival of a number of cooperative and politically committed touring groups, such as the San Francisco Mime Troupe, 7:84 and Joint Stock. This led to the rapid expansion of Off-Broadway and the London Fringe, leading to a not always useful two-layered theatrical culture. Britain finally saw the opening of its new National Theatre in 1976, while throughout Europe there sprung up a vast range of well-equipped, fully subsidized regional theatres, such as France's Théâtre Nationale Populaire, Milan's Piccolo Theatre, or the Schaubühne in Berlin. The challenge to subsidized theatre that was so much part of the climate of the 1980s led to an eventual shrinking in output, but was accompanied by the appearance of new voices from outside the powerful Dublin–London–New York axis, as well as the emergence of a series of significant women dramatists.

Of course, the production of new plays was only one part of the totality of theatrical activity. One of the most striking features was the large number of revivals of classical drama which were seen everywhere, especially in the second half of the century. Directors as diverse as Tyrone Guthrie, Peter Brook, Giorgio Strehler, Ariane Mnouchkine, Roger Planchon, Peter Stein, Deborah Warner and thousands of others all made great reputations for their productions of classical work, often to spectacular effect (and indeed, the very notion of a director was largely a twentieth-century invention).

While this undoubtedly made a great contribution to the art
of the theatre, it sometimes had the negative effect of mar-
ginalizing the new and the contemporary. There were also a
large number of adaptations of novels and poems, as well as
devised and improvised work which had no dramatist
involved. Performance and new kinds of live art emerged,
and had an increasingly strong influence on more traditional
text-based work. Operas were composed throughout the
century, including several standard-repertoire classics by
Giacomo Puccini, Leoš Janáček, Igor Stravinsky, Alban Berg,
Benjamin Britten and others. Perhaps most significant was the
triumph of that great twentieth-century innovation, the
musical.

The environment in which live theatre operated changed
in many ways. At the start of the century, the European and
American theatre was almost entirely unsubsidized, with only
German and French civic authorities taking on any responsibility. Following the Second World War, this changed rapidly, with the development of state and local subsidy throughout Europe, as well as in the Soviet Union. Only the United
States maintained its strictly commercial approach, with the
National Endowment for the Arts providing tiny amounts of
cash. In Europe, government support for the arts reached its
highest level in the 1970s, but took a dip when new, centre-
right governments cut subsidies, wishing to see the theatre
operating in a more mixed economy. The collapse of
Communism in 1989 entailed a sudden reduction in support
in the old Eastern Bloc, proving that freedom of expression is
often coupled with restriction of means. In Britain, the
advent of the National Lottery released large sums of new
money, but little sense of how it could affect the ongoing
health of the theatre.

The century also witnessed extremes of censorship and
freedom. Bernard Shaw had to wait many years to see the first
performance of *Mrs Warren's Profession* because it was about
prostitution. Bulgakov satirized the phone calls he received
from Stalin in his play *Molière* and Meyerhold 'disappeared'

in Stalin's purges. The dramatists and musicians of the Weimar Republic were considered 'decadent' by the Nazis and were either murdered or went into exile. Homosexual writers such as Terence Rattigan, Noël Coward and Tennessee Williams stayed 'in the closet' rather than have their work rejected. Bertolt Brecht was hauled up in front of the House UnAmerican Activities Committee and, once settled in East Berlin, enjoyed a tortuous relationship with the authorities.

However, the great cultural shake-up of the 1960s brought about the abolition of censorship in Britain in 1968. More importantly, it allowed for the great explosion of gay and lesbian drama from the 1970s on. It did not prevent the management of the National Theatre from being prosecuted for the overt sexual activity of Howard Brenton's *Romans in Britain* in 1980, and in Eastern Europe Václav Havel and other dissident playwrights were imprisoned and persecuted. But by the end of the century freedom of expression was pretty much guaranteed throughout Europe and the United States, although some critics detected a new kind of censorship through subsidy.

At the end of the twentieth century and the turn of the millennium, despite competition from radio, television, cinema and the internet, the theatre remains a significant and vital art form. In order to reflect the new century with equal success, it will need to find the writers, directors, actors and impresarios with the same level of vision, talent, integrity and energy which made the twentieth century one of the great periods of world drama.

Stephen Unwin
2 February, 2001

The fifty greatest plays?

It is important to emphasize that this is not a guide to the fifty *greatest* plays of the twentieth century. Instead, it focuses on fifty plays we feel were significant, as a way of giving an introduction to the different kinds of work the century produced. The selection was difficult, even when we gave ourselves strict criteria: no musicals, no operas, no adaptations of novels and no revivals of classics. We decided to concentrate on text-based work, while acknowledging the huge contribution made in other forms. We decided that only one play by a single writer should be included and have ranged as evenly across the decades as possible, so as to give some sense of the breadth of work produced.

We wanted the book to reflect diversity, particularly in the last thirty years, but are aware that only six of the plays are by women and just three are by black writers. One possible explanation for this is that, unlike poetry and the novel, theatre is capital-intensive, and has, as such, been monopolized by figures from the dominant groups. We are also aware that the selection consists largely of plays from Britain, Ireland and the United States, with only a few written in languages other than English, and very few from outside Europe or America. However, we wanted the guide to be genuinely useful and to feature plays which might well be revived or studied. If the emphasis is popular and mainstream, it is because these are plays that audiences are likely to encounter.

Believing that plays reflect the world in which they are written, we have tried to set each one within its particular historical and theatrical context. The heart of each chapter is a short critical essay, and we have also given an outline of the play's performance history. We have provided a chronicle of a thousand plays of the twentieth century to give a sense of what else was being written at the time. Dating plays is always difficult: we have used the date of first performance through-out, except when there is a significant gap between writing and première.

Stephen Unwin, Carole Woddis

La Ronde
(*Reigen*)
Arthur Schnitzler

1900, first performed 1920

> *Historical and theatrical context*

Turn-of-the-century Vienna attracted geniuses of all kinds. As capital of the vast but decaying Austro-Hungarian Empire, it was the seed-bed for one of the great flowerings of European culture. In music, Gustav Mahler and Richard Strauss were at their height and the young Arnold Schoenberg was exploring the atonality which was to characterize the Second Viennese School. Painting was dominated by artists such as Egon Schiele, Gustav Klimt and Alphonse Mucha, while literary circles included Hugo von Hofmannsthal, Hermann Broch, Stefan Zweig and Karl Kraus. In 1900, Sigmund Freud published his seminal *The Interpretation of Dreams*.

Viennese culture drew on the great achievements of nineteenth-century France, but carried its own distinct tone: erotic and morbid, scientific and voyeuristic, interested in the subconscious and critical of the *status quo*. It is one of the ironies of history that the person who did more than anyone else to destroy this flowering – Adolf Hitler – applied (twice) to study as an art student in Vienna and resorted to painting postcards when he was turned down.

Arthur Schnitzler (1862–1931) came from a comfortable Jewish medical family, and – like his almost exact contemporary Anton Chekhov – trained as a doctor. His more than twenty plays, which are often described as 'boulevard' pieces – light, well constructed and effortlessly erotic – include *Anatol* (1892), *Playing with Love* (1895), *The Green Cockatoo* (1899), *The Legacy* (1899) and *Professor Bernhardi* (1912). He also wrote numerous short stories and novels.

> *About the play*

The title of Schnitzler's masterpiece is hard to translate. '*Reigen*' means a 'round' in a dance, but a 'round' has other connotations in English, and so the French title *La Ronde* is usually adopted. The central action is a sexual dance, in which partner is handed on to partner, across the classes and throughout society: it is a '*ronde*' which connects each character to the next and eventually circles round on itself.

The play is written in ten scenes and features ten characters: five men and five women. In the short first scene we see a Viennese prostitute picking up a private soldier near the river. The tone is rough and their motives are simple. In the next scene we see the same soldier meet a working-class housemaid in the Prater on a Sunday evening. They hardly know each other's names but soon go off and have sex in the park. Afterwards he smokes a cigar and she wants to know if he is fond of her. Grudgingly, he agrees to walk her home, but slopes off to meet a blonde. In the third scene the housemaid is seduced (almost raped) by a young gentleman when he is left alone with her in the house. He in turn is visited by a middle-class married woman, who arrives thickly veiled, full of anxiety, saying that he had promised 'to be good', uttering all the clichés of the tempted wife. But once they share a glazed pear she is seduced. He begs for her love and behaves like a little boy. Despite her initial caution, she soon declares 'so I'm having an affair with a respectable woman'.

By the fifth scene the 'respectable woman' is in her bedroom with her husband, who protests that he still loves her and declares that one of their periods of 'platonic friendship . . . is about to end'. Young women like her, he says, have a 'clearer conception of the true nature of love'. But she wants to know about the whores he has had sex with in the past, and wonders whether married women ever sell themselves. Having made love, he recalls their first night together in Venice, secure in the (false) knowledge of her innocence and fidelity. But soon he is having dinner in a private room with a '*süße Mädel*' – one of those lower-middle-class 'sweet young things' who are such a Viennese speciality. She is flirtatious and bubbly, innocent and provocative. She swoons – declaring that someone must have drugged her wine – and they have sex. She is desperate to know if he loves her, but it is time for her to go home to her mother.

In the seventh scene the 'sweet young thing' visits a poet's room. It is dark but he refuses to light the lamps. He says he loves her ('it's wonderful when girls are stupid') and wants to know if she loves him in return. After having sex, he says that he is a famous playwright called Biebitz, but then admits he is only a shop assistant who plays the piano in a bar. In the next scene, the poet (who actually *is* Biebitz) is with a famous actress in an inn 'two hours from Vienna'. Amazingly, it transpires that she is both religious and sexually forward, and there is a tremendous comic sequence leading up to their coupling, with memories of her past lover Fritz all too present.

The last two scenes of the play see the actress being visited in her bedroom by a rather awkward young count, an amateur philosopher who has an aversion to sex before breakfast. But she soon seduces him and can twist him round her little finger. In the final scene, the count finds himself in the squalid room of the prostitute from the first scene. He is appalled, but when she wakes up he asks her about her 'revolting life'. Suddenly he sees something in her eyes that reminds him of someone from his past, and as he leaves, he says to himself:

> Wouldn't it have been beautiful if I had only kissed her eyes? That would have been an adventure. It was not to be.

Morning is breaking over Vienna, and the '*ronde*' has come full circle.

Although brutally erotic in its effect (sexual activity is marked in the script by a row of dashes, when the curtain is meant to be lowered and music played), *La Ronde* is not mere pornography. It is characterized above all by Schnitzler's attempt at a kind of documentary realism, full of the everyday details of Viennese life, which lays bare the duplicity and cruelty of Vienna's class system. Schnitzler's point is that different levels of society behave in different ways, but that sex, like death, is the great leveller. The young gentleman expresses the profound (if also banal) truth which lies so sweetly at the heart of the play:

> Life is so empty – so meaningless – and then – so short – so terribly short! – There is only one joy . . . to find a human being who loves one.

One of the key psychological changes in the twentieth century (especially in Europe and America) was in attitudes to sexuality: from repression at the beginning, to unprecedented freedom at the end. While it is impossible to give a specific reason for this change, psychoanalytic explorations and the tone of *fin de siècle* Viennese art were key catalysts. Sigmund Freud himself came to acknowledge the depth of Schnitzler's insight into the psychology of sexual desire, and praised him as his '*alter ego*': Schnitzler's plays – and *La Ronde* in particular – go to the dark heart of heterosexual relations, and do so with consummate skill.

> In performance

La Ronde was published privately in 1900, 'to be read among friends'. In a letter, Schnitzler said he had written scenes which were 'totally unprintable, of no great literary value, but if disinterred after a couple of hundred years, may illuminate in a unique way aspects of our culture'.

The play was not premièred until 1920 in Berlin, in the more liberal atmosphere following the First World War. But it caused a furore and was used as a target for anti-Semitism by right-wing extremists. In 1921, the play's cast and management were prosecuted for causing a public nuisance and participating in obscene acts. Although they were eventually acquitted, the row led to the fifty-nine-year-old Schnitzler insisting that the play should never be performed again.

La Ronde was first performed in London in 1923 in a private house belonging to members of the liberal-minded Bloomsbury group. Virginia Woolf wrote that 'the audience felt simply as if a real copulation were going on in the room and tried to talk to drown the very realistic groans . . .' It was condemned by the Nazis as Jewish and decadent. In post-war Europe, productions were rare until the 1970s.

Thereafter the play was staged regularly, sometimes with just two performers, and often with great success. With the appearance of AIDS, the play regained some of its vivid power. David Hare 'freely adapted' it in 1998 under the title *The Blue Room*. This modern-dress version was performed with the film star Nicole Kidman at the Donmar Warehouse in London.

In 1950, the play was made into a remarkable film by Max Ophüls, with Gérard Philipe, Jean-Louis Barrault and Simone Signoret.

Quotations from Arthur Schnitzler, *La Ronde*, tr. Frank and Jacqueline Marcus, Methuen, 1982

The Dance of Death (Parts 1 and 2) (Dödsdansen)
August Strindberg

1900, first performed 1905 (Part 1), 1906 (Part 2)

> Historical and theatrical context

The first year of the century saw the formation of the British Labour Party, the Boer War at its height and the death of two giants of the nineteenth century: the German philosopher Friedrich Nietzsche and the Irish playwright Oscar Wilde. Meanwhile, Scandinavia was undergoing a quiet transformation, from a backward area on the edge of Europe to the home of social democracy that it was to become after the First World War.

August Strindberg's (1849–1912) tempestuous personal life provided him with the raw material for his highly confessional writings. He was a complicated character, prone to violent mood swings – from dark depression to wild elation – but also capable of great intellectual clarity. His relationships with women were almost always unhappy and he was married three times, each time ending in divorce.

A central element in Strindberg's development as a dramatist was his struggle against his fellow Scandinavian Henrik Ibsen (1828–1906), whose 'well-made plays' had been so successful in the 1880s and 1890s. Strindberg was looking to move beyond the tidy limitations of 'naturalism' and attempt something more complex. In 1907 he set up his own Intimate Theatre in Stockholm and wrote four plays specifically for it. These experiments were dismissed at the time, but have provided a model for the later development of small studio theatres all over the world.

Strindberg's more than fifty plays include *The Father* (1887), *Miss Julie* (1888), *Creditors* (1888), *The Stronger* (1888–9), *To*

Damascus, Parts I, II and *III* (1898, 1901), *Easter* (1900), *Queen Christina* (1901), *A Dream Play* (1902), *The Ghost Sonata* (1907) and *The Great Highway* (1907). His vast output also included short stories, poems, essays and theses, including *By the Open Sea* (1889–90) and *Inferno* (1896–1908).

> About the play

Edgar is the artillery captain of a garrison overlooking a harbour somewhere in Sweden. He is a middle-aged misanthrope who sits in his tower – a fortress which used to be a prison – drinking whisky, smoking cigars and trying to control the lives and feelings of all who come into contact with him. His wife describes him as 'a bully with a slave's mentality', as a vampire:

> [who] likes to sink his claws into other people's destinies, suck excitement out of other lives, batten on others, because his own life is so totally boring to him.

Edgar has a brutal sarcastic wit and a strong sense of his own independence ('I've had nothing but enemies all my life, and they've helped me on my way, not harmed me'), but he also has a powerful sense of the finality of death:

> It's true that when the mechanism runs down you're a barrowload of shit to scatter over the garden, but as long as the cogs go round you must kick and fight, with your fists and your feet.

In short, Edgar is a monster with few redeeming features.

His companion in this misery is his wife, Alice, an ex-actress (two out of three of Strindberg's own wives were actresses) from a rich family, tight with her money, abusive of the servants and full of hatred for her husband:

> What shall I say? That I have sat in this tower for a life-time, a prisoner, kept from life by a man I have always hated, and whom I now hate so boundlessly that the day he died I would laugh for joy!

They have two surviving children: an adult son, and their daughter Judith. Their marriage is at boiling-point on the eve of their silver wedding anniversary.

Edgar's cousin Kurt arrives at the garrison to take up the post of quarantine master. Years earlier, Kurt had left his wife and lost his children as a result, and now Edgar repeatedly insists that Kurt saddled him with Alice. Her hopes for Edgar's death are about to be fulfilled when Edgar gets her to play 'The March of the Boyars' on the piano, and he dances to it and collapses (Strindberg originally wanted to use Saint-Saëns's music for his *Danse Macabre* but changed his mind when he discovered that Ibsen had used it in *John Gabriel Borkman*). He lies sick on the sofa, talking with Kurt about the meaning of life and the finality of death. The next morning – in a touch which stretches credulity – the junior officers send flowers to congratulate him on his illness, and Judith tells him that she cannot come to visit him. Edgar soon reveals to Kurt that it was he who told Kurt's wife how to get sole custody of his children.

Edgar gives up drinking and the prospect of death causes him 'to rethink his views on life'. He says he met Kurt's estranged son in town and invited him to the island where he will be under his command. He tears up his will (which would have left everything to Alice) and says he has deposited a petition for divorce. Alice throws her ring at him and tells Kurt that Edgar had tried to kill her by pushing her into the sea. She also says that Edgar has been involved in financial corruption and confides to Kurt that she wants to blow the whole place up and be free.

Later that evening, Edgar is 'making preparations to go': destroying cigars, whisky, love letters and pictures of his wife, and surrounding himself with candlelight. Meanwhile, Alice and Kurt have become involved in an erotic dance:

> Since I saw you as you really are, in all your nakedness, since lust distorted my sight, I realize the full power of evil – it makes the ugly seem beautiful, the good seem ugly and weak.

She fantasizes about freedom and when she makes plain to Edgar her relationship with Kurt, he draws his sabre, performs a 'dance of death' and collapses. But Edgar reveals that he invented everything that happened in town, and Kurt rejects Alice and leaves. Husband and wife are left together again, wondering whether 'life is serious or just a hoax?', and as the curtain falls they agree, to our horror, to celebrate their silver wedding.

Part Two – which is a separate play but which shares the same principal characters – opens in Kurt's house, where Judith ('a little flirt with plaits down her back and skirts that are too short') is teasing Kurt's son, Allan. But Judith already has a fervent admirer – an unnamed lieutenant – and there seems no future for Allan:

> I'm already your slave, but you aren't content with that,
> your slave has to be tortured and thrown to the dogs.

When Kurt arrives, he talks about the pleasure of being reunited with his son, but Alice warns Kurt of Edgar's continued malice towards him.

Edgar soon undermines Kurt's quarantine methods and criticizes him for having pulled out of a savings scheme he has set up. He also tries to get Judith married off to an old colonel and Allan is in despair. Edgar tells Kurt that his investments have failed and that he is going to have to sell everything he has, and soon buys his house. Allan is about to be sent off to Lapland (having had his commission bought by Edgar) when Judith declares her love for him. Meanwhile, Kurt realizes that his financial situation prevents him from entering parliament and Edgar announces his intentions to do so himself. Kurt acknowledges that everything Edgar has done to destroy him is like 'an everyday transaction between fellow citizens', but Judith has sent a message of rejection to the colonel, and Edgar has a stroke when he hears the news. By the end, all he can do is 'slobber unintelligibly' while Alice curses his dying body, saying a 'garden would be too good a resting place for this barrowload of muck'. His last words are 'forgive them for they know what they do', and as the play ends, the others realize the strange, appalling grandeur behind Edgar's malevolence.

The Dance of Death is deeply flawed, aesthetically and dramatically as well as morally and spiritually. Many of its psychological motivations are left unexplained and it has an alarming tendency to loop back on itself or lurch forward uncontrollably. Yet its ferocious, desperate, almost comically macabre quality makes it one of the key works of a century full of real-life horrors and despair.

> In performance

Part One of *The Dance of Death* was first performed in Cologne in 1905, and was seen with *Part Two* for the first time in Berlin later that year. It received its Swedish première at Strindberg's Intimate Theatre in 1909.

Max Reinhardt staged both plays together in Berlin in 1912. They were first performed in London in 1924, but it was not until Laurence Olivier and Geraldine McEwan played both together in one evening in 1965 at the Old Vic that *The Dance of Death* began to be recognized in the English-speaking theatre.

Quotations from August Strindberg, *Plays: Two*, tr. Michael Meyer, Methuen, 1982

The Cherry Orchard
(*Вишнёвый сад*)
Anton Chekhov

1903, first performed 1904

> Historical and theatrical context

Anton Chekhov (1860–1904) was not only a great short-story writer and dramatist, but also a practising doctor and social reformer. This brought him into contact with all parts of Russian society: the desperate poverty of the peasantry, the insecurities of the servant class and the changing roles of the professions, the intelligentsia and the landowners, all of which characterized turn-of-the-century Russia. The Russo-Japanese war (which culminated in the defeat of the Russian Imperial Navy) broke out in January 1904, and 1905 saw the violent suppression of the first Russian Revolution, which Lenin called a 'dress rehearsal' for the Bolshevik seizure of power in 1917.

By the time he came to finish his last and greatest play, Chekhov was a national figure. As well as his magnificent short stories, his plays included *Ivanov* (1887), *The Wood Demon* (1889), *The Seagull* (1895), *Uncle Vanya* (1899) and *Three Sisters* (1901). *The Cherry Orchard* was written in Yalta, where Chekhov was living for the sake of his health, and was sent to Konstantin Stanislavski, the director of the Moscow Art Theatre, with whom he had a long (if stormy) working relationship. Chekhov died of tuberculosis within six months of the play's première.

> About the play

The Cherry Orchard dramatizes the clash between the old values of the nineteenth century and the emerging energies of the twentieth, and locates that clash in real and fallible human beings. Chekhov achieves an unprecedented level of dramatic objectivity, in which the fragility of all human endeavour is glimpsed and is placed beyond the reach of moral judgement.

Madame Ranevskaya is returning from Paris to her estate in the Russian country. She is met by Lopakhin, a merchant who has left his peasant roots and is now 'almost' a millionaire. He informs her that her large cherry orchard will have to be sold, so that she can pay her debts. He urges her to lease out the land and buildings, to avoid losing her childhood home, but she refuses to listen. Lopakhin snaps the property up at an auction and the cherry orchard is cut down. At the end, Ranevskaya sets off once more for Paris, never to see her childhood home again.

Ranevskaya is convinced she has sins to answer for and that her suffering is deserved. Her husband died, her lover abandoned her and her son drowned in the river. Now she has a vision of her dead mother, dressed in white, standing amongst the cherry trees and she tells the 'eternal student' Trofimov:

> You can look boldly ahead, because you can't see anything to be frightened of, you're not expecting it, no, because life, real life, is still hidden from your young eyes. So you're braver, more honest, more profound than us, but just stop to think, if you have a generous bone in your whole body, show me some compassion. I was born here, you know, my mother and father, my grandfather lived here, and I love this house. I can't conceive of my life without the cherry orchard, and if it has to be sold now, well, you might as well sell me along with it.

Ranevskaya's grief is aristocratic and comic; but it is also human and touching.

Lopakhin is neither a lout nor a revolutionary. He is trying his best for Ranevskaya (whom he adores), and is proud of what he has achieved. He declares:

If only my father and grandfather could rise up out of
their graves, and see all that's happened – how their little
Yermolai, their abused, semi-literate Yermolai, who used
to run around barefoot in winter – how that same
Yermolai has bought this estate, the most beautiful spot
on earth. Yes, I've bought the land on which my father
and grandfather were slaves, where they weren't even
allowed into the kitchen.

Chekhov is careful to balance the sympathy. Lopakhin is frustrated, and for all his money he is still unable to write prop-
erly. But the historical process which the play embodies is
relentless, and Lopakhin's men start chopping down the
orchard even before Ranevskaya has gone.

Trofimov declares that work is the great liberator and that
the landowning class must suffer to expiate the sins of the past.
But he is an intellectual and a prude who does not understand
love. He has a vision of the whole of Russia as a garden and
declares that happiness is coming soon, but Chekhov knows it
will be as ephemeral as the moon reflected in a flowing river.
Trofimov looks into the future with confidence, but is in no
sense rational. He declares that he is beyond love and insists
that Ranevskaya face up to the truth of her life – but he is an
innocent who does not even have a lover. He insists, ominously, that the ruling class needs to atone for its past sins, but is
merciless in teasing the peasant Lopakhin. His attempt to live
without money is both touching and absurd. When he storms
out in anger at Ranevskaya, he falls down the stairs. Trofimov
is both a visionary and a fool.

Ranevskaya's brother Gaev is the perfect foil to her emotional quicksilver. He resorts to grandiloquent and sentimental speeches, which he suddenly breaks off in order to play
imaginary billiards. He is a delightful, ineffectual figure
whose optimism and garrulity knows no bounds – right till
the end, he is convinced that his aunt in Yaroslavl will come
up with the money which will save the estate, but we know
that this is unlikely.

Ranevskaya's adopted daughter Varya looks after the house. Her love for Lopakhin is never reciprocated. She tries to hold together what cannot be held together. Only the prospect of a nunnery offers her any peace. Ranevskaya tries to engineer a last-minute romantic ending, but Lopakhin lacks the courage and Varya is left weeping for her life. Anya, Ranevskaya's seventeen-year-old daughter, shows all the characteristics of youth. Her epiphanic moment with Trofimov at the end of Act Two – under the moon, beside a flowing river – is as moving as it is ephemeral. Her conviction that another orchard can be planted is touching but unlikely, as is her announcement that she is going to start a new and better life.

These protagonists are surrounded by figures of similar complexity, all hedged round with Chekhov's customary irony. Charlotta, Anya's German governess, masks her loneliness under a cover of magic tricks and aggressive despair. When she pretends to be cradling a baby – which promptly disappears – we see closer into the heart of her misery. When considering what to do at the end, she simply says 'Who cares?' Yepihodov, the estate clerk, is accident prone and longwinded. He loves the upwardly-mobile maid Dunyasha and has proposed to her, but is in a state of perpetual anxiety. His awkwardness expresses itself in his melodramatic and idle threat of suicide. Dunyasha loves Ranevskaya's young servant Yasha, who breaks her heart and lives only for himself. The eighty-seven-year-old footman Firs has been working in the house for many years. He calls the emancipation of the serfs 'the great disaster'. At the end of the play he is left alone, dying. The impoverished landowner Simeonov-Pishchik can only think about money and eventually gets a cash windfall. Each one of these figures embodies his or her own unique contradictions.

The Cherry Orchard features some of Chekhov's most audacious and complex stage poetry. In Act One the sun is coming up, but it is only two o'clock in the morning and the cherry blossom is ghostly white in the early morning sun. When the shepherd's pipe is finally heard, everyone has gone to bed.

The beauty of the open countryside by sunset in Act Two is contrasted with the town in the distance. Everything is put into context by the arrival of the tramp, with his song of the Russian poor: a new world is arriving in the form of an urban proletariat who will confront the landowners and sweep them all away. The ball in Act Three brings Ranevskaya's grief and Lopakhin's triumph into the most powerful juxtaposition, heightened by the crescendos of the Jewish band and the dancers. As the house is being closed down in Act Four, everyone speaks of a new life, some with confidence, some with terror. In the distance you can hear the cherry orchard being cut down, but nobody (except Yasha) drinks the champagne. Money is being made, but Firs is locked up inside the empty house. Wherever you look, contradictions abound.

With its tenderness and its wisdom, its comedy and its heart, its perfect stage poetry and its magnificent set pieces, *The Cherry Orchard* is not simply the first great play of the twentieth century, but almost certainly its greatest. Life is laid out on Chekhov's anatomist's table and shown for what it is.

> *In performance*

The Cherry Orchard was premièred at the Moscow Art Theatre on 17 January 1904 (Chekhov's forty-fourth and last birthday) amid much celebration of Chekhov's genius, but the author, who was very ill by this time, only watched Act Four. It was directed by Konstantin Stanislavski (who also played Gaev) with his usual emphasis on studied naturalism and high emotion. Ranevskaya was played by Chekhov's wife, Olga Knipper. Chekhov attended some of the rehearsals and was concerned to stress his conception of the play as a comedy. It was a qualified success, but the next day Chekhov wryly commented: 'Yesterday my play was on, so I'm in a bad mood'.

The Cherry Orchard was first produced in England by George Bernard Shaw in 1911. It has subsequently been tackled by nearly all the great twentieth-century directors. Recent productions include Peter Gill's at the Riverside

Studios (1978) with Judy Parfitt and using his own translation; Peter Brook's (1981) with Natasha Parry; and, best of
all, Peter Stein's production with Jutta Lampe, last seen at the
1997 Edinburgh Festival.

As well as the standard academic translations by Ronald
Hingley and Elisaveta Fen, freer versions include Trevor
Griffiths's explicitly Marxist take on the play, Michael Frayn's
adaptation, David Mamet's clipped, American version and
Stephen Mulrine's very speakable translation.

Quotations from Anton Chekhov, *The Cherry Orchard*, tr. Stephen
Mulrine, Nick Hern Books, 1998

The Voysey Inheritance
Harley Granville Barker

1903–5, revised 1913 and 1934

> Historical and theatrical context

The beginning of the twentieth century revealed Britain in a strangely ambivalent mood. The death of Queen Victoria in 1901 marked the beginning of the end of the British Empire – and yet Britain was still the leading Great Power and ruled more than a quarter of the world's population. The economies of America and Germany were flourishing and Germany in particular seemed to be doing more to share its new-found wealth with the workers who had created it. Complacency was combined with unease, and the chief legacy of the decade and a half leading up to the First World War was social reform, under Liberal Prime Ministers Herbert Asquith and David Lloyd George.

Harley Granville Barker (1877–1946) was one of the out-standingly progressive figures of early twentieth-century English theatre: as actor, director, essayist, campaigner and playwright. At the age of twenty-seven, with business manager J. E. Vedrenne, he established a repertory season with a group of actors to present new and classic plays at the Royal Court and the Savoy (1904–7). Soon, repertory theatres sprang up in Birmingham, Liverpool and Manchester in imitation. In 1907, with William Archer, he wrote a *Scheme and Estimate for a National Theatre*, which Laurence Olivier turned to when he set up the National Theatre half a century later.

Granville Barker's plays were influenced by Henrik Ibsen, Maurice Maeterlinck and George Bernard Shaw, in whose social dramas he had acted and who served as his mentor. His dynamic approach to acting and directing (he introduced the modern concept of the director to Britain) and the fluid,

speakable dialogue of his plays amounted to nothing less than
a theatrical revolution. Granville Barker's vision laid the
foundation stone for the subsequent flowering of British theatre
in the twentieth century.

Granville Barker's other plays include *The Marrying of Ann
Leete* (1901), *Waste* (1907), *The Madras House* (1910), *Rococo*
(1911), *The Secret Life* (1919–22) and *His Majesty* (1923–8).
His *Prefaces to Shakespeare* (1942–7) are still widely read.

> About the play

The confident, buccaneering, elderly Voysey is a wealthy and
successful family solicitor with chambers in Lincoln's Inn
Fields. He has engineered it that his third son, the highly
principled, almost priggish young Edward Voysey, should
discover that the firm he is due to inherit has been embez-
zling its clients' trust funds for more than thirty years. When,
in the first act, Edward confronts Voysey with this, he is not
in the least embarrassed, adding that he had to cover up for his
own father's misdeeds. Indeed, with characteristic bravado,
Voysey declares that he is proud that his clients have never
noticed anything amiss. Edward threatens to leave the firm
and have nothing more to do with his father. But Voysey, with
supreme confidence ('Business now-a-days is run on the lines
of the confidence trick'), argues that his dishonest actions
have their own integrity. He urges Edward to consider:

> how simple it would have been for me to go to my grave
> in peace and quiet and let you discover the whole thing
> afterwards.

He makes Edward's appeal to what is right appear naïve and
dangerous:

> My dear Edward, you've lived a quiet, humdrum life up to
> now, with your poetry and your sociology and your
> agnosticism and your ethics of this and your ethics of that!
> . . . and you've never been brought face to face with any

really vital question . . . And it's for your own sake and not
for mine, Edward, that I do beg you to . . . to . . . be a man
and take a man's view of the position you find yourself in.

When Edward resists, his father 'lets fly with a vengeance':

But I'm in a corner . . . and am I to see things come to
smash simply because of your scruples? Hadn't I the same
choice to make? D'you suppose I didn't have scruples? If
you run away from this Edward, you're a coward.

It is the future of the firm that is at stake and Voysey needs
Edward to continue his corruption. As the first act closes,
Edward is invited down to the family home in Chislehurst,
where he will:

find the household as if nothing really has happened.
Then you'll remember that nothing really has happened.
And presently you'll see that nothing need happen, if you
keep your head.

The second act takes place in the dining-room at
Chislehurst, 'a very typical specimen of the English domestic temple'. The women have withdrawn and Voysey is with
the men, smoking cigars and cracking nuts. His second son,
Major Voysey, whose voice is 'like the sound of a cannon', is
arguing the case for military conscription; the rich George
Booth, an old friend of Voysey's who has been 'bent on
nothing but enjoying himself', advises that young men
should 'keep to the middle of the road'; Mr Colpus, the vicar,
a 'harmless enough anachronism', fusses around; Denis
Tregoning, the fiancé of Voysey's forthright daughter, Ethel,
is taunted for his failings; and Edward sits at the far end of
the table, 'not smoking, not talking, hardly listening, very
depressed.'

Alice Maitland, a family friend to whom the hesitant
Edward has never quite managed to become engaged, arrives,
followed by Voysey's eldest daughter, the put-upon Honor,
and the 'hard and clever' writer Beatrice, the wife of Voysey's

youngest son, the painter, Hugh. Voysey advises Booth on his investments but catches a chill strolling in the garden. Edward tells Voysey that he will stay on at the firm, but wants to 'put things straight', 'unobtrusively', but his father is not impressed. His mother, the half-deaf, kindly Mrs Voysey is worried about her husband's health.

Several months later (Act Three), Voysey is dead. Edward has become head of the firm and gathers the family together at the funeral to tell them the true situation: Voysey was a swindler and there can be no inheritance. They are joined by Voysey's eldest son, Trenchard, a succesful barrister and QC, who had fallen out with his father years earlier, and the major's wife, Emily. The family is horrified and, with great skill and irony, Granville Barker exposes the various moral equivocations they, and particularly Edward's three brothers, indulge in to minimize the loss of their creature comforts. Edward himself tells Alice that he is prepared to make a clean breast of it, to confess all and go to prison: she exclaims in admiration that he is 'suddenly . . . a different man'.

In the fourth act, Edward is now head of the firm. He refuses to pay his father's 'confidential clerk' Peacey his £200 Christmas bonus, usually paid in exchange for his silence. Edward's brother Hugh turns up, looking for money, full of artistic vision and outlandish talk. He is going to separate from Beatrice and set out on his own to 'tramp the world'. When Booth appears, saying he wants to withdraw his considerable securities, he is devastated when Edward points out that 'the greater part of what is so neatly written down in this little book doesn't exist'. Booth can hardly believe that he too has been swindled and leaves, threatening to prosecute Edward.

The fifth act takes place on Christmas Eve. Booth has spoken to Mr Colpus and they have decided not to prosecute Edward 'so long as the repayment of their lost capital is a first charge upon the surplus earnings of the firm'. Meanwhile, the family is taking Beatrice and Hugh's impending separation very badly and in a tremendously funny scene a family row blows up in which the play's ironic analysis of the morality of the Edwardian upper-middle class is brilliantly aired. When the two 'new women', Beatrice and Alice, are left with Edward, they agree that they loved 'Pater . . . in spite of all'. Edward tells them of Booth's intention to 'bleed [him] sovereign by sovereign', saying that he will be 'struck off the Rolls . . . no more Lincoln's Inn'. But Alice declares her love for him ('you're ten times the man he ever was') and he finally manages to propose marriage. As the curtain falls, Edward is left sitting alone, 'conscious of new strength'.

Some have called *The Voysey Inheritance* a political play, others a drama of private conscience. Bernard Shaw called it 'a single situation in five acts', maintaining itself for three hours at a pitch which an 'ordinary constructed play attains for about five minutes at the end of the last act but one'. The critic Michael Billington described it as 'the first Marxist play in English'. What is certain is that under the guise of a conventional family saga, centred around a young man's coming of age, Granville Barker delivered a stinging attack on Edwardian bourgeois society and the moral duplicity that lay behind the accumulation of its wealth.

> In performance

The Voysey Inheritance received its première on 7 November 1905, as part of the Barker–Vedrenne season at the Royal Court. The play ran for six matinées. It soon played evenings and enjoyed a further four-week run, with Barker taking on the role of Edward. The revised version was produced in 1935, with George Devine, who was to found the English Stage Company at the Royal Court in 1956, as Colpus. It was co-directed by the author and Harcourt Williams.

Subsequent productions include Jane Howell's at the Royal Court in 1966, which triggered a broader Granville Barker reappraisal, and two in-the-round productions in 1989 – one by Gregory Hersov at Manchester's Royal Exchange, the other by Richard Eyre in the Royal National Theatre's

Cottesloe Theatre. William Gaskill's touring production was part of a Granville Barker retrospective at the 1992 Edinburgh Festival.

Quotations from Harley Granville Barker, *Plays: One*, Methuen, 1993

The Playboy of the Western World
J. M. Synge

1906, first performed 1907

> Historical and theatrical context

As in so many other small European nations, the early years
of the century in Ireland witnessed an intense debate about
Irish national identity. This was to lead to the Easter uprising
of 1916 against the British, the war for independence which
followed, the declaration of the Irish Free State in 1921, the
Irish Civil War of 1922–3 and Éamon de Valera's eventual
IRA victory in 1923. It also led to the division of Ireland into
the independent republic and Northern Ireland, a province
of the British state.

In drama, emergent nationalism took the form of revolt
against the contemporary English theatre, as well as against
realism, and some playwrights pursued a mystical notion of a
Celtic Renaissance. In 1902, the Irish National Theatre
Society was founded. The prospectus of the Irish Literary
Theatre said:

> we hope to find, in Ireland, an uncorrupted and imagina-
> tive audience, trained to listen by its passion for oratory –
> we will show that Ireland is not the home of buffoonery
> and of sentiment, as it has been represented, but the home
> of an ancient idealism.

J. M. Synge (1871–1909) was a highly educated Irish
Protestant, who had travelled widely in Europe, but heeded
W. B. Yeats's advice to go to the Aran Islands and describe
what he saw. Thus, although a native Irishman, Synge was an
outsider to its peasant culture. By the time he came to write
The Playboy of the Western World, he had already written *In the
Shadow of the Glen* (1903) and *Riders to the Sea* (1904), which

D. H. Lawrence was to describe as 'probably the genuinest bit of dramatic tragedy, in English, since Shakespeare'.

> About the play

The 'western world' of the title is the remote and wild north-west coast of Ireland. The play takes place in a 'shebeen' – a shabby, illegal public house – over one autumn evening and the following day. A young man, Christy Mahon, bursts in, declaring that he has killed his father. Everybody is impressed, especially Pegeen Mike, the landlord's young daughter, and her father offers Christy a job protecting the illegal whisky ('poteen') from the British authorities. Pegeen is soon quarrelling with the Widow Quin (a thirty-year-old woman who has 'buried her children and destroyed her man') over where Christy should stay and who would be the better partner for him. Christy sums it up at the end of Act One:

> Well, it's a clean bed and soft with it, and it's great luck and company I've won me in the end of time – two fine women fighting for the likes of me – till I'm thinking this night wasn't I a foolish fellow not to kill my father in the years gone by.

By the next morning, Christy is enjoying himself. Three local girls turn up, fascinated by this handsome stranger, laden with presents and food. Widow Quin arrives and Christy tells them his extraordinary tale. He says his father wanted him to marry an old woman, 'a walking terror from beyond the hills', and so he killed him:

> He gave a drive with the scythe, and I gave a lep to the east. Then I turned round with my back to the north, and I hit a blow on the ridge of his skull, laid him stretched out, and he split to the knob of his gullet.

A powerful erotic charge soon develops between Pegeen and Christy. The cowardly and religious Shawn, who is due to marry her, is desperate for Christy to leave. Widow Quin soon declares her own intentions. Suddenly, unexpectedly and comically, Christy's father, Old Mahon, appears, alive and well, with a bandaged head, hunting for his son. When the others manage to get him to leave, Christy emerges from his hiding place, devastated now that he knows that Pegeen will reject him. Once again, Widow Quin tries to entice him, as the girls return to take their hero off to the horse-racing on the beach.

Later in the day, two local farmers are complaining about Christy. Mahon returns, exhausted and apparently in despair:

> It's a hard story, I'm saying, the way some do have their next and nighest raising up a hand of murder on them, and some is lonesome getting their death with lamentation in the dead of night.

Meanwhile, Christy has won the horse race and the people carry him in triumph to the shebeen. In an extraordinarily poetic scene, Christy proposes to Pegeen:

> When the air is warming, in four months or five, it's then yourself and me should be pacing Neifin in the dews of night, the times sweet smells do be rising, and you'd see a little, shiny, new moon, maybe sinking on the hills.

When Pegeen's father returns drunk from a wake, he announces that she must marry Shawn. When she resists, her father tries to get Shawn to fight Christy, but when Christy sends Shawn packing, he joins their hands and blesses their marriage. Mahon enters with Widow Quin, and he and Christy leave the shebeen to fight. Christy soon returns, apparently victorious, but the crowd now want to hang him and manage to get a noose tied round his neck. They are about to drag him off when Mahon comes in again, apparently risen from the dead a second time. Father and son head off together, with Christy declaiming:

> Ten thousand blessings upon all that's here, for you've turned me a likely gaffer in the end of all, the way I'll go

romancing through a romping lifetime from this hour to the dawning of the judgement Day.

But Pegeen has summed up the serious side of the play:

> I'll say a strange man is a marvel, with his mighty talk; but what's a squabble in your back yard, and the blow of a loy, have taught me that there's a great gap between a gallous story and a dirty deed.

and it is Pegeen who is left alone with her grief, having lost 'the only Playboy of the Western World'.

Throughout *The Playboy of the Western World*, Synge heeded his own words: 'on the modern stage one must have reality, and one must have joy'. It is the channelling of unrestrained energy within a highly controlled form, the balance struck between ecstasy and sobriety, ridicule and respect, the outpouring of 'an imagination that is fiery and magnificent and tender' that makes the play such a rich work. Synge's own declared intentions are more than matched when it comes to the play's language:

> In a good play every speech should be as fully flavoured as a nut or apple, and such speeches cannot be written by any one who works among people who have shut their lips on poetry.

The Playboy of the Western World is both a celebration and a challenge to conventional notions about the Irish peasantry and, using both naturalistic dialect and highly artificial poetry in a fine and intricate balance, it is a theatrical and comic tour de force. As one of the key dramatic contributions to the great and challenging discussion about Irish identity, *The Playboy of the Western World* is an admirably complex and rewarding masterpiece.

> *In performance*

Synge was already suffering from Hodgkin's Disease by the time *The Playboy of the Western World* received its première on 26 January 1907 at the recently founded Abbey Theatre in Dublin. It was greeted with scenes of hysteria. Lady Gregory said that 'there was a battle of a week', and Yeats praised it as:

> Picturesque, poetical, fantastical, a masterpiece of style and of music, the supreme work of our dialect theatre, [Synge's] *Playboy* roused the populace to fury.

The seemingly innocent lines 'what'd I care if you brought me a drift of chosen females standing in their shift itself?' caused the correspondent of *The Freeman* to describe the play as 'an unmitigated libel on peasant men and, worse still, upon Irish peasant girlhood'. On the second night, cries were heard in Gaelic of 'kill the author' – Irish nationalists thought the play a slur on the Irish national character. Synge died two years later, but his play has outlived its many critics.

The play is very difficult to stage, and a modern production needs to strike a fine balance. As Synge himself wrote:

> Although parts of it are or are meant to be extravagant comedy, still a great deal that is in it and a great deal more that is behind it is perfectly serious when looked at in a certain light. This is often the case, I think, with comedy, and no one is quite sure today whether Shylock or Alceste should be played seriously or not. There are, it may be hinted, several sides to *The Playboy*.

It has been frequently performed in Ireland, Britain and the rest of the world. 1984 was a year full of revivals, with productions by Garry Hynes and Lindsay Anderson, as well as Mustapha Matura's Caribbean version, *The Playboy of the West Indies*. It has become a repertory classic and was revived by the Royal National Theatre in 2001.

The Playboy of the Western World has had a huge influence on subsequent Irish drama, and its poetic language and realistic view of fantasy is echoed in the work of Sean O'Casey and Samuel Beckett, as well as more recent Irish dramatists such as Brian Friel, Conor McPherson, Sebastian Barry and Martin McDonagh.

Quotations from J. M. Synge, *The Playboy of the Western World*, Nick Hern Books, 1997

Rutherford and Son
Githa Sowerby

1912

> *Historical and theatrical context*

Beneath their calm surface, the years leading up to the First
World War were a time of transition in Britain. Perhaps the
most significant social movement was the impassioned and
sometimes violent struggle for female emancipation and the
vote. The suffragettes were single-minded and effective in
their protests, which ranged from chaining themselves to
railings to hunger strikes. 1912 saw hundreds of women
attacking shops in London and throwing stones in Downing
Street. Married women over thirty were allowed to vote for
the first time in the 1918 General Election.

These years also saw an increase in the number of women
in positions of influence in the theatre. In 1907, Annie
Horniman established the first repertory theatre at the
Gaiety in Manchester, whilst Emma Cons and later her niece,
Lilian Baylis, were laying the foundations of what was to
become the centre of Britain's theatrical establishment at the
Old Vic Theatre in Waterloo. The Actresses' Franchise
League was founded in 1908. In 1913, Inez Bensusan took
over the Coronet Theatre for a Women's Theatre season and
Edy Craig's Pioneer Players, formed in 1911 and dedicated to
experimental work, allowed women to exercise their skills in
all areas.

This was the time of the 'New Woman', an idea influenced by Ibsen's heroine Nora in *A Doll's House*, who leaves
her husband so as to be true to herself. Enlightened male
dramatists such as George Bernard Shaw, Arthur Wing
Pinero and Harley Granville Barker were all sympathetic
to this notion, but although they 'created admirable, inde-

pendent, self-determining women', they 'denied them any sort of reality'. It remained for the women writers to do this.

Originally a writer of children's books (her first attempt at a play was called *Little Plays for Little People*), Githa Sowerby (1876–1970) wrote five more plays: *Before Breakfast* (1912), *A Man and Some Women* (1914), *Sheila* (1917), *The Stepmother* (1924) and *The Policeman's Whistle* (1934), but none of them matched her first triumph.

> About the play

The Rutherford and Son of the title is a North of England family firm of glassmakers. Rutherford ('the Guv'nor') has worked hard to build it up:

> I've toiled and sweated to give you a name you'd be proud to own – worked early and late, toiled like a dog when other men were taking their ease – plotted and planned to get my chance, taken it and held it when it come till I could ha' burst with the struggle.

But Rutherford is getting old, and the firm is in debt, affected by industrial unrest and cheap competition: 'Rutherford's is going down – down – I got to pull her up somehow'.

It is deep winter and the Rutherford home is cold and uncomfortable. Rutherford's eldest son, John, has recently returned from the south with his new wife, an office girl called Mary – a marriage condemned by Rutherford Senior as unworthy of his family's social standing. John is 'delicate-looking and boyish in speech and manner' and is recovering from an illness. They have a sick baby, Tony, who Mary dreams of giving a better life. Rutherford has two other children: his second son, Richard (Dick), an overworked curate, and his daughter, the thirty-six-year-old Janet, whom Rutherford has kept on as an unpaid housemaid. With his own elderly sister, Ann – a bitter, mean, conventional woman – Rutherford rules the house with an iron grip.

Young John is sceptical about the firm's morality and speaks of the worship of Moloch in the Old Testament:

> Out of every family they set aside one child to be an offering to him when it was big enough, and at last it became a sort of honour to be dedicated in this way, so much so, that the victims gave themselves gladly to be crushed under the great wheels.

It is clear that John's father has always blocked him and gives him neither position nor salary. But John has invented a metallurgical process which will make his fortune. He declares that he does not want to inherit the firm, and challenges his father to buy the patent ('I've got something to sell and you want to buy it, and there's an end'). But Rutherford is determined to steal his son's invention and John is weak and pliable.

At the beginning of Act II, Dick tells his father that he has been offered a senior curacy elsewhere. But Rutherford feels nothing but 'silent antagonism' towards Dick's calling:

> You can't make a silk purse out of a sow's ear – you were no good for my purpose, and there's an end.

Mrs Henderson, the mother of a lad caught 'pilfering money', arrives to plead for his reinstatement. When Rutherford tries to send her away, she shocks him by saying:

> You think yourself so grand wi' your big hoose, and your high ways . . . You wi' your son that's the laughing stock o' the parish, and your daughter that goes wi' a working man ahint your back!

The news of Janet's secret affair with his trusted foreman Martin cuts Rutherford to the bone. He sends for Martin, who enters, unaware of what has happened, and asks him for the secret of John's metallurgical invention. With great reluctance, Martin agrees: 'It's for Rutherford's'. When Janet appears, Rutherford confronts her and tells her to leave the next morning ('I'll have no light ways under my roof . . . Your

name shan't be spoke in my house . . . never again'). But Janet
defies her father and insists that they are all 'common' at
heart:

> Whatever Martin's done, he's taken me from you. You've
> ruined my life, you with your getting on. I've lived in
> wretchedness, all the joy I ever had made wicked by the
> fear o'you . . . Now you know!

The next morning Janet is strangely relieved and says that
they were 'to win through to happiness after all'. Martin has
been 'turned away' by Rutherford after working for him for
twenty-five years, but is convinced that Rutherford was in the
right. At one point he says: 'it was a great love ye gave me –
you in your grand hoose wi' your delicate ways. But it's broke
me.' She thinks they should leave together ('we'll begin again
. . . You and me, free in the world'); but he insists on staying
with 'the Master'.

 When John hears that Martin has given Rutherford the
receipt for his invention, robbing him of his last chance to
make his fortune, he takes money from his father's cash box
('I tell you it's mine, by right') and decides to leave the house
for ever. He refuses to listen to Mary's plea to act more
rationally, for the child's sake, but accepts that he should leave
them behind.

 With all three of his children gone, Rutherford has lost the
thing he most wanted – a son to carry on the family name.
But Mary strikes the devil's own bargain, in the only terms
the old man will understand:

> A bargain is where one person has something to sell that
> another wants to buy. There's no love in it – only money –
> money that pays for life. I've got something to sell that
> you want to buy . . . my son . . . Give me what I ask, and
> in return I'll give you – him.

With this cool, pragmatic deal, Mary secures a better life for
her son. Rutherford accepts what he recognizes as a business
deal and in the last moments of the play, as 'the little lad'

wakes up, a new softness seems to have entered Rutherford's heart.

Although Sowerby's father worked in the glass trade, *Rutherford and Son* is more than autobiography. With great insight, it anatomizes women's roles both within and outside the family and lays bare the patriarchal cruelty at the heart of industry and the 'family firm'. Sowerby's courage in addressing these issues in 1912 should not be underestimated; her sheer dramatic skill makes the play a landmark in the drama of a century in which many women finally gained the position and respect they deserved.

> *In performance*

Despite her lack of dramatic experience, Githa Sowerby enjoyed a huge success with *Rutherford and Son*. Presented for just three matinée performances at London's Court Theatre, opening on 31 January 1912, critical and popular acclaim was such that it went on to transfer twice – to the Little Theatre and the Vaudeville – and received 133 performances in all. After that, it disappeared from view until it was revived by Lewis Casson for BBC Radio in 1952.

There were two fringe productions by Mrs Worthington's Daughters in 1980 and Southern Lights in 1988, and Katie Mitchell directed the play at the Royal National Theatre in 1994 with the late Bob Peck as John Rutherford.

Quotations from Linda Fitzsimmons and Viv Gardener (eds.), *New Woman Plays*, Methuen, 1991

The Daughter-in-Law
D. H. Lawrence

1912, first performed 1967

> Historical and theatrical context

When D. H. Lawrence (1885–1930) wrote his three plays set during the industrial disputes of the Nottinghamshire coalfields, British Trade Union membership had reached an astonishing three and a half million. Miners were among the most politically conscious members of an increasingly militant working class, as the ten-month strike in 1911 by the South Wales Miners demonstrated. 1912 also saw the sinking of the *Titanic*, often seen as an emblem of the hubris of the British ruling classes.

In 1912, Lawrence was a young, unknown writer: his first novel, *The White Peacock*, had been written in 1911 and he was working on *Sons and Lovers*, which was to be published in 1913. His early poems had been accepted by the radical *English Review*, whose editor had encouraged Lawrence to write about 'the other half' – advice which was to have a huge effect on the subsequent shape of Lawrence's career.

Lawrence's own sense of dramatic innovation is clear from a letter to Edward Garnett in 1913:

> I believe that, just as an audience was found in Russia for Tchekhov, so an audience might be found in England for some of my stuff, if there were a man to whip 'em in. It's the producer that is lacking, not the audience. I am sure we are sick of the rather bony, bloodless drama we get nowadays – it is time for a reaction against Shaw and Galsworthy and Barker and Irishy (except Synge) people – the rule and measure mathematical folk . . . Damn my impudence, but don't mislike me. But I don't want to write like Galsworthy, nor Ibsen, nor Strindberg, nor any of them, not even if I could.

His other plays include *A Collier's Friday Night* (*c.*1909) and *The Widowing of Mrs Holroyd* (1911) which, together with *The Daughter-in-Law*, came to be known, in theatre circles at least, as 'the Lawrence Trilogy'. Lawrence is one of the century's greatest novelists, but he should be remembered as one of its finest dramatists as well.

> *About the play*

In *The Daughter-in-Law*, Lawrence takes one of his first steps in his lifelong investigation into the complex relationships between men and women. Although the play is set against the background of industrial action, at its centre is a set of acutely felt observations about love, families and sexual relationships.

Mrs Gascoigne's two sons both work down the mines. Joe, the younger, still lives with his mother, although he keeps threatening to leave for Australia. He is a joker, a show-off, who beneath his charm and childishness has an independent streak. His older brother, Luther, is slower, more surly, and struck with a deep sense of his own worthlessness. Both sons are in thrall to their dominant mother.

Six weeks before the action of the play begins, Luther married the middle-class Minnie, a nursery governess from Manchester. The marriage was reluctant on both sides, a making-do in the absence of any better option. Mrs Gascoigne is soon told that another girl – Bertha Purdey – is four months pregnant by Luther. It is agreed that the much better-off Minnie should find the money to support the baby and buy Bertha's silence (people will say that the father was 'one o' them electricians as was along when they laid th'wires under th'road down to Batsford').

Luther comes home from a day down the pit. He is filthy and insists on eating his dinner without washing. Minnie finds this both shocking and attractive. When Luther tells her about the plan to strike, she cannot understand what he is up to. Luther is appalled when Bertha's mother tells him about her daughter's pregnancy and says: 'Married I am, an' I wish I worna.' Later that night Luther comes in from the pub, drunk not just on beer but on his own self-loathing and sense of Minnie's superiority. When Minnie is told about Bertha, she agrees to help financially. But in a blazing row, Minnie blames his mother for everything: 'It's your mother's doing. *She* mollycoddled and marded you till you weren't a man – and now – I have to pay for it'. When Minnie leaves the house, it is not clear if she will ever return.

To everyone's surprise, Minnie comes back from Manchester two weeks later. The miners are now on strike and Joe and Luther have been involved in stopping strike-breaking. Joe draws a parallel between their strike and Minnie's absence and offers to find another girl to look after Luther. Minnie declares, somewhat provocatively, that she has spent £120 on a ring and three prints. Even when the men were working, this would have been an extravagance. In a strike it is almost criminal, and in a fit of rage Luther throws the prints into the fire. In the final act, Mrs Gascoigne tells Minnie that men are always trouble ('it's risky work, handlin' men'), but Minnie wants Luther back. Luther arrives with his head cut and running with blood: he has stopped the strike-breakers. In the last moments of the play, Minnie declares her love for Luther and provides him with his salvation.

The Daughter-in-Law is driven by two conflicts which were to be extensively explored in much of Lawrence's work. The first is class, and in the marriage of Luther and the better off 'daughter-in-law' there is a devastating picture of the clash between the uneducated industrial working class, and the self-improving, emerging lower-middle class. Lawrence captures the humiliation and the solidarity of poverty, as well as the attractive mobility but highly individualistic nature of the new class, with great precision and sympathy.

The other clash is between men and women: the casual fraternity of Joe, Luther and the striking coal-miners is set against the powerful and controlling but nourishing and erotic force of mother and wife. Like all of Lawrence's work, the play is sympathetic towards the male experience and it shows how, through the struggle of the strike and his confrontation with Minnie, Luther can come to manhood. But it also expresses the suffering of women, their capacity for love and the continued pains and joys of motherhood.

The Daughter-in-Law is one of the first great plays about the working class. It draws on a hidden tradition in English drama, first glimpsed in the medieval mystery plays and those scenes in Shakespeare in which working men and women, in their own dialect, speak their hearts and souls. It is a kind of writing which sets the working class within the material world in which they live, but presents their daily lives and struggles to be transcendent and even mythical. D. H. Lawrence's plays, and *The Daughter-in-Law* in particular, provide an alternative wellspring to the subsequent flood of English twentieth-century drama.

> In performance

The Daughter-in-Law received its world première more than fifty years after it was written, on 16 March 1967, in a Royal Court production directed by Peter Gill and designed by John Gunter. The following year, the three plays of the Lawrence Trilogy were seen together and proved a huge critical and popular success. It is quite possible that without the Royal Court these beautiful plays, written in the common voice, might have remained academic rarities. Peter Gill's production was generally regarded as definitive and has influenced a whole generation of directors and writers – Gill was obviously the 'man to whip'em in'.

The Daughter-in-Law is often revived in Britain, but the dialect makes it impossible to translate and it has hardly crossed the Channel. We are not aware of any US professional productions.

Quotations from D. H. Lawrence, *Three Plays*, Penguin Books, 1960

Heartbreak House
George Bernard Shaw

1914–19, first performed 1920

> Historical and theatrical context

Heartbreak House was written in a Britain preoccupied with
the ongoing carnage of the Western Front. In just four years,
nearly a million British soldiers were killed and more than
two million were wounded. New weapons and bad leadership
brought about an unprecedented military disaster. The First
World War was one of the great catastrophes of the twentieth
century and its repercussions were felt for many years.

This was a world that was changing rapidly. A small but
growing Labour Party began to make itself heard. The suffragettes were making advances in the Votes for Women
campaign. Unrest threatened the stability of the British
Empire, particularly in India and Ireland, and the 1917
Bolshevik Revolution in Russia sent shivers throughout the
ruling classes of Europe.

London's theatre seemed determined to ignore this. Apart
from a few topical plays, a spirit of determined frivolity
dominated right through into the 1920s. George Bernard
Shaw (1856–1950) – Irishman, Fabian, wit and theatrical
genius – turned this to his own advantage. As a highly successful theatre critic, he was aware – perhaps too aware – of
the different approaches in contemporary theatre. His ability
to combine a lightness of touch with penetrating social analysis helped him create a new kind of dialectical – and didactic
– theatre that is both provocative and entertaining.

Shaw's prolific output includes: *Widowers' Houses* (1892),
Arms and the Man (1894), *The Devil's Disciple* (1897), *Mrs
Warren's Profession* (1902), *Man and Superman* (1905), *Major
Barbara* (1905), *The Doctor's Dilemma* (1906), *Caesar and*

Cleopatra (1907), *Pygmalion* (1913), *Back to Methuselah* (1922), *St Joan* (1923), *The Apple Cart* (1929), *Too True to be Good* (1932) and *The Millionairess* (1936). His essays on politics, music and the theatre (especially his *Quintessence of Ibsenism*) have been influential.

Shaw was awarded the Nobel Prize for Literature in 1925, but turned down a peerage on principle.

> About the play

There is some dispute over the date of *Heartbreak House*. Shaw himself wrote that the play was 'begun when not a shot had been fired'. Some of it was certainly written one weekend in 1916 at Charleston – the Bloomsbury Group's country house in Sussex – from where the guns of the Somme could faintly be heard. Shaw regarded the play as his *King Lear*, but as his subtitle – 'a fantasia in the Russian manner on English themes' – implies, the play owes more to Chekhov, whom he revered, than to 'Shakespear', whom he scorned.

The absent-minded inventor Captain Shotover is eighty-eight, 'an ancient but still hardy man with an immense white beard'. He lives in a large country house (part of which he has made to resemble a ship) and has two daughters: the free-spirited Hesione Hushabye, who lives with him ('I keep the house: she upsets it'), and Lady Ariadne Utterword, an apparently respectable middle-aged woman who has lived abroad with her 'numskull' husband ('governor of all the crown colonies in succession') for twenty-three years. Both women are very beautiful.

The first act consists of a series of arrivals. The first is Ellie Dunn, a young, penniless, highly principled innocent. She is greeted by the elderly Nurse Guinness, but ignored by Shotover. Ellie is going to marry 'a perfect hog of a million-aire', 'Boss' Mangan. Hesione is appalled and promises to get Ellie out of it. But Ellie argues that Mangan invested capital in her father's failed business and that marrying her is his reward. Ellie confesses that she is in love with 'Marcus

Darnley', but when 'Darnley' turns up it quickly emerges that he is in fact Hesione's husband, Hector, who soon falls in love with the 'accursedly attractive' Lady Utterword. Meanwhile Shotover is trying to invent a secret weapon. By the time Lady Utterword's layabout lover Randall turns up, the house is rapidly resembling a 'ship of fools'.

Act Two takes place after dinner. Mangan reveals to Ellie that, far from saving her father, he deliberately ruined him, 'as a matter of business'. He also reveals that he is 'in love' with Hesione. But Ellie is adamant:

> Come, Mr Mangan! you made a business convenience of my father. Well, a woman's business is marriage. Why shouldn't I make a domestic convenience of you?

and hypnotizes him into falling asleep. Hesione tries to dissuade Ellie's eccentric and idealistic father Mazzini and flirts with him, but he turns out to be 'the one man I met who could resist me when I made myself really agreeable'. Ellie is furious:

> When I want all the strength I can get to lean on: something iron, something stony, I dont care how cruel it is, you go all mushy and want to slobber over me.

But, deep down, she is heartbroken. However, Mangan has overheard the whole conversation between the two women and is heartbroken too:

> Are all women like you two? Do they never think of anything about a man except what they can get out of him?

He declares that his engagement to Ellie is over. But suddenly Hector comes in, having discovered (and nearly killed) a burglar. There is a philosophical conversation about the rights and wrongs of robbery until, in a stroke of comic genius, it is revealed that the burglar was once married to Nurse Guinness. When left alone with Shotover, Ellie describes what she feels:

It is a curious sensation: the sort of pain that goes mercifully beyond our powers of feeling. When your heart is broken, your boats are burned: nothing matters any more. It is the end of happiness and the beginning of peace.

But Lady Utterword is having a row with her lover and Hector and Randall fight each other, despairing of the possibility of love between men and women.

Act Three takes place in the garden. It is a 'lovely night', but Hesione can hear 'a sort of splendid drumming in the sky'. Hector declares:

I tell you, one of two things must happen. Either out of that darkness some new creation will come to supplant us as we have supplanted the animals, or the heavens will fall in thunder and destroy us.

In his melancholy, Mangan declares that he does not actually have any money at all and also reveals that he is working for the government. Hesione says that it 'matters very little which of you governs the country so long as we [herself and her sister] govern you'. Ellie announces that 'there seems to be nothing real in the world except my father and Shakespear'. To everybody's astonishment, Ellie also announces her intention to marry Shotover, to 'give my broken heart and my strong sound soul to its natural captain, my spiritual husband and second father'. She goes on:

There is a blessing on my broken heart. There is a blessing on your beauty, Hesione. There is a blessing on your father's spirit. Even on the lies of Marcus there is a blessing; but on Mr Mangan's money there is none.

And Ellie comes up with the play's title:

This silly house, this strangely happy house, this agonizing house, this house without foundations. I shall call it Heartbreak House.

Shotover predicts England's catastrophe:

the splintering of her rotten timbers, the tearing of her
rusty plates, the drowning of the crew like rats in a trap.

Soon, the distant rumble of a bombing Zeppelin is heard.
The house takes a hit in the gravel pit where Shotover's
dynamite is stored, killing Mangan and the burglar, leaving
Ellie radiant at the prospect of the bombs coming again
'tomorrow night'.

Heartbreak House has such a restless, ludic quality, with
people constantly coming and going, striking poses, uttering
opinions and falling in love that one contemporary likened it
to 'pure Marivaux'. But this dazzling comedy of manners is
also a drama of destruction and, as so often in Shaw, its face-
tiousness masks human despair. Its allusions to *King Lear* and
the Trojan War are a closer guide to its author's intentions.

Shaw saw himself above all as a moralist. In *Heartbreak
House*, his attack is levelled at a powerful and privileged group
– bankers, politicians and businessmen, as well as artists,
idealists and intellectuals – who, through their own folly and
self-absorption, left the way clear for 'the philistines and
barbarians'. At times, Shaw's eagerness to please seems at odds
with his coruscating purpose. But the play magnificently artic-
ulates Shaw's prophetic sense of a nation adrift, heading for
the rocks. His vision remains as pungent as ever, challenging
us to make the connection between our own indolence and
the emergence of barbarism all around us.

> *In performance*

Heartbreak House was not well received on its British publication in 1919 and Shaw gave the play to the newly incorporated
American Theatre Guild, who presented the world première
on 10 November 1920 at the Garrick Theater in New York,
where it ran for 100 performances over almost five months.

The play had to wait until 1921 for its British première, in
a production co-directed by Shaw and the Irish playwright
J. B. Fagan at the Court Theatre in Sloane Square. It was

critically panned (one wag dubbed it 'Jawbreak House'), but was treated more kindly on a second outing in a cut version, though it still only played for sixty-three performances. Its reputation was saved by James Agate, who found it 'exhilarating and deeply moving'.

Recent revivals have included John Schlesinger's at the Old Vic (1975), and John Dexter's (1983) and Trevor Nunn's (1992), both at the Theatre Royal Haymarket. Calling it 'the century's original state-of-England play', the writer David Hare found his own resonance in a production at London's Almeida Theatre (1997), revealing a quality which Shaw is sometimes accused of lacking: emotion.

Quotations from George Bernard Shaw, *Heartbreak House*, Penguin, 1964

Six Characters in Search of an Author
(*Sei Personaggi in Cerca d'Autore*)
Luigi Pirandello

1921

> *Historical and theatrical context*

Italy was in turmoil after the First World War. It had secured
a place at the Paris Peace Conference as a victor, but only at
huge human cost. National sentiment had been satisfied by
the recovery of disputed areas in the north of the country, but
Italy still looked to the past to forge its future. In Benito
Mussolini it found a strong man who promised to revive the
glory of Ancient Rome while applying no-nonsense solutions
to the economic and social problems facing this backward
country.

Luigi Pirandello (1867–1936), one of the first 'modernists',
was a complex character. Along with other influential Italian
artists, he joined the emerging Fascist party in 1924 and,
despite maintaining that politics and art should be kept separate, was close to Mussolini and a friend of Italian Fascism
for the rest of his life. A practical man of the theatre, he ran
his own company, Il Teatro d'Arte in Rome, from 1925 to
1928, where he forged a new dramatic style which combined
the native traditions of *commedia dell'arte* with Stanislavsky's
psychological method. His work was inspired by the great
advances in European science (particularly Einstein and
Freud) and was influenced by his countrymen, Rosso di San
Secondo and Luigi Chiarelli, whose *teatro del grottesco* examined the co-existence of comedy and tragedy and the existential and surreal possibilities of mirrors and masks.

Pirandello's forty or so other plays include *Right You Are –
If You Think So* (1917), *The Rules of the Game* (1918), *Henry IV*
(1922), *The New Colony* (1928), *Lazarus* (1929), *As You Want*

Me (1930) and *The Mountain Giants* (1938). Several of these were adaptations from the many short stories he wrote between 1900 and 1918. *Six Characters in Search of an Author* is part of a trilogy that also includes *Each in His Own Way* (1924) and *Tonight We Improvise* (1929).

Pirandello was awarded the Nobel Prize for Literature in 1934.

> About the play

1918 was a watershed year for Pirandello. His wife was committed to a mental asylum, causing him guilt and despair. But his career was taking off and royalties allowed him to give up teaching. His passionate belief in the power of theatre, along with hostility towards meaningless spectacle, prompted him to ask fundamental questions about the relationship between theatre and life, illusion and reality, and the 'mystery of artistic creation'. To do this, Pirandello returned to the well-trodden, endlessly fascinating conceit of a 'play-within-a-play'.

Six Characters in Search of an Author takes place on a stage set up for rehearsals. A technician is banging in nails, chatting to the Stage Manager. Actors turn up and when the Director arrives, the rehearsals begin. The dialogue is rich with the everyday details of the theatre: the Leading Lady is late; the Director marks out an imaginary room; actors complain about the text (Pirandello's own *Rules of the Game*); the Director spouts dramatic theory which nobody understands, and so on. People laugh, cigarettes are smoked and the feel is utterly realistic.

But then six extraordinary figures appear in the auditorium. Pirandello suggests that the characters should wear masks, each fixed in a single sentiment: the remorseful Father, the grieving Mother, the vengeful Stepdaughter and the contemptuous Son, as well as a gloomy Boy of fourteen and his four-year-old Sister. They have come 'in search of an author'. They say they have a story and challenge the Director and the actors to represent them, 'because inside us we carry a drama full of pain'. The Father announces that they want to live 'for eternity' in 'them', the actors.

The characters soon reveal an intense family drama and the actors and the Director become a rapt audience. The Father, it seems, sent the Mother away, to go and live with another man by whom she had a second family – the Stepdaughter and the two small children. The Son, too, had been sent away because the Mother did not seem strong enough to cope with him. The Father is now filled with remorse: 'I always had these odious aspirations towards a certain moral sanity.'

It emerges that the Father used to follow his Stepdaughter back from school when she was a little girl. Years later, in dire poverty, the Mother took a menial job at Madame Pace's hat shop, a cover for the brothel where her daughter works. The Father, 'led by the wretched needs of the flesh', was just about to have sex with his Stepdaughter when the Mother came in and saw what was happening. The Son is implicated, too, in her descent into street-prostitution: his resentment drove her over the edge. The Director is intrigued by the story and the Father tells him that he should be the Author:

> What's needed is someone who will copy it down, since he would have it all in front of him – in action – scene by scene.

The Director calls a twenty-minute break, and the actors are left astonished: 'He expects us to improvise a play . . . like in the commedia dell'arte.'

Act Two starts with the Director and Stage Manager improvising a setting for the hat shop. The Director has prepared an outline and tells the Prompter to record in shorthand what is said. The play is cast and the Stepdaughter, who is to be played by the Leading Lady, increasingly behaves like a leading lady, while the Father is concerned with how the Leading Man will 'play me as I really am'.

Suddenly, to everyone's astonishment, 'the fat old hag' Madame Pace appears, speaking a jumble of languages, and the scene begins to be played out. While the Director seizes on Madame Pace's comic potential, the Mother spits out her anger and the Father points out that the scene cannot start with the Mother present. The Director declares that 'everything is useful', but the Stepdaughter drives Madame Pace away.

For a moment, the Father and the Stepdaughter enact what happened with total conviction. But when the actors come to perform it, the characters continually object and the gap between acting and life is dramatized in almost scientific terms. A row develops over who the scene really belongs to and what the play is for. The Stepdaughter gets to the heart of it:

> But how, I beg you, tell me how could he act out all these 'noble' remorses of his, all of his 'moral' torments, if you decide to spare him the horror of finding himself one fine day, after having invited someone to remove her dress, a dress of recent mourning, in the arms of a woman, a fallen woman, that same little girl, sir, that little girl he used to go and watch coming out of school?

At this, the Mother's anguish erupts and, as she enacts her scream when she saw what was happening in the shop, the Director brings the curtain down on the fictional first act.

While they consider how the second act should unfold, the Father asks the Director difficult existential questions, advising him not to trust in his own reality because 'it is destined to reveal itself as an illusion'. But the Father is jealous of the Director because his 'immutable reality' as a character cannot change and he is denied life by his creator. Here, Pirandello explores his concern with the workings of the writer's imagination: 'what scenes we proposed to him', as the Stepdaughter says.

Soon the Stepdaughter has persuaded the Director to stage the technically difficult scene in the Father's house and garden. The Son is very reluctant. The Stepdaughter sets up the young girl playing by the pool. The Sister drowns herself, and the Boy draws a revolver and shoots himself. As the play ends, four of the Characters, but ominously not the two dead children, exit through the auditorium, leaving the spectators stunned: 'it's make-believe', say the actors; it is 'reality', insists the Father. The Stepdaughter's scornful laughter is heard going out into 'real life'.

With its profound analysis of the fluidity of human personality, *Six Characters in Search of an Author* is one of the unique achievements of twentieth-century drama. It combines Freud's psychoanalytical insights with Einstein's new physics and is written with a panache and wit that makes it hugely enjoyable. In a time of moral and psychological relativism, Pirandello's masterpiece appears as one of the founding texts of postmodernism. Sometimes dismissed as too cerebral, the play expresses a distinctly modern kind of pain.

> In performance

Six Characters in Search of an Author caused a sensation at its first performance at the Teatro Valle in Rome in 1921. Max Reinhardt produced the play in Berlin in 1922 and Georges Pitoëff's Paris production in 1923 was a *succès de scandale*. The British première of the play was by the Stage Society in February 1922, at London's Kingsway Theatre.

Famous productions seen in Britain include Italy's Compania dei Giovanni in 1965 as part of the RSC's World Theatre Season at the Aldwych and Anatoli Vasiliev's adaptation seen at the London International Festival of Theatre in 1989. Ralph Richardson and Barbara Jefford appeared as the Father and Stepdaughter at the Mayfair Theatre in 1963, and Jefford returned to play the Mother in Nicholas Wright's translation at the National Theatre in 1987, which also featured Ralph Fiennes as the Son. The Abbey Theatre, Dublin staged a successful version by Thomas Kilroy in 1996. Most recently, a new translation by David Harrower called *Six Characters Looking for an Author* enjoyed critical success at the Young Vic, London in 2001.

After an early flurry, the play's popularity dwindled. Its fluid, agile language is difficult to translate, and productions find it hard to fulfill Pirandello's demand that it should not be 'the false truth of the stage but the positive, undeniable truth of life' that shines through.

Quotations from Luigi Pirandello, *Six Characters in Search of an Author*, tr. Mark Musa, Penguin, 1995

Juno and the Paycock
Sean O'Casey

1924

> Historical and theatrical context

Sean O'Casey (1880–1964) completed *Juno and the Paycock* in
1924. In the Irish Civil War of 1922–3 the government of the
recently independent Irish Free State led by Michael Collins,
and the Irregulars of the IRA (Irish Republican Army) under
Éamon de Valera, had fought each other almost as fiercely as
they had fought the British. The Irregulars had refused to
accept the new government's peace treaty with Britain and
this bitter and bloody struggle culminated in the assassination of Collins and the victory of the IRA. In essence, the
Civil War was fought between pragmatism and absolutism,
which the 'diehards' (the IRA) eventually won.

The play is the second part of what became O'Casey's
Dublin Trilogy – it came after *The Shadow of a Gunman* (1923)
and before *The Plough and the Stars* (1926). The trilogy was
written for the Abbey Theatre and its predominant style is
realistic, portraying daily lives in Dublin during the wars of
independence. Its surface is naturalistic and its analysis is
based on the premise that environment is the key element in
character and destiny. The three plays are written in a carefully scripted Dublin dialect (which can make them hard to
read), but they are also rooted in the popular traditions of
music-hall and melodrama. The trilogy is powerful drama
which works superbly well in the theatre.

Sean O'Casey's other, less naturalistic plays include *The
Silver Tassie* (1929), *Within the Gates* (1934), *Purple Dust*
(1940), *Red Roses for Me* (1942) and *Cock-a-Doodle-Dandy*
(1949).

> About the play

At the heart of *Juno and the Paycock* is the great, and some would say eternal, struggle between men and women. The play presents the world of male folly, arrogance and war and sees it as disastrous and charming, destructive and seductive in equal measure. Against that, it sets a female way of doing things which is quite different: pragmatic and rooted in the tough realities of daily life, but continually overwhelmed by the consequences of male folly. The play sets these two principles at each other's throats, and releases this conflict in both comic and tragic terms.

The male principle is embodied in 'Captain' Boyle, the strutting 'paycock' (peacock) of the title. O'Casey is careful to show him as a greedy, lazy, charming drunk. He never was a captain, and is ignorant and illiterate: an unemployed fantasist who considers himself above politics and the troubles of the world. Together with Joxer, his best friend and drinking buddy, he is a bar-room philosopher of the worst kind. Their antics resemble a music-hall double act. When, early in the play, Jerry Devine the socialist arrives with news of a job for Boyle, he is too lazy to try for it. When schoolteacher Charlie Bentham announces the death of Boyle's second cousin and tells him of his imminent wealth, Boyle immediately runs up a huge bill on credit, without ever verifying that his fortune will come through.

Disaster strikes when, two months later, the money has still not arrived. Bentham has disappeared to England. Creditors are calling and it emerges that no money is going to come from the will. The furniture gets taken away and even Joxer betrays Boyle (by stealing his last bottle of stout). At the end of the play, ignorant of the disasters that have struck his family, Boyle comes in drunk after a night in the pub with Joxer, and exclaims that 'th' whole worl's . . . in a terr . . . ible state o' . . . chassis!'

Boyle's wife Juno is cut from a very different cloth. She is

struggling to survive and keep her family and dignity together. She can be tough and intimidating and has a tremendous
desire for things to be better, but she is also at times a working-class snob. Her perspective on the world is limited by her
wish to provide for her family. Her husband describes her as
'always grousin'' and she is as limited in her down-to-earth
attitude as Boyle is in his flights of fantasy. Despite all this,
her struggle is presented as an heroic one.

The Boyles have two children. Unlike their parents, they
are both genuine idealists, prepared to sacrifice themselves
for their principles. The son, Johnny, lost his arm in the 1916
Easter Rising and has no truck with the political ignorance of
his father or the domesticity of his mother. At the beginning
of the play he is stricken with guilt and is anxious and restless
throughout. By the end, it is clear that he has been involved
with the Diehards and has betrayed their neighbour, Robbie
Tancred. This inevitably leads to Johnny's own death and the
heart of O'Casey's tragedy. Although the son's seriousness
and devotion to the political cause is set in strong contrast
with his father's frivolity, Boyle's fantasies and Johnny's
commitment are not actually that far apart: both lead to
catastrophe.

At the start of the play, the Boyles' daughter Mary is on
strike in protest at a colleague's unfair dismissal. She is also
coming of age, courting first the socialist Jerry Devine and
then the schoolteacher Charlie Bentham. When, at the end,
Jerry Devine returns and declares his love to Mary, he soon
reveals that his socialist concern for others is not universal
when he discovers that she is pregnant by Bentham. By the
close of the play, she reaches the conclusion that:

> There isn't a God, there isn' a God; if there was He
> wouldn't let these things happen.

Part of the greatness of the play lies in the way that O'Casey
sets this family tragedy within the context of the Irish civil
war. For all O'Casey's socialism and basic sympathy with the
nationalist cause, it is the expression of atheistic pacifism

which is the most striking political statement in the play. When a tailor rebukes Juno for not having enough respect for the dead, her answer is direct:

> Maybe, needle Nugent, it's nearly time we had a little less respect for the dead, an' a little more regard for the livin'.

For all its surface realism, the play is much more than either a naïvely naturalistic work capturing the realities of a Dublin family's life, or a piece of radical agitprop. It is a work of great artistry, with the classical myth of the goddess Juno and her philandering husband Jupiter woven into the fabric. O'Casey subtitled the play 'a tragedy in three acts' and the critic James Agate in 1925 said it was 'as much a tragedy as *Macbeth*, but [one] taking place in the porter's family'. It follows a classical three-act form and is beautifully structured and proportioned.

But that does not do justice to the greatness of O'Casey's achievement. Most important is the sheer force of O'Casey's vernacular poetry, which brings all this together and expresses it with overwhelming emotional power. One example will have to suffice:

> Maybe I didn't feel sorry enough for Mrs Tancred when her poor dead son was found as Johnny's been found now – because he was a Diehard! Ah, why didn't I remember that then he wasn't a Diehard or a Stater, but only a poor dead son! It's well I remember all that she said – an' it's my turn to say it now: What was the pain I suffered, Johnny, bringin' you into the world to carry you to your cradle, to the pains I'll suffer carryin' you out o' the world to bring you to your grave! Mother o' God, Mother o' God, have pity on us all! Blessed Virgin, where were you when me darlin' son was riddled with bullets, when me darlin' son was riddled with bullets? Sacred Heart o' Jesus, take away our hearts o' stone, and give us hearts o' flesh! Take away this murdherin' hate, an' give us Thine own eternal love!

At the start of the twenty-first century, it is shocking just how resonant this still sounds.

> *In performance*

Juno and the Paycock received its première on 3 March 1924 at Dublin's Abbey Theatre and quickly became the most popular play in its twenty-year history. It received its London première in late 1925 and Alfred Hitchcock made a film of the play in 1930. In 1966, Laurence Olivier directed it for the National Theatre at the Old Vic, and in 1980 Judi Dench played Juno for the RSC. The play has been performed throughout the world and has become an essential part of the popular repertoire.

Quotations from Sean O'Casey, *Three Dublin Plays*, Faber and Faber, 1998

Journey's End
R. C. Sherriff

1928

> ### Historical and theatrical context

The human cost of the First World War was enormous: over eight million men killed and thirty million captured or wounded. But the trenches also had devastating political effects on the participating states. In Germany and Russia a poisonous and unstable brew of revolution and nationalism emerged, while the stunned victors, particularly France and Britain, were left with a determination to avoid repeating these horrors. 'The long truce' (1918–39) was simply a gap in the hostilities, and the First World War led inevitably to the Second.

'The war to end all wars' also shattered lingering Victorian and Edwardian notions of chivalric idealism. It was the subject of some of the century's most evocative poetry – by Siegfried Sassoon, Rupert Brooke and Wilfred Owen – but took some time to appear in dramatic form: Shaw's *Heartbreak House* was written to the sound of the Somme in the distance, but is more concerned with those responsible for the war than with the 'poor bloody infantry'. It was not until ten years after the armistice that the two great dramatic works about the soldier's experience of the war appeared: Sean O'Casey's *The Silver Tassie* (1929) and R. C. Sherriff's *Journey's End* (1928).

The enormous success of *Journey's End* came as a surprise to R[obert] C[edric] Sherriff (1896–1975), a Surrey-born insurance worker and retired army captain. Though some of his stage plays – which included *Badger's Green* (1930), *St Helena* (1936), *Home at Seven* (1950), *The White Carnation* (1953) and *The Long Sunset* (1955) – enjoyed moderate success, none achieved the scale or lasting appeal of *Journey's End*. However, Sherriff went on to carve out a distinguished career as screenwriter of such film classics as *Goodbye, Mr Chips* (1939), *Lady Hamilton* (1941), *Mrs Miniver* (1942), *No Highway* (1950) and *The Dam Busters* (1955).

> *About the play*

As a serving officer for a year on the Western Front, R. C. Sherriff knew all about the men who fought there, and it is this that gives his writing its authenticity. The result is that *Journey's End*, in three tightly written acts, rich with the details of the daily routine, shot through with the trauma of the conditions and violence that is all around, shows more eloquently than any news footage the experience of life, and death, in the trenches.

The play takes place in a British officer's dugout 'fifty yards' behind the front line 'before St Quentin' and just one hundred and fifty yards from the German front line. It is March 1918, on the eve of the German offensive at Cambrai, in which the British were to lose more than 75,000 men. Captain Hardy, an officer from another regiment, is about to go on leave and is chatting to Osborne ('about forty-five – physically as hard as nails', nicknamed 'uncle'), the Company's second-in-command. The rather stilted, almost jolly dialogue alerts us to the incongruous, matter-of-fact attitudes of men grown inured to a world gone mad around them.

Raleigh, a new officer arrives. He is nineteen and 'only left school at the end of last summer term'. He chats with Osborne about 'rugger and school' and it emerges that he asked to be sent to this company in particular because it is led by Stanhope, his school hero, who is also engaged to his sister. But Osborne is concerned:

> You see, he's been out here a long time. It – it tells on a man – rather badly –

The newcomer is struck by how 'frightfully quiet it is', but, as Osborne points out, 'a hundred yards from here the Germans are sitting in their dugouts, thinking how quiet it is'. When Raleigh admits that he finds the landscape 'almost romantic', the veteran tells him that he 'must always think of it like that if [he] can'.

Dennis Stanhope is only twenty-one, but already old ('despite his stars of rank he is no more than a boy'). He is unhappy about Raleigh's arrival and is anxious about his fiancée finding out the truth about him:

> She thinks I'm a wonderful chap – commanding a company. She doesn't know that if I went up those steps into the front line – without being doped with whisky – I'd go mad with fright.

Stanhope decides to censor Raleigh's letters to her. He will:

> Cross out all he says about me. Then we all go west in the big attack – and she goes on thinking I'm a fine fellow for ever – and ever – and ever.

When he does read one of the letters he finds himself described as 'the finest officer in the battalion'. The fact is that although Stanhope's nerves are shattered and he drinks heavily to cover it up, he has been at the front for three years and is a first-rate officer. The psychological effects of combat on even the most courageous of men are revealed through Stanhope's contradictory behaviour.

Hibbert is a young officer who is showing all the symptoms of shellshock. When he turns down food on account of his 'neuralgia', Stanhope interprets it as cowardice:

> How long's he been out here? Three months, I suppose. Now he's decided he's done his bit. He's decided to go home and spend the rest of the war in comfortable nerve hospitals. Well, he's mistaken . . . No man of mine's going sick before the attack. They're going to take an equal chance – together.

When Hibbert threatens to desert, Stanhope pulls a gun on him. He says he will shoot him, but make it look like an accident. He appeals to Hibbert's *esprit de corps* and sense of loyalty to others:

> If you went – and left Osborne and Trotter and Raleigh and all those men up there to do your work – could you ever look a man straight in the face again – in all your life!

A kind of light relief comes from the jovial, cockney Second Lieutenant Trotter (who has apparently 'put on weight during his war service') and the chirpy 'soldier servant' Mason, who provides a semblance of normality by serving up cups of tea that taste like onions and food whose provenance he will not admit. When he makes 'yellow soup', Osborne insists they must have pepper on it and Trotter jokes:

> War's bad enough with pepper – but without pepper – it's – it's bloody awful.

Like Brecht and Kipling (and Napoleon before them), Sherriff understands that an army marches on its stomach. As well as endless jokes about food, there is talk about the beauty of the sunrise, or Trotter's garden at home, or Osborne's reading of *Alice's Adventures in Wonderland*, or Trotter's chart to make the six days they have to spend at the front seem to pass more quickly. It is these realistic touches which give the play so much of its depth.

Stanhope instructs a sergeant major to lay wire down either side of the dugout, turning it into a fortified island, in preparation for the imminent German attack. He will not contemplate retreat: 'Our orders are to stick here. If you're told to stick where you are you don't make plans to retire.' A Colonel arrives to order a 'raid' to take prisoners and find out what is going on behind the enemy lines. It is decided that Osborne will take Raleigh along with him. The Germans have sarcastically tied red rags on either side of the gap in the wire and Stanhope asks why the raid cannot take place at night. As the last minutes tick away, Osborne and Raleigh are left together, Raleigh tempted by the prospect of the MC (military cross) but Osborne wanting to talk of other things: *Alice in Wonderland*, Raleigh's home, or the chicken Mason has got them for their dinner that evening. And off they go into the 'pale evening sunset', bound together, heroic in a strangely understated way. They manage to capture a German soldier, but Osborne is killed, 'while he was waiting for Raleigh'.

As the night draws in, Stanhope and Trotter get drunk, smoke cigars and tell obscene stories. Stanhope snaps at Hibbert, who has been showing them pornographic post-cards. To Stanhope's fury, Raleigh prefers to be with the 'men': 'My officers are here to be respected – not laughed at.' But Raleigh is appalled by Stanhope's apparently callous behaviour, unaware that Stanhope is even more shocked by Osborne's death than he is. Choked with tears, Stanhope asks him: 'You think there's no limit to what a man can bear?'

The last scene takes place just before dawn. Mason has prepared 'sambridges' for the officers and Stanhope ensures that 'the men' have 'a decent drop of rum'. As the dawn breaks, German shells begin to explode all around them. Hibbert is dragged off to the front line by Mason, who appears fully armed for the first time. Raleigh is carried in by the sergeant major, badly wounded in the back, and his hero Stanhope stays with him until he dies. The shelling intensi-fies, the dugout suffers a direct hit, its roof collapses and as the curtain falls, the earth buries Raleigh's body.

Journey's End is remarkably free of polemic. There is no talk of patriotism or anti-German feeling. Although Sherriff shows how Britain's class system persisted even at the front line, and touches on the sheer futility of the war effort, there is little sense of Sherriff telling us what to think. Modern audiences may mock the play's understated heroics and its cheerful camaraderie, but *Journey's End* is written with such authority and dramatic skill that there is little doubt that it will continue to be an eloquent witness to one of the century's darkest moments.

> *In performance*

Journey's End was rejected by many managements before securing a Sunday evening performance by the Incorporated Stage Society at London's Apollo Theatre on 9 December 1928, when the young Laurence Olivier played Stanhope. George Bernard Shaw used his influence to help get the play produced at the Savoy in 1929, where it was a tremendous success. It has been frequently revived, particularly by amateur groups, and was a great hit on Broadway. *Journey's End* was made into an Anglo-American film in 1930.

Quotations from R. C. Sherriff, *Journey's End*, Gollancz, 1929

The Front Page
Ben Hecht and Charles MacArthur

1928

> Historical and theatrical context

The Front Page was written at the height of the 1920s, a time of tremendous optimism in the United States, when the economy was booming, individualism was rampant, newspapers were sensationalist, crime was glamorous and the disaster of the Great Depression – triggered by the Wall Street Crash of 1929 – had not yet struck.

Chicago, where the play is set, was enjoying a literary renaissance, with writers mythologizing the city's reputation for crime and violence. The New York theatre was brash and commercial, with work by George S. Kaufman, Moss Hart and Noël Coward holding the stage prior to the emergence of the more heavyweight dramatists of the thirties such as Clifford Odets and Eugene O'Neill.

The Front Page was the first of Ben Hecht's (1894-1964) and Charles MacArthur's (1895–1956) collaborations. Others include *Twentieth Century* (1932) – a satirical comedy about New York society – *Ladies and Gentlemen* (1939) and *Swan Song* (1946). They also set up a film production company together, and wrote numerous essays, short stories, and screenplays. Ben Hecht was a reporter for the *Chicago Journal* and the *Chicago Daily News* and this experience gives *The Front Page* its authenticity.

> About the play

The play is set in the press room of the Chicago Criminal Courts, and features eight crime reporters working for a range of national and local papers. It is 8.30 at night. Some of the men are playing poker, phones are ringing and they are all cracking jokes, oblivious to the human drama they are meant to be reporting. The atmosphere is thick with poker, journalism and the law; the language is ribald, sharp-witted and cynical.

It quickly emerges that a Communist, Earl Williams, has been condemned to hang on a trumped-up charge of killing a black man, so that the racist Mayor can attract the black vote and win the election. The execution has been set for 7.00 the following morning. There are all the usual grotesque preparations: the ritual of the last dinner (sponsored by a local restaurant), the testing of the gallows and the hyping-up of the criminal (and 'red') danger to the City. The journalists want Williams's execution brought forward so that they can get the story into their first editions.

Walter Burns is the hard-boiled editor of the *Herald Examiner* and is trying to find one of his correspondents, Hildy Johnson. But Hildy is about to marry his girlfriend, Peggy, and is catching a train to New York with her that evening so that he can take up a new and better-paid job in marketing. A series of brilliantly drawn cameo characters visit the press room: Mrs Schlosser, the jealous wife; Woodenshoes, the intellectual cop; Diamond Louie, the mobster (who embodies the complex link between the press and organized crime); Jennie, the scrubwoman; Mollie Malloy, the local tart (who curses the newspapermen: 'it's a wonder a bolt of lightning don't come through the ceiling and strike you all dead!'); and the corrupt Mayor and Sheriff, who are only interested in votes. Hildy is saying goodbye to his colleagues for the last time when shouts and sirens announce a jail break: Earl Williams has escaped! As the curtain falls, Hildy phones through to Walter with the story.

At the start of Act Two, Williams's reprieve arrives, but the Mayor bribes the bearer of the reprieve (one Mr Pincus) to leave. It soon transpires that Williams shot his way out with the Sheriff's own gun: Hildy paid 'two hundred and sixty bucks' for this information and desperately wants his 'marriage money' back from Walter. Diamond Louie will only lend him $150 and the train to New York is due to leave in fifteen minutes. Hildy is alone when suddenly Williams himself comes crashing through the skylight. Hildy rings Walter in excitement but pressure is building from Peggy on the other line. Williams declares 'It's better to die for a cause than the way most people die' and Mollie hides him inside a rolltop desk. When the other journalists return to phone through their copy, there is ribald suspicion about what Hildy and Mollie were up to in the press room, and they both get involved in an increasingly farcical protection of Williams's hiding place. The journalists soon decide that Williams may be in the building and decide to search it. Peggy's mother, Mrs Grant, comes in furiously, and accuses Hildy of talking a 'lot of gibberish' about catching a murderer. The others immediately turn on Hildy to find out what he is hiding, but Mollie soon distracts their attention by jumping out of a window twenty foot above the gound (and surviving). Walter arrives and Mrs Grant is hysterical. Peggy comes to fetch Hildy and, as Walter is gleefully clearing the front page for his exclusive, she storms off, shouting: 'You never did love me.'

Act Three starts minutes later. Walter and Hildy have to get the desk (and Williams inside it) out of the press room and into the *Examiner* office. When a journalist called Bensinger arrives (in whose desk Williams is hiding), Walter offers him a job – with a pay rise and a byline – to get him out of the room. Diamond Louie comes in: he had been driving Mrs Grant and they crashed into a police patrol. Hildy presumes she is dead and that he is responsible and telephones all the hospitals to find her. He is just about to set off when the Sheriff and the deputies turn up. They threaten Hildy and find Williams's gun (which the Sheriff recognizes because it is his own). Mrs Grant arrives with two policemen, claiming she has been kidnapped, while Walter discovers that Butch, who was going to come and move the rolltop desk, is in bed in a hotel with a blonde. Mrs Grant accuses Walter of being in charge of the kidnap and tells the Sheriff there is a murderer hiding in the room. A farcical climax is reached when the Sheriff's three bangs on the desk are answered by Williams's three bangs inside it. Guns are drawn, phone calls are made and newspaper stories are concocted. The Mayor enters and Walter tries to frighten off the Sheriff. Mr Pincus returns, drunk, with Williams's reprieve. Walter and Hildy slap a charge of bribery on to the Mayor and the Sheriff, who release them. Peggy appears and Hildy swears he will stop writing for newspapers and they leave for New York. Walter gives Hildy an engraved watch as a memento, but phones the New York police to get them to arrest him on arrival for having stolen it.

The Front Page is an astonishingly well-crafted farcical romance and the brilliance of its (admittedly dense) plotting cannot be overstated. It is also a powerful political and social satire, whose main target is newspapers and the way they concentrate only on what they think is interesting or matters ('Who the hell's going to read the second paragraph?'). Its great innovation is its brilliant quick-fire wit, its dazzling theatricality and its virtuosity in interweaving so many different characters and stories. It uses a startling technique of overlapping dialogue which gives a powerful illusion of reality. Quite often there are three or four conversations going on at the same time, often with an unheard voice at the other end of the phone. All of this gives a sense of a vast and complex society, with each individual having his or her own life story and preoccupations. Even the smallest part is written with a specific vernacular feel and the play looks forward to the brilliantly intricate dialogue of writers such as Tennessee Williams, Clifford Odets, Arthur Miller, David Mamet and Sam Shepard, as well as to high-quality American television like *Hill Street Blues* or *ER*. If the 'American Century' is characterized by the triumph of the common man, it is plays like *The Front Page*, and the great tradition of realistic American drama that emerged in its wake, that best expresses it.

> *In performance*

The Front Page was premièred at the Times Square Theater, New York City, on 14 August 1928, in a production directed by George S. Kaufman. It was revived at the Old Vic in London in 1972 and at the Donmar Warehouse in 1997. It is a mark of the play's great popularity that it has been used as the basis for three films – in 1930, in 1940 (as *His Girl Friday*, directed by Howard Hawks), and in 1974 (adapted by Billy Wilder, with Jack Lemmon and Walter Matthau) – as well as a musical (*Windy City*) in 1982. The play is rarely revived, perhaps because of its large cast.

Quotations from Ben Hecht, Charles MacArthur, *The Front Page*, Samuel French, 1928

Private Lives
Noël Coward

1929, first performed 1930

> *Historical and theatrical context*

The England for which Noël Coward (1899–1973) wrote his
most successful play was for the most part oblivious to the
darkness that was about to confront it. W. H. Auden came to
call the 1930s 'a low dishonest decade', and even in 1929 the
signs were ominous: the Nazis had become the second-
largest party in Germany, depression and unemployment
paralysed the economies of Europe and America, while in the
Soviet Union Stalinism was tightening its deadly grip. But
this was also the time of luxury travel, Hollywood's golden
age and the style and glamour of the 1920s. In certain privileged circles, the frivolity and freedom of the 1920s – the
'flappers' – were still all the rage.

By 1929, Coward was a major theatrical figure, renowned
for his comic wit, theatrical iconoclasm, and commercial
appeal. He was wealthy and admired, and extraordinarily
popular. His prolific output includes *The Vortex* (1924), *Fallen
Angels* (1925), *Hay Fever* (1925), *Bitter Sweet* (1929), *Cavalcade*
(1931), *Design for Living* (1933), *Tonight at 8.30* (1935),
Present Laughter (1939) and *Blithe Spirit* (1941). He also wrote
the screenplay for the film *Brief Encounter* (1944).

> *About the play*

Noël Coward wrote *Private Lives* in 1929 in Shanghai, while
recovering from influenza. He had the idea for the play one
sleepless night in the Imperial Hotel in Tokyo:

> The moment I switched out the lights, Gertie [the actress
> Gertrude Lawrence] appeared in a white Molyneux dress

on a terrace in the South of France and refused to go again until four a.m., by which time *Private Lives*, title and all, had constructed itself.

The result is one of Coward's most brilliantly constructed plays. Written in three taut acts, it has four central characters – two men and two women – and all the symmetrical balance and psychological intrigue of an eighteenth-century comedy of manners.

Act One is set on the double balcony of a hotel in Deauville. Sibyl and Elyot are on the first evening of their honeymooon. This is his second marriage, and she is questioning him about his first wife, Amanda. Little do they know that in the neighbouring suite Amanda is also on her honeymoon, talking with her new husband, Victor:

> I suffered a good deal, and had my heart broken. But it wasn't an innocent girlish heart. It was jagged with sophistication. I've always been sophisticated, far too knowing. That caused many of my rows with Elyot. I irritated him because he knew I could see through him.

In a moment of comic perfection, Amanda and Elyot spot each other and are appalled, both declaring that they want to leave immediately with their new spouses. But Victor and Sibyl are equally astonished and soon both pairs of newly-weds have blazing rows.

Amanda and Elyot meet a second time, and when the orchestra plays a tune they both remember (prompting Elyot's famous line 'Strange how potent cheap music is'), the old relationship resumes: emotional and bad-tempered, erotic and savage, romantic and provocative. We quickly see that this couple is addicted to each other and that Coward's portrait cuts to the heart of the contradictions so often implicit in such relationships. So as to stop arguing they invent 'a catchword', ('Solomon Isaacs', soon shortened to 'sollocks') which 'when either of us says it, automatically cuts off all conversation for at least five minutes'. By the end of Act One they have eloped, leaving Victor and Sybil together, looking for their spouses and sharing a cocktail.

Act Two takes place in Amanda's flat in Paris. Almost the entire act is taken up with an extended conversation between Amanda and Elyot which switches in seconds from powerful declarations of romantic love to arguing and bickering with a ready wit and a vicious tongue. They love and hate each other in equal measure. The play is remarkable above all for the quality of their dialogue and there is a sequence in Act Two which manages to catch so many of the shifting truths of love that it is worth quoting at length:

Elyot What does it all mean, that's what I ask myself in my ceaseless quest for ultimate truth. Dear God, what does it all mean?

Amanda Don't laugh at me, I'm serious.

Elyot You mustn't be serious, my dear one, it's just what they want.

Amanda Who's they?

Elyot All the futile moralists who try to make life unbearable. Laugh at them. Be flippant. Laugh at everything, all their sacred shibboleths. Flippancy brings out the acid in their damned sweetness and light.

Amanda If I laugh at everything, I must laugh at us too.

Elyot Certainly you must. We're figures of fun alright.

Amanda How long will it last, this ludicrous, overbearing love of ours?

Elyot Who knows?

Amanda Shall we always want to bicker and fight?

Elyot No, that desire will fade, along with our passion.

Amanda Oh dear, shall we like that?

Elyot It all depends on how well we're played.

Amanda What happens if one of us dies? Does the one that's left still laugh?

Elyot Yes, yes, with all his might.

Amanda That's serious enough, isn't it?

Elyot No, no, it isn't. Death's very laughable, such a cunning little mystery. All done with mirrors.

Amanda Darling, I believe you're talking nonsense.

Elyot So is everyone else in the long run. Let's be super-ficial and pity the poor philosophers. Let's blow trumpets and squeakers and enjoy the party as much as we can, like very small, quite idiotic schoolchildren. Let's savour the delight of the moment. Come and kiss me darling, before your body rots and worms pop in and out of your eye sockets.

Amanda Elyot, worms don't pop.

The Act ends with Amanda and Elyot declaring their undying hatred of each other ('I hope to God I never set eyes on you again as long as I live'), fighting on the floor in 'paroxysms of rage', while Victor and Sibyl look on, appalled, from the door.

Act Three takes place the following morning. Victor and Sybil are asleep on sofas set outside Amanda's and Elyot's door. Amanda's maid Louise (a wonderful cameo part, speaking only French but managing to set the squabbling quartet into relief) arrives with breakfast. Amanda and Elyot appear from their separate bedrooms and declare that they are going away, separately and for ever.

Sibyl's and Victor's conventionality emerges as a perfect foil to Amanda and Elyot's idiosyncrasies and although Coward himself was dismissive about their characterizations, they are an essential element in his structure. Sibyl is a nice woman who cries a lot and has no sense of humour. When

Victor manfully challenges Elyot to a fight, Elyot's response is:

> Listen a minute, all this belligerency is very right and proper and highly traditional, but if only you'll think for a moment, you'll see that it won't get us very far.

There is a discussion about the possibility of divorce and both couples dismiss the idea. Sybil and Victor insult each other ('stop it! stop it! You insufferable great brute') and Amanda and Elyot go off together. The curtain comes down on Sibyl hitting Victor and him shaking her 'like a rat'.

The greatness of *Private Lives* lies in the balance it strikes between wit and seriousness, joy and despair, pleasure and pain. It catches the gauche absurdity of romantic attachment, the contradictions of intimacy and the overwhelming power of erotic attachment. The play is daring in its approach to love and marriage and got Coward into trouble with the censor. When many artists were turning their attention to public and social issues, Coward deliberately focused on personal experience. It is a measure of its worth that seventy years later, when so much of that politically committed art can feel dated, Coward's masterpiece still speaks so clearly to a modern audience.

> In performance

Private Lives received its world première on 18 August 1930 at the King's Theatre, Edinburgh in a production directed by Coward himself, who also played Elyot. Gertrude Lawrence played Amanda and the young Laurence Olivier portrayed the unimaginative Victor. The play received mixed reviews at the Phoenix Theatre in London, where it opened on 24 September 1930, but soon became a popular hit and went to Broadway the following year.

With its razor-sharp wit and mercurial shifts in tone, the play presents a formidable challenge to actors. Coward wrote later:

I have seen many actresses play Amanda, some brilliantly, some moderately and one or two abominably. But the part was written for Gertie and, as I conceived and wrote it, I can say with authority that no actress in the world ever could or ever will come within a mile of her performance of it.

The play was filmed in 1931 with Norma Shearer and Robert Montgomery. It was revived in 1963 at Hampstead Theatre Club, helping to revive Coward's career and prompting one critic to call it the 'funniest play to have adorned the English theatre in this century'. John Gielgud directed it in 1972 with Maggie Smith and Robert Stephens, and the play was seen on Broadway in 1982 with Richard Burton and Elizabeth Taylor. It is regularly revived in Britain and has saved many a repertory theatre from bankruptcy. It was staged at the Royal National Theatre in 1999, with Juliet Stevenson as Amanda, as part of the Coward centenary celebrations.

Quotations from Noël Coward, *Plays: Two*, Methuen, 1979

Tales from the Vienna Woods
(Geschichten aus dem Wiener Wald)
Ödön von Horváth

1931

> Historical and theatrical context

The Austria in which the Hungarian-born Ödön von
Horváth (1901–38) wrote *Tales from the Vienna Woods* was a
democratic republic built on the ruins of the Hapsburg
Empire. Its capital, Vienna, was the home of Sigmund Freud
and the Second Viennese School – the atonal music of Arnold
Schoenberg, Anton Webern and Alban Berg. For more than
thirty years it had enjoyed an extraordinary cultural flowering. By 1931, however, it was in social and economic turmoil
– dramatically shown by the bankruptcy of the Credit
Anstalt Bank in 1931 – opening the way for the accession of
the authoritarian Catholic President Dollfuss in 1932 and
Hitler's *Anschluss* (annexation) in 1938.

The play draws on the traditions of the *Volksstück* – a difficult
term to translate, which refers to the Austrian folk dramas of
authors such as Nestroy and Raimund. Horváth declared:

> Quite deliberately I am destroying the old folk-play, both
> in its form and its ethos – and I am attempting to find the
> new form of the folk-play. In doing so I turn more to the
> tradition of the folk-singers and folk-comedians than to
> the author of the classical folk-plays.

Horváth's plays are absolutely free of the Nazi associations of
Volk; indeed he deliberately exploited these traditional forms to
write deadly anatomies of the mentality that led to Fascism.

By the time of his death, in exile in Paris, in a freak accident
at the age of thirty-six, Horváth had written some of the great
plays in the German language: *Italian Night* (1930), *Faith*,

Hope and Charity (1931–2), *Casimir and Caroline* (1932), *Don Juan Comes Back from the War* (1936) and *Figaro Gets a Divorce* (1937), as well as his novel *Youth without God* (1937) – a chilling analysis of the appeal of Fascism to young people. In his pocket was found a fragment of his unfinished novel *Adieu, Europa*:

> Why was it that I had to leave my home?
>
> What did I stand up for? I never took part in politics. I stood up for the rights of the human being. But perhaps my crime was that I found no solution.
>
> I go on writing my feuilleton and I don't know the answer. I don't know it yet.
>
> The sea roars. New waves and still more new waves keep on coming. Again and again and again.

> About the play

The play's motto is 'Nothing gives so strong an impression of infinity as stupidity', and Horváth manages to blend a romantic yearning for the seeming infinity of the Vienna Woods with a desolate satire on bourgeois stupidity. If his work lacks the savage cruelty of his contemporaries Karl Kraus or Bertolt Brecht, it has a kind of sweetness which is as insidious as the songs which weave through the play and perhaps provides a truer picture of the attraction of the 'sentimental stupidity' which was to lead so disastrously to Austria's embrace of Fascism.

Act One opens in the Wachau, a popular holiday district outside Vienna. The young gambler Alfred is visiting his mother and grandmother. He is accompanied by a young widow called Valerie, whose relationship with Alfred is increasingly rocky. Meanwhile, in Vienna, a middle-class girl called Marianne is about to be engaged to Oskar, the young owner of a butcher's shop. But when she sees Alfred from the window, she falls in love with him instead. Marianne's father, however, has arranged a picnic 'by the beautiful Blue Danube' to celebrate her engagement. When an earnest student called Erich appears, he and Valerie indulge in a casual and almost unpleasant flirtation. Marianne's father also flirts with Valerie, but when Erich draws his gun, Valerie falls for him instead. Later that evening, still beside the river, Marianne and Alfred kiss. She breaks off her engagement to Oskar in front of everyone and declares her love for Alfred.

A year later Alfred and Marianne are living together in cheap lodgings and have a baby. They have no money and are in trouble. Alfred is trying to sell cosmetics and has stopped betting on horses. His friend von Hielinger gets Marianne a job with a baroness who runs a dancing club (a thin disguise for a brothel). The baby, meanwhile, is in the Wachau with Alfred's mother and grandmother, who refuse to give Alfred any money unless he marries Marianne or goes away to France. But Valerie and Erich have fallen out and Alfred visits her on his way to France. Oskar is still obsessed with Marianne and is intent on vengeance. Marianne goes to confession but refuses to repent of her illegitimate child. At the end of Act Two she asks:

> If there is a God . . . what's to become of me, God? Dear God, I was born in Vienna 8 and I went to the local secondary school, I'm not a bad person . . . are you listening? What's to become of me, God?

Act Three opens in a tavern during the Viennese wine festival. Everybody is drunk, singing songs, eating too much, breaking the furniture and rowing with each other. An American comes in – he has come home to 'old Vienna' – and when it starts to rain, the whole party is led off to Maxim's. There, they are entertained with tableaux vivants and Marianne is recognized as one of the naked dancers. Marianne's father disowns her and she threatens to throw herself in front of a train. The American offers to pay for Marianne's favours but she refuses, tries to steal his money and is fired.

Alfred soon appears at his mother's place: he has not gone to France and has spent his grandmother's money on gambling. The child is seriously ill because the grandmother has been careless in looking after him. Valerie and Erich soon split up and Erich returns to Kassel, while Oskar's revenge on Marianne grows. Marianne's father makes a chilling prophesy: 'I'm telling you now: very soon there's going to be another war. There just has to be! There'll always be wars.' Valerie's response is 'True. But that would mean the end of our civilisation as we know it.' Alfred tries to make it up with Valerie, who is still angry with him. Marianne is on remand and Oskar offers to marry her, but Marianne goes back to her father, saying 'when it really comes down to it, I don't give a shit. What I'm doing, I'm doing for Leopold [her son], because none of this is his fault.' But in the last scene of the play, the boy has died and Alfred's mother and grandmother are writing a letter to explain. Marianne arrives with her father, is given the letter and tries to kill the grandmother. She has suffered terribly and she and Oskar are left, a couple desperately tied together, while Johann Strauss's sugary waltz 'Tales from the Vienna Woods' swells in the background.

Tales from the Vienna Woods is written with an extraordinary attention to detail. It is Chekhovian in its dramatic counterpointing and filmic in its ability to gaze objectively at the intricate surface of things. It is punctuated with folk-songs and Viennese waltzes, and is as fine as gossamer but tough as old nails. The Austrian dramatist Peter Handke once declared that 'Horváth is better than Brecht', but in some ways it is a false opposition: Brecht's intention was explicitly revolutionary and his dramatic style is more jagged and provocative. It is perhaps more useful to see Horváth as Chekhov's descendant: a scientist not afraid of poetry and a dramatic poet of unique power and understanding.

> In performance

Tales from the Vienna Woods received its première at the Deutsches Theater in Berlin, with Peter Lorre and Carola Neher in the roles of Alfred and Marianne, in November 1931, the same year that Horváth was awarded the prestigious Kleist-Preis. The Nazis regarded Horváth as 'degenerate' and it was not until the 1960s that his plays enjoyed the kind of attention they deserved in Austria and Hungary. Now his work is regularly performed throughout Europe and *Tales from the Vienna Woods* is generally regarded as his masterpiece.

Horváth's reputation in Britain was enhanced in 1977, when Christopher Hampton's translation of the play was premièred at the National Theatre, in a production directed by Maximilian Schell. It was only in the 1980s that the British theatre began to recognize his true worth and even today revivals of his work are rare. Christopher Hampton's own play *Tales from Hollywood* entertainingly imagines Horváth among the palm trees of Los Angeles, rubbing shoulders with other brilliant central European refugees from Hitler.

Quotations from Ödön von Horváth, *Tales from the Vienna Woods*, tr. Christopher Hampton, Faber and Faber, 1977

Blood Wedding
(*Bodas de sangre*)
Federico García Lorca

1932, first performed 1933

> Historical and theatrical context

Spain enjoyed an outbreak of political and social liberalism in the early 1930s. Following the fall of the dictator Primo de Rivera in 1930, cultural and educational reform were in the air, as was a determination to drag this conservative, Catholic country into the modern world. This was cut short by the Spanish Civil War (1936–8) when, despite the best endeavours of an international movement of workers, artists and intellectuals, the fledgling Republic was defeated by Spanish Fascists, unopposed by the Western democracies but with the active support of Nazi Germany. Appalling atrocities were committed on both sides and General Franco's victory had consequences throughout Europe.

Poet, playwright, and theatre director Federico García Lorca (1898–1936), along with his friends the surrealist painter Salvador Dalí, the film-maker Luis Buñuel and the composer Manuel de Falla, was at the centre of Spain's cultural and social foment. He founded and was artistic director of the government-funded touring company, La Barraca, set up to tour the countryside with a company of student actors and bring the masterpieces of the Spanish Golden Age – Calderón, Lope de Vega and Cervantes – to the peasantry. With this theatre company, he developed a highly effective and uncluttered theatrical style, using gesture, dance, song and intense poetry.

As well as several volumes of poems (including the much admired *Gypsy Ballads*), Lorca's plays include *The Butterfly's Evil Spell* (1919), *The Shoemaker's Prodigious Wife* (1926), *Mariana Pineda* (1927), *The Love of Don Perlimplin* (1928), *The*

Public (1929), *When Five Years have Passed* (1929), *Yerma* (1934), *Doña Rosita the Spinster* (1935), *The House of Bernarda Alba* (1936) and *The Destruction of Sodom* (1936, private reading only and now lost).

Lorca was murdered by Franco's troops in Granada in August 1936 and his body was never found.

> *About the play*

Although the Granada-born Lorca came to be regarded as the leading Spanish poet–playwright of the twentieth century, he was very much a European writer influenced by the trends of his time. As a homosexual, his plays speak powerfully of individuals whose desires conflict with the forces of social convention. *Blood Wedding*, the first of his trio of Andalusian rural tragedies, is his masterpiece, the most accomplished integration of the poetic and the dramatic, the symbolic and the real, the lyrical and the concrete, and represents a distinctive theatrical breakthrough. He wrote it in the summer of 1932, while obsessively listening to a Bach cantata, as the first attempted military coup against the Republic was taking place.

Blood Wedding has its roots in an incident Lorca read of in a Madrid newspaper in which a young man ran off with a bride from Almería on the night before her wedding and was killed by the Bridegroom's cousin. Although, as Lorca's brother, Francisco, said, the characters in the newspaper 'have been converted into anonymous beings who possess a country's generic character', the realities of this story, with its financial greed and its sexual desire, its poverty and its violence, gave Lorca his inspiration.

Blood Wedding opens in the Bridegroom's home. His Mother is worried about his wish to marry a local girl. She is gripped by the desire to avenge her murdered husband and elder son ('A glorious man, an angel, his mouth like a flower, who goes out to his vines or his olives, to look after them, to care for them because they are his passed down to him from his fathers . . . And he never comes back') and she is opposed to the marriage ('Whenever I speak her name it's as if a stone hit me between the eyes'). A Neighbour soon confirms her worst suspicions: the girl used to have a lover, Leonardo, a member of the Felix family who murdered her menfolk.

The second scene is set in Leonardo's house, with his wife (the Bridegroom's cousin), their baby and his mother-in-law. The women sing a lullaby about a horse with a dagger of silver in his eye – which is soothing but heavy with symbolic inference. Leonardo has been spotted on the 'other side of the plain', and (in a highly sexual metaphor) has 'exhausted his horse'. The women know about Leonardo's passionate affair with the Bride. Soon word comes of the Bridegroom's wealth, and Leonardo is upset. The words of the lullaby go to the heart of it:

> Down by the river,
> Down by the river,
> Blood is pouring
> Stronger than the water.

The third scene takes place in the Bride's house. The Bridegroom and his Mother are visiting. The Bride's Father thinks the wedding is a good idea and they agree on a day. But the Bride can hardly disguise her reluctance, especially when a servant tells her that Leonardo had come visiting her on horseback at night.

Act Two starts early on the morning of the wedding. The Bride feels she is 'withering away', and speaks of 'Black clouds. An icy wind blowing, here, deep inside.' Suddenly Leonardo appears and confesses:

> What good did my pride do me – not seeing you, and knowing you were lying awake night after night. None! It only poured blazing coals over me. You think time heals and that walls shut away but it's not true.

And then, with great delicacy, songs and poetry, the guests arrive to take the Bride off to church. Leonardo and his wife are left in despair.

Before the wedding party, the Bride's Father and the

Bridegroom's Mother talk of the land, of children and of grandchildren. People dance and drink and appear to be happy. But suddenly they find out that Leonardo and the Bride have vanished: 'They've gone. They've run away. She and Leonardo, on a horse. Like a whirlwind. Her arms around him.' In words that could come from Shakespeare's *Romeo and Juliet*, the Bridegroom's Mother gives commands: 'The bloody days are back. Both families! You with yours. Me with mine. Get after them! Get after them!'

Act Three starts in the forest. Three woodcutters talk about what has happened:

> The Bridegroom will find them, moon or no moon. I saw
> him rush off. Like a raging star. His face the colour of
> ashes. He carried the fate of his family.

And when the moon ('a young woodcutter with a white face') rises, it speaks:

> Tonight there'll be blood
> To warm my cheeks.

But the moon disappears, an old Beggar Woman emerges out of the darkness:

> The coffins lie open.
> The white sheets are spread
> For heavy bodies
> With their throats cut.

The Bridegroom appears, bent on murder and revenge, but the Beggar Woman takes him off. Leonardo and the Bride appear and declare their passion for each other, but both know that he will have to die. The scene ends with one of the most mysterious stage directions in drama:

> Exeunt embracing. Moon appears, with blue light. Violins
> – two screams and violins stop. Beggar Woman appears,
> back to audience. Opens cloak, centre stage.

In the final scene of the play two girls dressed in blue are in a white room, winding skeins of red wool. They sing about the deaths of Leonardo and the Bridegroom. The Mother-in-Law advises the Wife to know nothing about what happened: 'On your bed / Put a cross of ashes / Where his pillow was.' The Beggar Woman tells the girls that the bodies are being brought back. The Bridegroom's Mother is mourning for her son ('Other mothers will go to their windows, lashed by the rain, looking for the faces of their sons. Not me'), when the Bride comes in to offer herself up to the Mother's fury, but also to explain her actions:

> I was a woman on fire. Inside and outside ablaze with agonies. Your son was a single drop of water that I hoped would give me children and health: the other was a dark big river, carrying torn-up trees, that brought me the sound of its reeds and its song. And I was going with your son, your little boy of cold water. But the other sent thousands of birds that stopped me and dropped frost into the wounds of this poor, shrivelling woman, this girl possessed by flames.

The Mother declares that the Bride is not to blame, that revenge would be pointless:

> What do I care about your death? What do I care about anything? Blessed be the wheat, because my sons lie under it. Blessed be the rain, because it wets the faces of the dead. Blessed be God, because he lays us all together, so we can rest.

And at the end all three women are left stating once again the bald, inescapable, tragic facts:

> With a knife
> With a small knife
> On an appointed day
> Between two and three in the morning
> Two men who were in love
> Killed each other.
> With a knife

Commentators have detected Ibsen, Shakespeare or even Euripides in the play's form and obsessions. Certainly J. M. Synge's *Riders to the Sea* (1904) had an influence on Lorca's depiction of stoical, maternal grief. Despite the play's uniquely Andalusian quality, there is something classical about this dazzlingly simple tale of two mismatched lovers in an unforgiving world being inexorably driven by their animal passions towards a fate which they are powerless to avoid.

> *In performance*

Blood Wedding had its première in Madrid's Teatro Beatriz on 8 March 1933, in a production directed by Lorca himself, and was immediately hailed as the author's most significant work to date. Its success in Spain was followed by a triumphal season in Buenos Aires, where Lorca was called 'the ambassador of Spanish culture in Latin America'. This was followed by productions in New York in 1935 and France in 1938. The play received its British première in 1947.

Recent British productions have included Communicado's Scottish-dialect production in 1988, Yvonne Brewster's multiracial version at the National Theatre in 1991 and Tim Supple's 1997 production at the Young Vic in Ted Hughes's remarkable translation. But *Blood Wedding* has proved notoriously elusive for British companies to pull off successfully.

Lorca's play has spawned versions in various other art forms: Carlos Saura's acclaimed flamenco film in 1981, a ballet (by the American Ballet Theatre) in 1953 and two operas.

Quotations from Federico García Lorca, *Blood Wedding*, tr. Ted Hughes, Faber and Faber, 1996

Murder in the Cathedral
T. S. Eliot

1935

> Historical and theatrical context

The mid-1930s saw an extraordinary flourishing of cultural activity throughout Britain and America, mostly in response to the alarming political and social developments in Europe. The Nazis passed the notorious Nuremberg laws in 1935, which were to provide the legal basis for Hitler's persecution of the Jews, while in Italy Mussolini's Fascist thugs were flexing their muscles. The ground was being laid for the Spanish Civil War (1936–1938), in which the struggle against Fascism was first waged and in which so many artists and intellectuals were to become involved.

The American-born Anglo-Catholic T[homas] S[tearns] Eliot (1888–1965) was not the first major poet to be attracted by the notion of reviving verse drama. Most of the Romantic poets – Wordsworth, Byron, Shelley, Keats and Tennyson (who wrote his own dramatic version of *Becket*) – had all experimented with it, with distinctly mixed results. The novelist Christopher Isherwood collaborated with the poet W. H. Auden on *The Dog Beneath the Skin* (1935) and *The Ascent of F6* (1936), left-wing plays very different from T. S. Eliot's Christian drama of sacrifice and individuality, but which similarly address public issues in dramatic verse.

By the time T. S. Eliot wrote *Murder in the Cathedral*, he was already established as a major poet. His poems include 'The Love Song of J. Alfred Prufrock' (1915), *The Waste Land* (1922) – widely regarded as his masterpiece – 'The Hollow Men' (1925), 'Ash-Wednesday' (1930) and *Four Quartets* (1935–42). He experimented with poetic dialogue in *Sweeney Agonistes* (1932) and dramatic choruses in *The Rock* (1934), a scenario for a pageant on behalf of London's churches. His later plays include *The Family Reunion* (1939), *The Cocktail Party* (1950), *The Confidential Clerk* (1954) and *The Elder Statesman* (1958). He was also the author of numerous influential critical essays – particularly on the Elizabethan and Jacobean dramatists – and his book of children's poetry *Old Possum's Book of Practical Cats* (1939) was the inspiration for the successful musical *Cats*.

> About the play

T. S. Eliot was commissioned by the Bishop of Chichester to write a play for the 1935 Canterbury Festival. It was Eliot's idea to dramatize the assassination of Thomas Becket, Archbishop of Canterbury, in his own cathedral on 29 December 1170. The story of the highly intelligent, politically involved Christian martyred by the state struck a chord. In searching for the appropriate form, Eliot drew on the Greeks – especially Aristophanes, Euripides and Aeschylus – more than Shakespeare. The most important influence, however, was the highly irregular, conversational verse found in the English medieval drama *Everyman*.

The influence of the Greeks is most evident in Eliot's use of a chorus of poor women, whose role is part expository, part amplification of thoughts, part changing colours and moods. At the start of the play, their function is to mediate between the audience – the non-believers – and the belief that is being dramatized. As the play goes on, they become increasingly involved. They also speak some of the greatest verse in the play:

> Since golden October declined into sombre November
> And the apples were gathered and stored, and the land
>   became brown sharp points of death in a waste of water
>   and mud,
> The New Year waits, breathes, waits, whispers in darkness.

On his return to Canterbury from Europe (where Becket has been undertaking negotiations between the Pope and the King), Thomas is confronted by four tempters. These are all succesfully overcome, but his murderers are on the way and the chorus can sense it:

> I have smelt them, the death-bringers, senses are quickened
> By subtle forebodings; I have heard
> Fluting in the night-time, fluting and owls, have seen at
>   noon
> Scaly wings slanting over, huge and ridiculous . . . I have
>   felt
> The heaving of earth at nightfall, restless, absurd. I have
>   heard
> Laughter in the noises of beasts that make strange noises:
>   jackal, jackass, jackdaw; the scurrying noise of mouse
>   and jerboa; the laugh of the loon, the lunatic bird.

The climax of the drama is reached when Thomas deliberately opens the door to his murderers:

> Unbar the door! unbar the door!
> We are not here to triumph by fighting, by stratagem, or
>   by resistance,
> Not to fight with beasts as men. We have fought the beast
> And have conquered. We have only to conquer
> Now, by suffering. This is the easier victory.
> Now is the triumph of the Cross, now
> Open the door! I command it. OPEN THE DOOR!

At which point Thomas is killed and there is a great chorus of lamentation:

> Where is England? where is Kent? where is Canterbury?
> O far far far far in the past; and I wander in a land of barren
>   boughs: if I break them, they bleed; I wander in a land
>   of dry stones: if I touch them they bleed.
> How can I ever return, to the soft quiet seasons?

After the murder, Eliot pulls off a tremendous theatrical trick: he has the four knights turn to the audience and ask us for our judgement. In many ways, these requests are astonishing and present the state in all its powerful rationalism.

They reach forward to the modern world in a startlingly attractive way and convincingly frame the criticism of Thomas as a 'monster of egotism'. Eliot's technique echoes Brecht's notion of *Verfremdung* (making the familiar strange) and as a result we look at the martyrdom afresh.

The Third Priest argues that Thomas's death has strengthened the church, which 'is fortified / By persecution: supreme so long as men will die for it.' and tells 'weak sad men' that:

> In the small circle of pain within the skull
> You still tramp and tread one endless round
> Of thought, to justify your action to yourselves,
> Weaving a fiction which unravels as you weave,
> Pacing forever in the hell of make-believe.

Eliot celebrates the refutation of normal life and insists on separation and sacrifice. If the play stands for a kind of political quiescence and the need for a ritualized blood sacrifice if society is to be renewed, it also expresses powerful wisdom:

> Go to vespers, remember me at your prayers.
> They shall find the shepherd here; the flock shall be
>   spared.
> I have had a tremor of bliss, a wink of heaven, a whisper,
> And I would no longer be denied; all things
> Proceed to a joyful consummation.

The play brilliantly dramatizes Eliot's anxiety about the individual and society and the role of the conscience in a world which is misguided and wrong. He also asks whether you should oppose that society or submit to your faith and become a sacrificial victim – an all too vivid subject for a writer of individuality and conscience in a dark and difficult time.

Whatever the play's political and religious convictions, at the heart of *Murder in the Cathedral* is Eliot's appropriation of the language and forms of Christian ritual and of the living drama of the Catholic mass (the play even includes a sermon – the weakest writing in it). What Eliot has written is not so much a play as a liturgy of martyrdom, devised to be enacted in the very cathedral where that martyrdom took place. The verse is successful because of its roots in liturgical verse and the play's brilliant dramatic structure – as in Aeschylus or Racine – allows for a remarkable level of concentrated focus. It is for his lyric and epic poetry that T. S. Eliot will above all be remembered; yet in a century whose drama was dominated by varieties of prosaic naturalism, Eliot's drama, and *Murder in the Cathedral* in particular, should take an honourable, if rather unusual, position.

> *In performance*

The first performance of the play took place in Canterbury Cathedral on 15 June 1935 as part of the Canterbury Festival. The producer (i.e. director) was E. Martin Browne and Becket was played by Robert Speaight. The play has been revived many times since, although not often professionally, and the film of the original stage production was the most frequently broadcast play on television in the 1940s and 1950s.

With some notable exceptions, by the end of the century the attempt to revive poetic drama had become very unfashionable. Never mind that poetic drama had dominated the two greatest periods in dramatic literature (the Greeks and Shakespeare): after the war, it came to be seen as quaint and incapable of reflecting the complex and prosaic realities of the modern world.

There is a debate about the contribution made by Eliot to the cause of poetic drama. While some see his sacramental tone as providing a useful blueprint, others detect a powerful streak of intellectual élitism which has prevented verse being taken seriously as an instrument of dramatic speech.

Quotations from T. S. Eliot, *Murder in the Cathedral*, Faber and Faber, 1935

Mother Courage and her Children
(Mutter Courage und ihre Kinder)
Bertolt Brecht

1939–41, first performed 1941, final draft 1949

> ## Historical and theatrical context

Bertolt Brecht (1898–1956) started writing *Mother Courage and her Children* in 1938, and completed the first draught shortly after Germany's invasion of Poland in 1939. It was one of the group of plays which Brecht wrote during the 'dark times' of the late 1930s and early 1940s while in exile in Scandinavia and America. Along with an acute sense of the horror of war, *Mother Courage* is informed by Brecht's Marxist view of war and Fascism as the logical outcome of capitalism.

The play is subtitled 'A Chonicle of the Thirty Years War' and in it Brecht drew on Schiller's *Wallenstein* and other eighteenth-century German historical dramas, as well as Shakespeare. Another important influence was Jaroslav Hašek's novel *The Good Soldier Schweyk*. The original German is tough but poetic, vernacular but never crude, the language of Luther's Bible, as well as of German folk-songs and fairy-tales, and is almost impossible to translate. The play's visual imagery is inspired by the paintings of Breughel and Hieronymous Bosch. Its dramatic technique is the culmination of Brecht's many experiments throughout the 1920s and 1930s, and with its episodic structure, inserted songs and deliberate open-ended jaggedness, the play is the summation of Brecht's notion of 'epic theatre'.

Brecht's other plays include *Baal* (1922), *The Threepenny Opera* (1928), *The Rise and Fall of the City of Mahagonny* (1928–9), *The Mother* (1930–1), *Fears and Miseries of the Third Reich* (1935–8), *The Resistible Rise of Arturo Ui* (1941), *The Good Person of Szechwan* (1938–41), *Mr Puntila and his Man*

Matti (1940–1), *Schweyk in the Second World War* (1941–5), *The Caucasian Chalk Circle* (1948), and *The Life of Galileo* (1937–9, 1945–7 and 1955–6). He also wrote some of the finest poetry in German, as well as numerous short stories, essays and diaries. His writings on the theatre are extensive and have proved extraordinarily influential.

> About the play

Anna Fierling (nicknamed 'Mother Courage') earns her living on the killing fields of the Thirty Years War, driving a cart from camp to camp, flogging boots and rum, sausages and pistols to the soldiers, striking bargains, lying and cheating, and sometimes even thriving. She is a formidable operator who can deal with anything that is put in her way. She is unsentimental, canny and shrewd. She is one of the 'little people', for whom religion and ideology are alien, who is simply trying to find a way of surviving. She lives off the war that surrounds her and she feeds it.

At the beginning of the play, Mother Courage is accompanied by her three children (all fathered by different men): her two sons, Swiss Cheese and Eilif, and her daughter, Kattrin, who is dumb. Swiss Cheese is the simple, honest one. Quite early on in the play he is given responsibility for a regimental cash box, which he apparently loses, and he is condemned to be shot. He could have been saved if Courage had not been haggling down the price of her cart. When his body is brought in for identification, Courage denies knowing him at all. Eilif is the brave one and is quickly recruited. He soon becomes a wartime hero for stealing cattle and is fêted by the general, but is eventually shot for committing the same crime in peacetime. Finally, Courage loses her beloved Kattrin, whom she always thought plain enough to avoid trouble, when in the climactic scene of the play, in an act of courageous folly, she climbs on to a roof and bangs away at a drum to warn a town of its imminent sacking and is shot for it. The last, and astonishing, image of this long and extraordinary play is Courage pulling her cart, all alone, striking up a brave song, still touting for business.

The challenge *Mother Courage* presents, for both audience and performer, is that Brecht has given us a character of tremendous complexity and asks us to be objective and critical of her. Towards the end of scene six, she speaks about how it is a 'long anger' that is needed, not a short one. This, she hints, is the anger which changes the world. But then, when business starts up again, she loses that insight and sets out again, trying to earn a living. What Brecht is asking is similar to the Christian notion of hating the sin but loving the sinner: we enjoy and admire Courage's toughness and shrewd wit, while at the same time despairing that she does not recognize the contradiction she embodies. War is created and sustained by human beings; it is not an impersonal fact of life. Brecht is trying to get us to see that and face its challenge head on.

The greatness of the play, however, and the reason why it is one of the enduring masterpieces of the century, lies in something more than its astonishingly well-drawn central character and its passionately held insights. For, like Shakespeare, Brecht's historical imagination, coupled with his startling dramatic technique, creates the illusion of an entire world caught in a terrifying and endless struggle between two sets of interchangeable masters, disguising themselves as different religions. In *Mother Courage*, Brecht has written a twentieth-century riposte to the classical drama of kings and queens, a history written 'from the bottom up', and he focuses in detail on real people – soldiers, peasants, tradesmen, prostitutes and even generals – finding ways of feeding themselves and surviving the insanity which surrounds them. His characters are often distorted and dehumanized by the world in which they live, but they are nevertheless astonishingly true to life and recognizable.

In his extensive notes on the play, Brecht said that *Mother Courage* was meant to show:

that in wartime the big profits are not made by little people. That war, which is a continuation of business by other means, makes the human virtues fatal even to their possessors. That no sacrifice is too great for the struggle against war.

Brecht firmly believed that it was not good enough to observe the world, but it was necessary to change it, and the restrained edginess of this note goes to the core of his intentions. What it does not express is the extraordinary realism of Brecht's treatment.

This realism tolerates no heroism and Brecht's analysis is merciless and unsentimental. At times, his vision can seem too harsh and uncompromising, too difficult for an audience to be involved in the kind of 'complex seeing' which he was so keen to promote. But when set against the background of a world collapsing into barbarism and war, *Mother Courage* is an extraordinary vision of the darkest moment of a very dark century. If the twentieth century has seen the worst warfare in history, Brecht's play is drama's greatest plea for peace and against Fascism.

> *In performance*

Mother Courage received its première in Zürich in April 1941, with Therese Giehse in the title role. Although Brecht was not able to see the production, he was unhappy with the critical response to the play as a 'Niobe-like tragedy' (in which the loss of the children is somehow 'natural' and 'inevitable') and he rewrote several scenes for his own production at the Deutsches Theatre in Berlin in January 1949. This great production, with his wife Helene Weigel in the title role, in Theo Otto's design and with Paul Dessau's extraordinary music, was the finest example of Brecht's own theatre practice and was seen all over the world, establishing at a stroke his international reputation. Despite (or perhaps because of) the dominance of this production (whose details were lovingly recorded in a *Modellbuch*), the play has become one of the twentieth century's greatest classics and has been performed throughout Europe and America. However, no production has come close to the astonishing emotional power and theatrical flair of Brecht's own.

Brecht's extensive theoretical writings are easily misinterpreted. His insistence that the audience should not 'hang up its brains with its coats in the cloakroom' has sometimes resulted in productions which are coldly analytical and fail to engage with the complex human beings which lie at the heart of his best work. Brecht's Marxism engaged in the contradictions and distortions imposed on human beings by the world in which they live. He wanted his work to provoke the desire that the world could and should be changed. His famous 'alienation' effect was an attempt to find a way to provoke his audience into understanding. But without the pleasures of poetry and feeling, such learning is impossible.

The English-language première was directed by Joan Littlewood for Theatre Workshop in 1955, with herself in the title role. Other notable British productions include Bill Gaskill's National Theatre production in 1965 with Madge Ryan as Courage, Howard Davies' production of Hanif Kureishi's version for the Royal Shakespeare Company in 1984 with Judi Dench, and Jonathan Kent's Royal National Theatre production of David Hare's translation with Diana Rigg (1995). The Glasgow Citizens' Theatre did a famous production in which the cart was a beaten-up car, and in the United States there have been versions which have set the play during the American Civil War.

Although respected in the English-speaking theatre, the play has never been a box-office hit, and the size of the cast, as well as the demands of the piece itself, makes revivals in Britain and America less and less common. It is still regularly performed in France and Germany.

Quotations from Bertolt Brecht, *Mother Courage*, tr. John Willett, Methuen, 1980

Long Day's Journey into Night
Eugene O'Neill

1939–40, first performed 1956

> Historical and theatrical context

In 1940, America's attitude to the war in Europe was ambivalent. President Roosevelt described the US as the 'arsenal of
democracy' – ready to provide Britain with weapons and
equipment – while at the same time assuring his people that
the US would not be actively involved. All this was changed
by the Japanese attack on Pearl Harbour and the US declaration of war (December 1941), but 1940 was a moment of
isolation, in which the old world seemed to be descending
into darkness while America kept herself aloof.

On his deathbed, the Irish-American Eugene O'Neill
(1888–1953) exclaimed: 'born in a goddam hotel room and
dying in a hotel room'. The son of a successful touring actor,
much of O'Neill's childhood was spent on the road. As a
young man, he suffered from tuberculosis. His mother
became addicted to morphine following the loss of Eugene's
younger brother in a painful birth. Eugene visited New York's
low dives and brothels, drank heavily and lived in flophouses.
He was married three times and neglected his own children,
just as he himself had been neglected.

In his development as a dramatist, O'Neill rejected the
commercialism that had brought his father wealth but
unhappiness, and was influenced by Strindberg. His early
works were staged by the Provincetown Players on Cape Cod
and in Greenwich Village, where O'Neill pursued his theatrical experimentation with considerable success. More than
most dramatists, O'Neill had a complex relationship with
productions of his own work, which he often found disappointing.

O'Neill's nearly fifty plays include *The Hairy Ape* (1921), *Mourning Becomes Electra* (1929–31), *The Iceman Cometh* (1939) and *A Moon for the Misbegotten* (1943). He was awarded the Pulitzer Prize a record four times – for *Beyond the Horizon* in 1920, *Anna Christie* in 1921, *Strange Interlude* in 1928 and *Long Day's Journey into Night* in 1956 – and the Nobel Prize for Literature in 1936.

> *About the play*

Eugene O'Neill sent the manuscript of *Long Day's Journey into Night* to his wife, Carlotta, on their twelfth wedding anniversary:

> Dearest: I give you the original script of this play of old sorrow, written in tears and blood. A sadly inappropriate gift, it would seem, for a day celebrating happiness. But you will understand. I mean it as a tribute to your love and tenderness which gave me the faith in love that enabled me to face my dead at last and write this play – write it with deep pity and understanding and forgiveness for all the four haunted Tyrones.

This most autobiographical of playwrights drew directly on his own family experiences in fashioning his masterpiece.

Long Day's Journey is set in James Tyrone's summer house in 1912. He is a succesful sixty-five-year-old actor – robust and confident, but always anxious about money – who spends most of his life on tour. The house is stuffed full of books, mostly plays, all read and re-read. His wife Mary is highly strung and suffers from a mysterious illness.

The Tyrones have two sons. The elder one, Jamie, is an actor, but only gets work through his father ('I never wanted to be an actor. You forced me on to the stage'). He suffers from 'premature disintegration': 'You've thrown your salary away every week on whores and whiskey!' The younger son, Edmund, is sick, possibly dying, and displays an 'extreme nervous sensibility'. Delicate and frail, he works as a journalist and has a streak of political anarchism.

Act One opens just after breakfast. Mary is looking healthier than she has for a long time. But Edmund has been going to the same cheap doctor – Harker – as Mary saw when she was ill. Tyrone is angry with Jamie's profligacy and complains of his two sons' 'ingratitude'. Jamie blames his father's meanness for his mother's sickness. Mary nurses Edmund like a baby but regrets that 'no respectable parent will let their daughters be seen with [her sons].'

Act Two introduces Cathleen, a warm-hearted Irish maid. Mary has been resting after a sleepless night, and appears almost unnaturally well. But her bitterness will out:

> None of us can help the things life has done to us.
> They're done before you realize it, and once they're done
> they make you do other things until at last everything
> comes between you and what you'd like to be, and you've
> lost your true self for ever.

They all have a whiskey – 'the best of tonics' – and drink to 'health and happiness'. But Mary is in despair, and as they go into lunch Tyrone challenges her: 'For the love of God, why couldn't you have the strength to keep on?' The doctor confirms that Edmund has consumption, prompting Mary to say:

> And yet it was exactly the same type of cheap quack who
> first gave you the medicine – and you never knew what it
> was until it was too late! I hate doctors! they'll do any-
> thing – anything to keep you coming to them.

When she leaves, Jamie says: 'the cures are no damned good except for a while' and Tyrone adds: 'Yes that's the way the poison acts on her always. Every day from now on, there'll be the same drifting away from us until by the end of each night —'. Like us, perhaps, Tyrone has begun to lose patience:

> For God's sake don't dig up what's long forgotten. If
> you're that far gone in the past already, when it's only the

beginning of the afternoon, what will you be tonight?

It soon transpires that Mary gave birth to a child (significant-ly) named Eugene who died, and that Edmund was intended as his replacement. Since then, she has lost her faith and her way. When the men go into town she is left alone:

It's so lonely here. You're lying to yourself again. You wanted to get rid of them. Their contempt and disgust aren't pleasant company. You're glad they're gone. Then Mother of God, why do I feel so lonely?

By the start of Act Three, Mary has been to town to fetch the morphine to which she has become addicted. The fog has rolled in 'from the Sound and is like a white curtain drawn down outside the windows'. Mary looks back on her life ('I really did have a good health once, Cathleen. But that was long ago'), saying that as a young girl she wanted to be a pianist or a nun, but met Tyrone, a romantic matinée idol, and gave up all her dreams. But when she is alone she admits:

You were much happier before you knew he existed, in the Convent when you used to pray to the Blessed Virgin.

Tyrone and Edmund return drunk. Jamie is still out drinking and Mary blames her husband for his alcoholism. But she says that she still loves him, and they remember their wedding and her 'soft, simmering satin' gown. But as the night draws in and the whiskey flows, her bitterness intensifies. Edmund tells his mother that he will have to go to a sanatorium, say-ing Tyrone wants to take her 'baby' away from her. But Edmund puts his finger on it when he says 'All this talk about loving me – and you won't even listen when I try to tell you how sick [I am]'. Eventually the truth emerges: 'It's pretty hard to take at times, having a dope fiend for a mother!' A foghorn sounds, Edmund leaves, Tyrone returns with more whiskey and Mary breaks down, uncontrollably worried about Edmund's health. Cathleen announces dinner and Mary goes upstairs to take more morphine.

Act Four takes place at midnight and the fog is thicker than ever. Tyrone is drunk, as is Edmund, and he berates his son for profligacy: 'the poorhouse is at the end of the road, and it might as well be sooner as later'. Edmund has been on the beach, in the fog. He wanted to 'be alone with myself in another world where truth is untrue and life can hide from itself'. They exchange snippets of poetry, about drink and oblivion. And they talk about Jamie 'hiding in a Broadway hotel room with some fat tart'. All the time, they are worried about Mary coming down, 'nothing but a ghost haunting the past'. They play cards and Edmund rages at Tyrone's treatment of his mother and that he is going to be sent to a state Sanatorium rather than a private one. But Tyrone talks of the poverty of his own youth: 'It was in those days that I learnt to be a miser', as well as of the artistic compromises he has made. And Edmund talks personally, and poetically, about his experiences at sea ('I will always be a stranger who never feels at home').

Suddenly Jamie returns, 'drunk as a fiddler's bitch'. He has been to see 'Fat Violet' and is uproarious and vulgar. When Jamie refers to their mother in a song, Edmund punches him and Jamie confesses his violent jealousy of her love for his brother. Soon Tyrone appears, as does Mary, looking like Ophelia in 'the Mad Scene', carrying her wedding dress. She says she wants to be a nun. That is the only way she can find peace.

Long Day's Journey is not a perfect work. The autobiographical freight the characters are expected to carry can make it ponderous and repetitive, as if the writer needs to rehearse the emotions from every single angle. It is much too long and lacks real dramatic conflict. And yet this whiskey-soaked American tragedy has an extraordinary, almost novelistic power: massive, sombre and inevitable. In its poetic, Shakespearian heart, the play captures the long day's journey of life from sunlight and health into the twilight and gloom of sickness and death.

> *In performance*

When O'Neill finished writing *Long Day's Journey into Night*, he left it with his publishers, insisting that it was so autobiographical it should not be published until twenty-five years after his death and that it should never be performed. His third wife thought differently and let Yale University Press publish it and gave a licence for it to be performed abroad. The result was that the play did not receive its première until three years after O'Neill's death, on 10 February 1956 at the Royal Dramatic Theatre in Stockholm. The first American production was at the Helen Hayes Theater in New York on 7 November 1956.

The play received its London première on 24 September 1958, with Anthony Quayle and Gwen Ffrangçon-Davies as the parents and Ian Bannen and Alan Bates as the sons. The National Theatre staged the play in 1971 with Laurence Olivier and Constance Cumming, and in 1991 with Timothy West and Prunella Scales. It was also staged in the West End in 2000, with Jessica Lange and Charles Dance.

Long Day's Journey into Night was made into a film in 1962, directed by Sidney Lumet, with Katherine Hepburn and Ralph Richardson.

Quotations from Eugene O'Neill, *Long Day's Journey into Night*, Jonathan Cape, 1956

An Inspector Calls
J. B. Priestley

1945

> Historical and theatrical context

1945 was possibly the most momentous year of the twentieth
century. The celebrations following the total defeat of Nazi
Germany were darkened by the discovery of the concentra-
tion camps, and the price of Japanese surrender was the
dropping of atomic bombs on Hiroshima and Nagasaki. The
terrible cost of a world war was counted, and Europe in particular found itself exhausted and broke.

In Britain, to many people's surprise, the great wartime
prime minister Winston Churchill was heavily defeated in
the 1945 General Election, and Clement Attlee's reforming
Labour Government came to power on a large majority and
the promise of a more egalitarian Britain. This was the most
explicitly left-wing government in British history, whose lasting monument was the National Health Service.

The Yorkshire-born, lifelong Socialist J[ohn] B[oynton]
Priestley (1894–1984) led an extraordinarily productive life
in which he published more than one hundred and twenty
books and countless articles and essays. His many plays
include *Dangerous Corner* (1932), *Time and the Conways*
(1937), *I Have Been Here Before* (1937), *When We Are Married*
(1938) and *The Linden Tree* (1947).

> About the play

An Inspector Calls is a curious mixture of conventional thriller
(a 'whodunnit') and philosophical essay. It is set in 1912, in a
fictitious town in the North Midlands called Brumley
(Birmingham – 'Brum' – crossed with Burnley, perhaps?). It

features the blustering patriarch Arthur Birling and his frosty upper-class wife, Sybil. They have money, status (he used to be mayor and she is from a good family) and a comfortable home. They also have two children: a tearaway, hard-drinking son, Eric, and a nervous and rather foolish daughter, Sheila. At the start of the play, the family is celebrating Sheila's engagement to Gerald Croft, the son of local aristocrats. Over a cigar, Arthur tells Gerald that:

> In twenty or thirty years' time – let's say, in 1940 – your son or daughter might be getting engaged – and I tell you by that time you'll be living in a world that'll have forgotten all these Capital versus Labour agitations and all these silly little war scares. There'll be peace and prosperity and rapid progress everywhere.

Birling is drawn as a cartoon capitalist – domineering, antiintellectual, highly emotional and comically misguided. His family exhibits all the neurotic repression commonly associated with the English ruling class.

After dinner, the maid announces the unexpected arrival of Police Inspector Goole. Goole soon announces that he has come to investigate the suicide that day of a young working-class girl named Eva Smith. He has reason to believe that all the Birlings are in different ways implicated, but he is careful to interview them individually, showing the photograph of the girl to only one member of the family at a time. Step by step, he shows the connections: Arthur fired Eva Smith from his company because she was agitating for better pay; Sheila got her sacked from the shop she worked in because she looked prettier in a blouse she wanted to buy; Gerald met her after she had changed her name to Daisy Renton and made her his mistress, but eventually dropped her, after she had experienced the greatest happiness of her life; and Sybil refused to help her when she came to see her women's charity because she called herself 'Mrs Birling' and said she was pregnant by a drunken young lad of the upper class. When Eric returns at the beginning of Act Three, he knows that his turn is next. He freely admits that he got Eva Smith pregnant and that she turned down his offer to marry him, along with the fifty pounds he had stolen from his father's office.

Each of these allegations drives powerful wedges between father and son, girlfriend and boyfriend, husband and wife. They also expose the glaring hypocrisy at the heart of the family. The responses are different: Arthur is worried about his reputation (and the damage caused to his prospects of a knighthood); Sheila is struck down with guilt and is full of a sense of the rightness of the Inspector's role and of their impending doom; Gerald comes clean and gains, at least in Sheila's eyes, some kind of dignity (though she breaks off their engagement); Sybil is haughty and condescending but is finally forced into silence when she realizes the network of responsibility; and Eric is contrite.

The climax is reached in Act Three:

Inspector I don't need to know any more. Neither do you. This girl killed herself – and died a horrible death. But each of you helped to kill her. Remember that. Never forget it. (*He looks from one to the other of them carefully.*) But then I don't think you ever will. Remember what you did, Mrs Birling. You turned her away when she most needed help. You refused her even the pitiable little bit of organized charity you had in your power to grant her. Remember what you did.

Eric My God – I'm not likely to forget.

Inspector Just used her for the end of a stupid drunken evening, as if she was an animal, a thing, not a person. No, you won't ever forget.

Sheila I know I had her turned out of a job. I started it.

Inspector You helped – but didn't start it. (*Rather savagely, to Birling*) You started it. She wanted twenty-five shillings a week instead of twenty-two and sixpence. You made her pay a heavy price for that. And now she'll make you pay a heavier price still.

Birling Look, Inspector – I'd give thousands – yes, thousands –

Inspector You're offering the money at the wrong time, Mr Birling. No I don't think any of you will forget. Nor that young man, Croft, though he at least had some affection for her and made her happy for a time. Well, Eva Smith's gone. You can't do her any more harm. And you can't do her any good now, either. You can't even say 'I'm sorry, Eva Smith'.

Sheila That's the worst of it.

Inspector But just remember this. One Eva Smith has gone – but there are millions and millions and millions of Eva Smiths and John Smiths still left with us, with their lives, their hopes and fears, their suffering, and chance of happiness, all intertwined with our lives, with what we think and say and do. We don't live alone. We are members of one body. We are responsible for each other. And I tell you that the time will soon come when, if men will not learn that lesson, then they will be taught it in fire and blood and anguish. Good night.

If the tone of this can seem rather didactic, it is also a genuinely moving statement which has its roots in the action preceding it. But despite this, Goole is a problematic figure. In many ways insufficiently characterized, he is asked to play Nemesis and even the best actor cannot disguise this transparent function. It is as if Goole's effect on others matters more to Priestley than his motivation or individuality.

After his departure, the family are left appalled and divided and there is some speculation about whether Goole was an inspector at all. It is only when Gerald points out that they cannot be absolutely sure that Goole was referring to the same girl that their spirits are lifted, but so also is our understanding of Priestley's point – that even if it had been five different girls, the Birlings would still have had a responsibility to others in society. When Arthur eventually hears from the hospital mortuary that a girl called Eva Smith 'had died after swallowing some disinfectant', they are left in profound shock, wondering what the consequences will be.

An Inspector Calls has its faults. For all its concern with the search for truth in a corrupt society, it has few of the psychological nuances that make the plays of Ibsen or Tennessee Williams so remarkable, and as a political drama it feels rather watered down when set alongside Brecht or Arthur Miller. Its dramatic punch can feel hackneyed and the final section of the play – after the Inspector's departure – is particularly difficult to take. The notion of the innocent victim and the wicked family is too black and white and the play exhibits an almost Christian streak of moral evangelism which can feel very awkward. And yet in the discussion about the relationship between the individual and society and the reconstruction of civilized society following the barbarism of the mid-century ('public men have responsibilities as well as privileges'), *An Inspector Calls* stands as a dramatic provocation whose English cussedness gives it a strange and peculiarly compelling moral power.

> *In performance*

An Inspector Calls received its world première in Russian in Moscow in August 1945. Its English-language première took place in October 1946, with Harry Andrews as Gerald Croft, Alec Guinness as the young Eric Birling and Ralph Richardson as the Inspector. The play has been revived many times, in Britain and elsewhere, and is always popular.

Stephen Daldry's expressionist production for the Royal National Theatre (1993) became one of the theatrical phenomena of the 1990s. Many felt that Daldry had dusted down an old rep 'warhorse' and shown it in its true political and theatrical colours; others felt that the expressionist staging underlined some of the play's weaknesses. It certainly revived interest in a dramatist who had often been dismissed as second-rate.

Quotations from J. B. Priestley, *Time and the Conways and Other Plays*, Penguin, 1969

Men Should Weep
Ena Lamont Stewart

1947

> Historical and theatrical context

Ena Lamont Stewart (born 1912) was a product of the Red Clyde, Glasgow's powerful left-wing movement which emerged during the First World War, reached its apogee in the 1930s, survived the Second World War and ensures that to this day Glasgow is still the most consistently left-wing city in Britain.

Men Should Weep came directly out of the 'golden age' of plays produced by Glasgow's Unity Theatre (founded in 1941), an amalgamation of several amateur groups aimed specifically at working-class audiences. Robert McLeish's The Gorbals Story (1945) and George Munro's Gold in his Boots (1947) were other plays from this time which continued the pre-war tradition of social realism of Joe Corrie's mining classic, In Time o' Strife (1927). Grinding poverty has scarred much of Glasgow's proud but embattled history, and daily life in its notorious slums, especially the Gorbals, was the subject of these plays.

Despite the success of Men Should Weep (and to a lesser extent her earlier Starched Apron in 1945), Ena Lamont Stewart's subsequent playwriting career never took off. Her later plays included After Tomorrow (1956) and Business in Edinburgh (1970), but her career was blocked by changing theatrical fashion and what she called 'the male chauvinism rife in Scottish theatre'. In 1982 she recalled: 'I've been accused of being a Communist and a man-hater in my time, yet all I was doing was writing about real people as I saw them.' Later generations of female Scottish playwrights owe much to her pioneering first steps.

> *About the play*

Men Should Weep is a *tour de force* of working-class naturalism.
Written in a dense and brilliantly observed Glaswegian dialect,
its three acts take place in the kitchen of John and Maggie
Morrison's tenement in the East End of Glasgow amid the
dire poverty and unemployment that racked the city in the
1930s. The subject is domestic: the way men and women in
their different ways find ways of surviving such deprivation.

Maggie has seven 'bairns' and the youngest, Bertie, is ill.
The others are hungry and unhealthy, the young ones riddled
with lice and filthy. Her oldest son, Alec, is well known to the
'polis' and her daughter Jenny is earning a reputation too.
Granny moans about being packed off to live with Maggie's
sister-in-law, Lizzie, and Maggie's own unmarried sister, Lily
(a 'spare hard-mouthed woman'), berates her for not keeping
up appearances and for living 'in this midden'. But Maggie is
battling through, doing what she can. It is poverty which is
the great enemy:

> Lily, money disnae stretch. Ye pit oot yer haun for yer
> change, and whit dae ye get? A coupla coppers. A ten
> shillingy note's no a ten shillingy note ony langer. I dinna
> ken whit they dirty rotten buggers in Parliament aree
> daein' wi ma money, but they're daein somethin.

Maggie's husband John is unemployed and spends most of his
time in the library. Their nosy, self-righteous neighbours tell
them (with some pleasure) that all the houses on Alec's street
have collapsed and the Morrisons are forced to take him in,
along with his young, sexually provocative wife, Isa. When Alec
turns up drunk, arguing with Isa, John blames himself for it: 'A
man's got nae right tae bring weans intae the world if he canna
provide them'. In a rare moment of calm, John and Maggie
share a tin of beans that was meant for the children, but when
Jenny comes in, with a 'couple of gins' inside her and announces
that she has a new job and is leaving home, they are devastated.

Act Two opens with the tight-fisted Lizzie coming to col-
lect Granny. Lily, Alec and Jenny all turn up, as do two
removal men, and in a scene rich with Glaswegian wisecracks,
Granny departs. But Maggie has been at the hospital. Bertie
has tuberculosis. When Jenny leaves, John expresses the
heart of the play:

> Christ Almight! A we've din wrong is tae be born intae
> poverty! Whit dae they think this kind o life dis tae a
> man?

Isa and Alec's marriage is in difficulty and they have resorted
to crime. Maggie comes in, exhausted from work, and is confronted by Alec's self-pity. But when Isa appears, she slaps her
and calls her a slut and then rows with John, saying that he
has done nothing to clean the place up ('Jessie business' he
calls it). But to her surprise, John takes Isa's side and Maggie
storms off, leaving Isa flirting with her husband. When
Maggie returns, she suddenly 'collapses in a storm of weeping' triggered by the state of Edie's shoes. As the curtain falls,
Maggie, with typical humour, sums up the way she feels:

> Heartburn! I wonder whit kind of a male idiot called indi-
> gestion heartburn? Ma Goad? I could tell him whit heart
> burn is! Ma Goad! Couldn't I no!

Act Three is set on Christmas Day. Maggie is determined to
make it special: 'This is the first Christmas I've had a decent
job for ten year; it's gonna be the best'. She is wearing a new
dress, the flat has been decorated, Ernie has got new football
boots and they have bought a 'wireless'. John has got a job at
last and has bought her a dashing red hat. They all have tea
and cakes to celebrate. Even Lily has softened and has helped
with stockings for the little ones. But deep down Maggie is in
despair: the hospital will not allow Bertie home until they are
satisified conditions there are more hygienic.

Isa has managed to find a place for Alec and her to live, and
they manage to repair their marriage. Jenny returns, well
dressed and obviously happy, and offers to give her mother

the money she has saved, to make a down-payment on a clean, rented flat near a park. John is appalled and his masculine pride as breadwinner and father is affronted. In his eyes, Jenny is 'living in sin' with her 'fancy man' and he rejects her money:

> If ye'd earned it, I'd be doon on ma knees tae ye. But ye're no better than a tart. We tried wur best tae bring you up respectable so's ye could marry a decent fella.

Lily, sometimes harsh in her judgements but always fiercely loyal to Maggie, will not let the opportunity go: 'It's no for *you*!' she says to John, 'It's for Bertie an the ither weans, ye pig-heided fool!' Maggie suddenly finds her voice, berating John for his double-standards:

> Whit wis I, when we was coortin, but *your* tart?. . . Aye, I wis your whore. An I'd nae winnins that I can mind o. But mebbe it's a right being a whore if ye've nae winnins.

She accepts the money and rebukes herself for having been so hard on John. But the light of optimism and hope is in her eyes and she will not be denied: 'Four rooms, did ye say, Jenny. Four rooms. Four rooms . . . an a park forbye! There'll be flowers come the spring!'

A better way of living is possible, *Men Should Weep* seems to imply, even in conditions of terrible poverty, if only we can get beyond ignorance and division. The play's depiction of the courage, humour and inventiveness of people living in near-destitution gives that socialist optimism a rare and compelling integrity.

> *In performance*

Men Should Weep was premièred on 30 January 1947 in the Glasgow Athenaeum, in a production directed by Robert Mitchell. It was an immediate success and subsequently played in Edinburgh, London and Glasgow's Theatre Royal, before disappearing from view. It was revived in 1982 as part of 7:84's 'Clydebuilt' Season of largely forgotten Scottish working-class plays. Giles Havergal's further revival for the Glasgow Citizens in 1998, in a theatre situated in the old Gorbals, showed that despite the waning of Scottish Communism, *Men Should Weep* could still resonate with a new generation.

Quotations from Ena Lamont Stewart, *Men Should Weep*, 7:84 Publications, 1983

The Maids
(*Les Bonnes*)
Jean Genet

1946/7, first performed 1947, revised 1954

> *Historical and theatrical context*

Following the Liberation in 1944, France was anxious to rebuild its future and put its recent, harrowing past behind it. The countryside was poor, industry was in ruins and morale was shattered. France's total defeat in 1940, the widespread French collaboration with the Nazis and her minor role in the defeat of Germany felt like a national disgrace. The United States launched the Marshall Plan in 1947 to help Europe rebuild its shattered infrastructure, but France – dominated by the Catholic Church and politically unstable – was still reeling from the Second World War.

Against this bleak background, the anti-establishment, blatantly erotic plays of Jean Genet (1910–86) – thief, prostitute, homosexual and poet – came as an explosion. Like the visionary Antonin Artaud, Genet was looking for a fluid and ritualistic form of drama such as existed in the oriental theatre. The French theatre, steeped in seventeenth-century classicism, was outraged as much by Genet's aesthetic daring as by his critiques of power and his amorality. But Genet became the darling of the left-wing intelligentsia and was dubbed 'Saint Genet' by the existentialist writer and philosopher Jean-Paul Sartre. When Genet was condemned to life imprisonment in 1948 for ten convictions for theft, Sartre's and Jean Cocteau's campaign led to a presidential pardon.

Abandoned by his working-class mother, reared by foster parents and sent to a reformatory at the age of ten, having been wrongly labelled a thief, Genet decided, in existentialist fashion, to become what he had been accused of being: a criminal. Always a champion of the underdog (prisoners, the Black Panthers and Palestinians among others), his politics proved no less influential than his literary achievements.

Genet's other plays include *Deathwatch* (1946), *The Balcony* (1956), *The Blacks* (1958) and *The Screens* (1961). His writings include *Our Lady of the Flowers* (1944), *Querelle of Brest* (1947), *The Thieves' Journal* (1949), three screenplays and the ballet scenario, *Adame Miroir* (1948). He also produced a film, *Un Chant d'Amour* (1950), with Jean Cocteau.

> About the play

The Maids takes place in a claustrophobic, flower-strewn, Louis-Quinze bedroom. Claire and Solange are sisters. In what is obviously a regular ritual, they take it in turns to play at being their 'Madame', wear her gorgeous clothes and order each other about. At the beginning, Claire, the younger, more highly strung one, is leading: 'When will you understand that this room is not to be sullied? Everything, yes, everything that comes out of the kitchen is spit!' she shrieks at Solange, the older, more dominant one, who is now playing the submissive 'Claire'. As much as 'Madame' insults and humiliates 'Claire', so 'Claire' in turn insults 'Madame', teasing her about her lover (Monsieur), who is in prison (as a result of incriminating letters they have sent to the police). 'The ceremony' is distinctly sado-masochistic, lush with eroticism and religious overtones. It also enacts the ambivalence they feel towards Madame – whom they both adore and want to see dead. They also keep stepping in and out of character and the audience is never quite sure who is playing what, when.

At one point Claire fantasizes about how she will share in Monsieur's glory as he is 'led from prison to prison'. At another, Solange speaks of how Madame's suffering has transfigured her:

> When she learned that her lover was a thief, she stood up to the police. She exulted . . . Did you see it? Her grief

sparkling with the glint of her jewels, with the satin of her gowns, in the glow of the chandelier!

Eventually, these fantasies reach their climax, when 'Claire' (Solange in reality) advances on 'Madame' (Claire) in order to strangle her. Suddenly an alarm clock sounds, the signal that the real Madame is about to return and the game must end. But they still have time to tease each other about their lovers and lament the opportunities they have missed to kill Madame. The phone rings. It is Monsieur; he has been released on bail by the judge and is waiting for Madame. The maids are terrified that their betrayal will be discovered.

Both are near to breaking-point. 'I can't stand it any more,' says Claire, 'I can't stand my hands, my black stockings, my hair.' 'I want to help you. I want to comfort you', replies Solange, 'but I know I disgust you. I'm repulsive to you. And I know it's because you disgust me. When slaves love one another, it's not love.' We come to realize that their games are a form of escapism from a horrible reality. They are determined to liberate themselves by poisoning Madame's camomile tea.

With the arrival of the real Madame, the tone changes. She is younger than the maids, more beautiful, arrogant and capricious. She can be both cruel and kind. Patronizingly, she offers the maids her cast-off dresses and furs; just as quickly, she takes them back. The maids shrivel and become obsequious in her presence. Madame notices the phone is off the hook and the maids are forced to tell her that Monsieur is waiting for her in a bar. Solange is sent to find a taxi while Claire goes to prepare the tea. When she returns, she tries to persuade Madame to drink it, but every device fails and Madame leaves.

Claire and Solange are in despair. Their only comfort is to return to their rituals. The sense of transgression is heightened by Solange insisting they perform in semi-darkness. This frightens Claire, who believes they are being watched. 'Let's get right into the transformation,' urges Solange.

Claire appears in Madame's white dress and Solange is dazzled. As 'Madame' she pours out a torrent of insults against servants. Meanwhile, Solange as 'Claire' takes a whip and forces 'Madame' to submit. Claire can feel Solange getting carried away and cries out for help. But Solange points out that no one can hear her yells, until finally Claire protests that she is ill and Solange leads her into the kitchen.

This time, it seems, Solange has killed Claire. She fantasizes about her new role as a criminal, her elevation in the eyes of the world, her seduction by the hangman as she climbs to the gallows. She has a vision of a procession of servants coming to watch her. At which point the door opens and Claire walks in. She insists on assuming her role as 'Madame' and drinking the cup of tea prepared for the real Madame. It is Solange's turn to see the danger and call a halt to the role-playing. But Claire persists. She urges Solange to be strong and keep 'us both alive'. She drinks the tea and dies; in her death she achieves liberation and, symbolically, eternal union with her sister. Solange fantasizes about it:

> She rings the bell. The porter yawns. He opens the door.
> Madame goes up the stairs. She enters her flat – but,
> Madame is dead. Her two maids are alive: they've just
> risen up free, from Madame's icy form. All the maids were
> present at her side – not they themselves, but rather the
> hellish agony of their names. And all that remains of them
> to float about Madame's airy corpse is the delicate per-
> fume of the holy maidens which they were in secret. We
> are beautiful, joyous, drunk, and free!

Based on the real-life, gruesome murder of a mother and daughter by their two maids in Le Mans in 1933, the play broke new ground in its use of lush, heightened prose and ritualized role-playing. Genet used specific details from the original incident, but the fluctuating relationship between the sisters, and with Madame, came to represent larger metaphors – the duality of the human psyche, a class-ridden French society and sexual ambiguity.

Like all Genet's plays, *The Maids* has sometimes been dismissed as an overheated gay fantasy. But that is to underestimate a play which, with its examination of class, criminality, desire and power relationships, has proved to be one of the most resilient texts of twentieth-century drama.

> *In performance*

The Maids was first performed in April 1947 at the Théâtre de l'Athenée in Paris, and became Genet's most successful play. Written at the request of Louis Jouvet, one of France's greatest actors and directors, the text used was a modified version of Genet's original. Graphic displays of taboo subjects such as sado-masochism and incestuous lesbianism left its first audiences stunned. Genet is thought to have written five versions of the play, two of which are missing. The standard English translation is Bernard Frechtman's, based on the text used in the 1954 revival by Tania Balachova, and said to be closer to Genet's original intentions than the one used by Jouvet. Martin Crimp wrote a fresh and colloquial version of the play in 1999.

The Maids has often been played by three men (Genet's preferred mode). It was turned into an opera by John Lunn in London in 1998 and retold by American dramatist Wendy Kesselman as a study in the suffocating conformity of French bourgeois life, *My Sister in This House*, in 1981.

The mime and dance artist Lindsay Kemp made a film, *La Ceremonie*, inspired by *The Maids* in 1999.

Quotations from Jean Genet, *The Maids*, tr. Bernard Frechtman, Faber and Faber, 1963

Waiting for Godot
(*En Attendant Godot*)
Samuel Beckett

1948–9, first performed 1953

> Historical and theatrical context

Samuel Beckett (1906–89) wrote *Waiting for Godot* in Paris in the late 1940s, and the moral despair which was the legacy of the Second World War lies at the heart of his dramatic masterpiece. Beckett had taken part in the French Resistance and the play's powerful sense of anonymous threat may owe something to that experience. The late 1940s also saw a new international awareness, which is apparent in the play's multinational 'universality'.

The philosophical background to *Waiting for Godot* was the existentialism dominant in French thinking at the time – particularly in the work of Jean-Paul Sartre and other avant-garde figures. But equally important was Beckett's own use of literary influences: James Joyce, Dante, the Bible and St Augustine, as well as the patter of Irish blarney, popular song, vaudeville and gallows humour. Beckett subtitled the play a 'tragicomedy in two acts', and the fusion of the tragic and the comic, the dignified and the grotesque, the formal and the vernacular, runs right through it.

By the time he wrote *Waiting for Godot* (the play was originally written in French) Beckett was well regarded, if largely in avant-garde literary circles, and was working on his great trilogy of novels: *Malloy*, *Malone Dies* and *The Unnameable* (1951–3). *Waiting for Godot*, however, was his first serious foray into drama. Part of his declared motivation was commercial – he was in dire financial straits – and the play's success came to provide Beckett with a degree of financial security for the rest of his life. It also provided him with a relief from the exhaustion of the Trilogy. The critical success of *Waiting for Godot* decided the direction of Beckett's dramatic career. His later works develop from what he discovered then: they refine it, intensify it, strip it down to its bare and tragic essentials. With *Waiting for Godot*, Beckett found his dramatic voice.

Beckett's subsequent plays include *All That Fall* (1956), *Endgame* (1957), *Krapp's Last Tape* (1958), *Happy Days* (1961), *Eh, Joe* (1967), *Not I* (1973), *Footfalls* (1976), *A Piece of Monologue* (1979), *Rockaby* (1980) and *Ohio Impromptu* (1981). His many novels include *More Pricks Than Kicks* (1934), *Murphy* (1938), *Watt* (1953), *How It Is* (1964), *Imagination Dead Imagine* (1966), *For To End Yet Again* (1975), *Company* (1979), *Ill Seen Ill Said* (1982) and *Worstword Ho* (1983). Beckett was awarded the Nobel Prize for Literature in 1969, and is considered by many to be the greatest writer of the twentieth century.

> *About the play*

Waiting for Godot has been described as a drama of inaction, in which 'nothing happens, twice'. Superficially, this summarizes the play well: its two acts share the same setting ('A Country Road. A Tree.'), occur at the same time of day ('Evening'), and share the same *dramatis personae*. It also misses the whole point of the play, which is a comic dramatization of anguish and of the possibility, however hard, of surviving it.

The play features two tramps, Estragon and Vladimir. They are bored, hungry and lost. To pass the time, they bicker with each other, joke, talk about their lives and abuse each other both physically and verbally, like two clowns in the circus ring or a music-hall double act. It transpires that they are waiting for someone. They are waiting for Godot:

Estragon Let's go.

Vladimir We can't.

Estragon Why not?

Vladimir We're waiting for Godot.

Estragon (*despairingly*) Ah! (*Pause*) You're sure it was here?

Vladimir What?

Estragon That we were to wait.

Vladimir He said by the tree. (*They look at the tree*) Do you see any others?

Estragon What is it?

Vladimir I don't know. A willow.

Estragon Where are the leaves?

Vladimir It must be dead.

Estragon No more weeping.

And so on.

Half-way through Act One, two strangers arrive. At first, Estragon and Vladimir presume that one of them must be the long-awaited Godot. Instead, the all-powerful Pozzo is being led in by his helpless servant Lucky, who is being taken to the fair to be sold. Pozzo's world is full of luxuries: a stool, a bottle of wine, some chicken, a pipe, a vaporizer and, most importantly, a servant, all of which are beyond the wildest dreams of the two tramps. Pozzo is *someone* – formal, pompous, cruel, piglike – while Lucky has nothing at all and lives in a state of abject despair. At first, Lucky appears to be dumb, until, on command, he launches into a long and convoluted speech about the existence or otherwise of a personal God: a parody of useless philosophical discourse and of the futility of seeking after meaning in life.

In Act Two Beckett springs a surprise. Tragedy has struck: Pozzo enters blind and Lucky is dumb. When Vladimir first sees the blind Pozzo, he says (with a rhetorical hyperbole which is in itself a cause for celebration):

Let us not waste our time in idle discourse! Let us do
something, while we have the chance! It is not every day
that we are needed. Not indeed that we personally are
needed. Others would meet the case equally well, if not
better. To all mankind they were addressed, those cries for
help still ringing in our ears! But at this place, at this
moment of time, all mankind is us, whether we like it or
not. Let us make the most of it, before it is too late! Let
us represent worthily for once the foul brood to which a
cruel fate consigned us! What do you say? It is true that
when with folded arms we weigh the pros and cons we are
no less a credit to our species. The tiger bounds to the
help of his congeners without the least reflection, or else
he slinks away into the depths of the thickets.

Despite the ultimate futility of life, and an absurd world
which has no meaning and no aim, there is, it seems, the possibility of human connectedness.

But that optimism is shortlived and when Vladimir and
Estragon interrogate Pozzo about what has happened, he
replies, furiously:

Have you not done tormenting me with your accursed
time! It's abominable! When! When! One day, is that not
enough for you, one day, like any other, one day he went
dumb, one day I went blind, one day we'll go deaf, one
day we were born, one day we shall die, the same day, the
same second, is that not enough for you? (*Calmer*) They
give birth astride of a grave, the light gleams an instant,
then it's night once more.

Vladimir goes further:

Was I sleeping, while the others suffered? Am I sleeping
now? Tomorrow, when I wake, or think I do, what shall I
say of today? That with Estragon my friend, at this place
until the fall of night, I waited for Godot? That Pozzo
passed, with his carrier, and that he spoke to us? Probably,
but in all that what truth will there be? . . . He'll know

nothing. He'll tell me about the blows he received and I'll give him a carrot. (*Pause*) Astride of a grave and a difficult birth. Down in the hole, lingeringly, the gravedigger puts on the forceps. We have time to grow old. The air is full of our cries. But habit is a great deadener. At me too someone is looking, of me too someone is saying, he is sleeping, he knows nothing, let him sleep on (*Pause*). I can't go on!

At which point a Boy (who had briefly appeared in Act One) enters to say that Godot will come tomorrow. Vladimir may despair, but we have to go on. The last two lines catch the essence of the play:

Vladimir Well? Shall we go?

Estragon Yes, let's go. (*They do not move.*)

Waiting for Godot has a parable-like luminosity, which gives it a strange timelessness, and its startling central image of two tramps under a tree on a country evening as the sun is beginning to set can seem like something out of St Matthew's Gospel, or Shakespeare, or a folk-tale. But it also contains a startlingly contemporary image of post-war Europe. Rank cruelty is brought face to face with a glimpse of two tramps in a prelapsarian paradise. It is in the exquisite counterpointing of these four characters that the play's kaleidosocopic meaning lies.

In *Waiting for Godot* Beckett created something unique. Its language is fresh, vernacular, elegant and raw. Its dramatic structure is flawless. Its tone shifts from the desperate to the ecstatic with extraordinary nimbleness. When asked what it all meant, Beckett said, ambiguously, 'Why do people have to complicate a thing so simple I can't make it out?' Hailed by some as the greatest play of the twentieth century, *Waiting for Godot* speaks of the modern human condition in a way unparalleled by any other writer.

> *In performance*

En Attendant Godot received its world première in early January 1953 at a small Paris theatre, under the direction of Roger Blin. Its English-language première took place at the Arts Theatre, London, on 3 August 1955, in Beckett's own translation, in a production directed by Peter Hall. The notices were mostly negative, until Harold Hobson and Kenneth Tynan turned it into a major success, with Hobson describing a road-to-Damascus experience. The play has been performed all over the world ever since.

Waiting for Godot should be genuinely funny in the theatre, particularly when played without the kind of pious seriousness which sometimes disfigures productions. The play's meticulously scored rhythmic patterns and repetitions need to be caught and its innate theatricality needs to be released. One useful approach to the language (although not approved of by Beckett himself) is to see the wisecracking between Estragon and Vladimir as 'blarney' (it plays beautifully with Irish voices) and to cast and direct Pozzo and Lucky with some understanding of class relations. This places the philosophical talk within an appropriately articulate but vernacular voice, and allows the audience to see the realism behind Beckett's purpose.

Despite Beckett's own protestations that *Waiting for Godot* is a 'bad play', it has had a quite extraordinary influence on twentieth-century drama and literature. Even Brecht was known to have been interested in it, and the play gained a strange afterlife in the chapter on *King Lear* in Jan Kott's influential book *Shakespeare our Contemporary* (1965). All of Beckett's plays have now been filmed and were first screened in 2001.

Quotations from Samuel Beckett, *Waiting for Godot*, Faber and Faber, 1956

Death of a Salesman
Arthur Miller

1949

> *Historical and theatrical context*

Arthur Miller (born 1915) wrote *Death of a Salesman* in an America in which the courage and determination of the Second World War was being displaced by the all-important business of making money. The economy was booming and America stood pre-eminent in both military and economic terms. And yet the US was consumed with anti-Communist hysteria, fed by the USSR's development of its own atomic bomb, the formation of NATO and the Berlin airlift.

Talking about the American theatre of the 1940s, Miller has written:

> I thought the theatre a temple being rotted out with com-
> mercialized junk, where mostly by accident an occasional
> good piece of work appeared, usually under some disguise
> of popular cultural coloration such as a movie star in a
> leading role . . . it was also a time when the audience was
> basically the same for musicals and light entertainment as
> for the ambitious stuff and had not yet been atomized, as
> it would be by the mid-fifties, into young and old, hip and
> square, or even political left and middle and right. So the
> playwright's challenge was to please not a small sensitized
> supporting clique but an audience representing, more or
> less, all of America.

It is the sense that in his great plays Miller is writing modern tragedies for an entire nation that makes them so startling; tragedies in which the hero is an ordinary man and the forces that bring him down are the stuff of everyday life.

Arthur Miller's other plays include *The Man Who Had All*

the Luck (1944), *All My Sons* (1947), *The Crucible* (1953), *A View from the Bridge* (1955), *After the Fall* (1964), *The Price* (1968), *The Archbishop's Ceiling* (1977), *The American Clock* (1980), *The Ride Down Mount Morgan* (1991), *The Last Yankee* (1993), *Broken Glass* (1994) and *Mr Peter's Connections* (2000). His screenplays include *The Misfits* (1961) for his then wife Marilyn Monroe, and *Playing for Time* (1980). His autobiography, *Timebends*, appeared in 1987.

> About the play

Arthur Miller's first hit (*All My Sons*) was written under the acknowledged influence of Ibsen and a naturalistic form and a realistic time scheme are part of its power. But with *Death of a Salesman* Miller was interested in trying out something new:

> *All My Sons* had exhausted my lifelong interest in the Greco-Ibsen form, in the particular manner in which I had come to think of it. Now more and more the simultaneity of ideas and feelings within me and the freedom with which they contradicted one another began to fascinate me.

In *Death of a Salesman*, this 'simultaneity' allowed Miller to concentrate an entire life into twenty-four hours, with memories and anxieties flooding the protagonist's brain, leading inevitably to the final crisis. Interestingly, Miller's original title was *The Inside of his Head*.

For all its formal innovation, *Death of a Salesman* tells a simple story. Willy Loman is a sixty-two-year-old travelling salesman, running up 80,000 miles a year on his car, working on commission and overstretched. His long-suffering wife Linda is worried:

> He drives seven hundred miles, and when he gets there no one knows him anymore, no one welcomes him. And what goes through a man's mind, driving seven hundred miles home without having earned a cent?

Willy is exhausted and keeps having accidents with the car.

Having discovered a rubber pipe in the basement, Linda is increasingly concerned that he might be trying to commit suicide.

Their two grown-up sons Biff and Happy have come home. Both are big strong men who have not made it in the world. Happy has a dead-end job and spends his time chasing girls. Biff cannot settle down, goes from job to job and is really only interested in working out west, on farms. Every time he comes home, he becomes locked in an old and unresolved struggle with his father.

The action starts at a moment of optimism in the family: the mortgage is nearly paid off and the boys are going to get a second chance, maybe set up in business together and 'lick the world'. Biff is going to visit rich Bill Oliver to see if he will invest in a new business selling sports clothes and Willy is going to talk to his boss Howard to see if he can get a desk-based job in New York. They are all caught up in the American dream: money is there to be made, there is justice on earth and everyone will get their due.

The men arrange to meet for a celebratory dinner that evening. When Howard refuses to give Willy the office-based job, Willy loses his temper and is fired. And when Bill Oliver does not recognize Biff, he storms off, stealing Oliver's pen. At the restaurant, Biff manages to tell the news to Willy, who is devastated. Meanwhile, Happy has met a couple of girls and the boys disappear into the night. When Linda discovers what has happened, she is furious and, in tones reminiscent of King Lear's charge of 'monstrous ingratitude', kicks the boys out of the house:

> You're a pair of animals! Not one, not another living soul would have had the cruelty to walk out on that man in the restaurant!

All this is laced with memories of better times, of Willy's childhood, of the days when he was known and respected throughout New England, of Biff and Happy as two young boys and of Willy's brother Ben, who made money in the past ('when I walked into the jungle, I was seventeen. When I walked out I was twenty-one. And, by God, I was rich!'). It is part of the greatness of the play that these flashes of optimism, these glimpses of a better world, most touchingly caught in Linda's devotion to her husband, stand out against a bleak and merciless world, in which money is the measure of all things and success the goal to which everyone aspires. And there is pain: memories of Willy's adulterous affair, as well as conversations with Charley the neighbour, who is doing so well that he lends Willy money and whose son Bernard is now a Washington lawyer.

When the dreams have finally collapsed, Willy decides to kill himself to get an insurance pay-off for Linda and to help set up the boys. This is his final heroic act: the last thing he can sell is himself. He declares: 'A man can't go out the way he came in, Ben, a man has got to add up to something.' Willy has predicted that his 'funeral will be massive', but in the play's moving last section, entitled *Requiem*, we are told that nobody other than the family was there.

Death of a Salesman exhibits considerable technical skill: sophisticated time shifts, complex storytelling techniques and a fine musical structure. The play is written in a simple, beautifully heard New York dialect, which at its greatest is the poetic voice of the common man. In a debate about the stature of the 'tragic hero', Miller wrote:

> I had not understood that these matters are measured by Greco-Elizabethan paragraphs which hold no mention of insurance payments, front porches, refrigerator fan belts, steering knuckles, Chevrolets, and visions seen not through the portals of Delphi but in the blue flame of the hot-water heater.

In *Death of a Salesman*, Miller has written one of the defining plays of the twentieth century. It goes to the heart of American capitalism and shows its effect on a real family – the pressure to be successful and surround yourself with material well-being, the treadmill of repayment, the alienation from nature and the meaninglessness of a lonely death. In Willy

Loman, Miller has drawn a tragic figure, contradictory and true, whose death carries with it all the 'pity and terror' of classical tragedy, but whose life is set in the everyday modern world which we all inhabit. As his wife says:

> Willy Loman never made a lot of money. His name was never in the paper. He's not the finest character that ever lived. But he's a human being, and a terrible thing is happening to him. So attention must be paid. He's not to be allowed to fall into his grave like an old dog. Attention must be finally paid to such a person.

> In performance

Death of a Salesman was premièred on 10 February 1949, at the Locust Street Theatre in Philadelphia in a production directed by Elia Kazan. Miller reported on it:

> As sometimes happened later on during the run, there was no applause at the final curtain of the first performance. Strange things began to go on in the audience. With the curtain down, some people stood to put their coats on and then sat again, some, especially men, were bent forward covering their faces, and others were openly weeping. People crossed the theatre to stand quietly talking with one another. It seemed forever before somone remembered to applaud, and then there was no end to it.

Although the play was a critical success, it was also regarded as a piece of Communist propaganda, with one woman, so Miller reported, calling it 'a time bomb under American capitalism'. Miller responded by saying:

> I hoped it was, or at least under the bullshit of capitalism, this pseudo-life that thought to touch the clouds by standing on top of a refrigerator, waving a paid-up mortgage at the moon, victorious at last.

Death of a Salesman was premièred in London in July 1949. In

1983 Miller directed his own production of the play in Beijing, amidst China's increasing embrace of capitalism. The play was made into a film in 1951, with a fine central performance from Fredric March, and has been produced, usually to great acclaim, in theatres all over the world.

Quotations from Arthur Miller, *Plays: One*, Methuen, 1988; *The Theatre Essays of Arthur Miller* Methuen, 1994; *Timebends*, Methuen, 1987

The Deep Blue Sea
Terence Rattigan

1950–1, first performed 1952

> *Historical and theatrical context*

By the time Terence Rattigan (1911–77) came to write *The Deep Blue Sea* at the age of forty, he was the undisputed king of a London theatre dominated by commercial predictability. His plays, whose careful, conventional structure he defended with a craftsman's pride, were written, as he said, to please a fictional Aunt Edna, who 'must never be made mock of, or bored, or befuddled, she must equally not be wooed, or pandered to or cossetted'. West End audiences, sunk in post-war austerity, wanted entertainment and Rattigan, with his consummately honed latter-day 'problem' plays, knew more than anyone else how to supply it.

Despite the emotional subtleties of many of his earlier plays, Rattigan was considered a successful lightweight. He came to be despised by the generation of dramatists who appeared in the mid-1950s and opposed all the values he embodied. But it is possible that 'the angry young men' had more in common with Rattigan than they realized, above all in their dislike of the intolerance and emotional restraint of the average English male. Like many homosexuals at the time (when homosexual acts were still illegal), Rattigan kept his sexuality a secret but expressed it, often in code, in his plays.

Terence Rattigan's other stage plays include *French Without Tears* (1936), *After the Dance* (1939), *Flare Path* (1942), *The Winslow Boy* (1946), *The Browning Version* and *Harlequinade* (1948), *Separate Tables* (1954), *Bequest to the Nation* (1970), *In Praise of Love* (1973) and *Cause Célèbre* (1977).

> *About the play*

The Deep Blue Sea had its roots in Rattigan's own experience. In 1949, he had fallen deeply in love with a young actor, Kenneth Morgan. But Morgan started seeing another man, the new relationship was not successful and Morgan took an overdose and gassed himself to death. Whether or not the rumour is true that Rattigan's first draft was about a gay man, Morgan's suicide provided Rattigan with a powerful opening image for his drama of the frustrated human heart.

As the play opens, Hester Collyer, a smart clergyman's daughter, has just tried to gas herself. She has left her barrister husband, Sir William Collyer, and is living with her lover, Freddie Page, a Battle of Britain veteran, now an alcoholic and unemployed test pilot, in a downmarket boarding-house in Ladbroke Grove – a far cry from her former Central London home. She is in despair at Freddie's failure to reciprocate the passion she feels for him.

Smelling gas, the other residents of the tenement break in and discover her. With admirable economy, Rattigan establishes their qualities: the kindly but no-nonsense caretaker, Mrs Elton; Philip and Anne Welch, the conventional young couple who live upstairs; and Mr Miller, the refugee ex-doctor. They discover an empty aspirin bottle and an envelope containing a suicide note. But Mr Miller soon brings Hester round. Meanwhile, in the absence of Freddie, Philip phones Collyer and tells him to come over. When pressed by Mrs Elton as to why she attempted suicide, Hester says:

> When you're between any kind of devil and the deep blue
> sea, the deep blue sea sometimes looks very inviting. It
> did last night.

When Collyer arrives, his conversation with Hester has all the intimacy and edginess of the estranged couple. Hester wants to know about their shared friends, but when he asks her why she left him, she rebukes him for talking to her as if she was in court. She admits that Freddie does not love her any more and Collyer comes close to asking her to return. Instead, Hester gives him one of her new paintings. Collyer leaves and moments later Freddie comes back. He has been away for the weekend, playing golf, spending money, meeting people who he thinks will give him some work. He hardly notices Hester's emotional state, but quickly realizes that he forgot her birthday. She deliberately lets him find her suicide note and as the curtain falls he starts to read it.

Act Two takes place that afternoon. Freddie is drinking whisky with his old RAF friend Jackie:

> My God – if all the men who forgot their wives' birthdays were to come home and find suicide notes waiting for them, the line of widowers would stretch from here to – to John o'Groats.

But Jackie suspects there must be 'something more' and Freddie admits that the physical passion he felt has gone. As he drinks, he becomes more maudlin, and rereads Hester's letter:

> The fault lies with whichever of the gods had himself a good laugh up above by arranging for the two of us to meet –

When Hester comes in, she tears up the note. She wants them to leave the flat because 'a man is coming' to buy one of her paintings. Freddie admits to Jackie that he is out of his depth:

> I hate getting tangled up in other people's emotions. It's the one thing I've tried to avoid all my life, and yet it always seems to be happening to me . . . Too many emotions. Far too ruddy many.

But Freddie has his sensitive side too: 'My sort never get a hearing. We're called a lot of rude names, and nobody ever thinks we have a case'.

Mr Miller comes in looking for Hester: his European

psychological insights are the opposite of the English repression he meets. Having seen Freddie leave, obviously drunk, Collyer arrives. Hester confesses:

> Lust isn't the whole of life – and Freddie is, you see, to me. The whole of life – and of death, too, it seems.

She explains how the affair started, while Collyer was playing golf. But Collyer also has his say:

> That this man you say you love is morally and intellectually a mile your inferior and has absolutely nothing in common with you whatever; that what you're suffering from is no more than an ordinary and rather sordid infatuation; and that it's your plain and simple duty to exert every effort of will you're capable of in order to return to sanity at once.

Much to their surprise, Freddie walks in. Collyer soon leaves, obviously upset at the state Hester is in, and Freddie tells her that he is going to South America to work as a test pilot. What is more, he is going to go alone, immediately. As Freddie says:

> I'm such a damn fool and that's been the trouble, or I should have done this long ago. That's it, you know. It's written in great bloody letters of fire over our heads – 'You and I are death to each other'.

Hester, with her eyes full of tears, calls out to him: 'Don't leave me alone tonight'.

But later that evening, Hester is alone. Mrs Elton and Ann Welch come in, and Ann tells Hester that Freddie has gone to a club with her husband, Philip. Mrs Elton confides in Hester that she is her favourite tenant; she also reveals that Miller was struck off for 'things unnatural' and now works as a bookmaker's clerk by day and in a hospital for infantile paralysis by night.

Collyer arrives, having heard about Freddie's departure. He wants her to come back, but she refuses:

I can't go back to you as your wife, Bill, because I no longer am your wife. We can't wipe out this last year as if it never happened . . . You aren't in love with me now, and you never have been . . . I'm simply a prized possession that has now become more prized for having been stolen, that's all.

He leaves – affectionate, dignified and desolate to the end.

Philip arrives. He claims to understand Hester, having had his own infatuation for an actress, which he cured simply by going away: 'the physical side is really awfully unimportant – objectively speaking'. Hester phones Freddie to get him to come back for a talk and shows Philip the shallowness of his advice. Miller soon interrupts Hester's second suicide attempt. He tries to get her to face up to her life and to find some purpose to it. He is apparently making some progress when Freddie enters to get his bag. There is little to be said and Freddie leaves. As the curtain falls, Hester packs one of Freddie's suitcases, and seems, perhaps, to be cured.

The remarkable achievement of *The Deep Blue Sea* is its frank and realistic acknowledgement of the true complexity of sexual relations. It is a brilliant analysis of desire and longing, rooted in the rigidities of 1950s English society, yet smouldering with eroticism. If Rattigan had written only this, his reputation as one of the century's most profound anatomists of love and heartache would be assured.

> In performance

The Deep Blue Sea has seldom failed to move and entertain its audiences. It opened at the Duchess Theatre in the West End on 6 March 1952, in a production directed by Frith Banbury, and was an immediate success, with Harold Hobson declaring it Rattigan's 'best play'. Some critics levelled charges of melodrama or berated Hester for her behaviour: the *Daily Mail* described her as 'perhaps in need of a good slap or straight talk by a Marriage Guidance Expert'.

The play gave Peggy Ashcroft, who played Hester, one of her most powerful roles (in rehearsal, the inner truth of the play – 'about sex in which sex is never mentioned' – made Ashcroft describe feeling as though 'I'm walking about with no clothes on'). Roland Culver was Collyer and an unknown actor, Kenneth More, played Freddie Page. It made him a star overnight.

Later, Celia Johnson and Googie Withers replaced Ashcroft as Hester, and Vivien Leigh played the part when it was filmed in 1954. Recent London Hesters have included Dorothy Tutin (Greenwich, 1981), Penelope Keith (Theatre Royal, Haymarket, 1988) and Penelope Wilton, unforgettably, directed by Karel Reisz (Almeida, 1992).

Quotations from Terence Rattigan, *The Deep Blue Sea*, Methuen, 1985

The Chairs
(*Les Chaises*)
Eugene Ionesco

1951, first performed 1952

> *Historical and theatrical context*

The German occupation of France (1940–4) had a profound
effect on French life. Following the humiliation of complete
defeat and the compromises imposed by the Vichy regime,
the choice seemed to be between resistance or collaboration. By 1944 faith in liberal progress had been scotched
and God was 'dead'. The only coherent position was a philosophy of pessimism – existential and full of despair. After
the war, the most perceptive artists and intellectuals became
aware of the scale of Soviet brutality, and Communism
appeared as morally bankrupt as Fascism. The Second
World War, with all its horrors, had raised the vexing question of responsibility and free will, in an apparently absurd
universe.

Existentialism had first been discussed in the 1930s. The
two key French figures, Jean-Paul Sartre and Albert Camus,
were both questioning Marxists who had fought in the
Resistance and who both wrote novels, essays and plays. One
of the key features of what the critic Martin Esslin came to
call 'The Theatre of the Absurd' was the reduction of language, characterisation and theatricality to its rawest form,
which often involved slapstick and the grotesque, as well as
philosophical speculation and jokes.

The Romanian-born Eugene Ionesco (1912– 94) moved to
Paris in 1942, having spent many years of his youth shuttling
betwen Paris and Bucharest. He was a ferocious anti-Fascist,
but also a virulent anti-Communist. He declared: 'It's not a
certain society that seems ridiculous to me, it's mankind.'

His other plays include *The Lesson* (1950), *The Bald Prima Donna* (1956) and *Rhinoceros* (1958).

> *About the play*

Ionesco describes his one-act masterpiece *The Chairs* as 'a tragic farce'. It is certainly an astonishing theatrical tour de force. It has very precise stage directions (which are ignored at the director's peril) and Ionesco even includes a diagram showing a semi-circular room, a raised rostrum, ten doors and two windows. The space is entirely empty at the beginning. We are in a house on an island, surrounded by water.

The cast consists of two very old people (an Old Man of ninety-five and his wife, an Old Woman of ninety-four), an Orator in his forties, and 'many other characters'. The Old Man is an orphan and is adored by the Old Woman. He also calls her 'Mummy', and she calls him 'poppet'. They share a sense of a perfect golden time which is now gone.

It is unclear when the play happens. The Old Man talks familiarly about Paris, but then says:

> There was such a place, only it turned to ruins. It was the city of light, only the light died, and had been dead for four hundred thousand years. There's nothing left of it now but a song.

We are in a world cut free of the constraints of naturalism – universal and abstract.

'Why don't you *be* something to cheer us up?' the Old Woman says to the Old Man at the beginning, 'Do "the two of us came"' game. But he replies:

> Seventy-five years of married life and every evening without exception you're still forcing me to tell the same old story, impersonate the same old Characters, . . . on and on and on. Can't we change the subject?

The Old Man announces that he has called a meeting, and has hired a professional Orator to convey his 'message'. A boat is heard drawing up outside, and the Old Man and Old Woman go off and are heard greeting a third person ('So pleased you could come. Mind you don't crumple your hat'). They reappear with their guest, a Young Lady, but, astonishingly, Ionesco says that she is 'invisible'. Yet the old people behave as if she is entirely real, fetching her a (real) chair, sitting her down, talking to her and listening to her imaginary story (which of course is silent).

The doorbell rings. An invisible Field Marshal comes in. The Old Woman fetches him a chair. He is introduced to the Young Lady. More boats draw up. The Fabulous Beauty of the Old Man's youth arrives ('Don't you realize? Joy, beauty, eternity itself might all have been ours . . . if only we had dared'). She is with her husband, who once was the Old Woman's flame. At one point the Old Woman:

> simperingly shows her thick red stockings, lifts her numerous skirts, reveals her moth-eaten petticoat, exposes her old woman's breasts. Then, hands on hips, head flung back, shrieking erotically, she thrusts her pelvis out, legs apart, and laughs the laugh of an old whore.

More invisible guests arrive and the Old Woman brings more chairs. There is a question about whether they had children together: the Old Woman speaks of a son, aged seven, who left, accusing them of 'killing all the birds'. Meanwhile the Old Man says that he 'left [his] mother to die alone in a ditch'.

Further invisible guests arrive, including three or four very tall journalists, and more chairs are brought for them. Still more guests, including children, arrive, followed by more and more guests, building up to a tremendous dumb-show climax:

> Then, for a long while, no more words. We hear the waves, the boats, the endless ringing . . . All the doors now open and close continuously of their own accord . . . **The old couple go from one door to another silently . . .**

The Old Man welcomes the guests . . . The Old Woman brings on chairs. The Old Man and the Old Woman meet and collide once or twice without interrupting the action.

Finally, the whole stage is completely full of invisible people. The Old Woman starts to sell programmes, and the Old Man tries to organize the crush. They find themselves trapped on opposite sides of the stage:

I'm frightened, sweetest heart, it's too crowded . . . we're so far apart . . . at our age we should be more careful . . . we might lose each other.

The guests talk to the Old Man about what he believes in and he spouts all the clichés of liberalism and Marxism as well as various philosophical platitudes. Both are desperate for the Orator to arrive: 'He'll explain everything . . . surely it's time.'

'My system is perfect', the Old Man says, 'provided you obey my instructions . . . We can save the world! . . . One truth for all . . . Since my authority is absolute! . . .' Suddenly the room is flooded with a brilliant light and the Old Man announces the arrival of 'His Majesty the King of Kings'. The Old Man's address to this imaginary 'Emperor' becomes more and more bizarre, as he speaks with great frankness of the humiliations and disasters of his life, his perpetual child-ishness and the new role of his wife as 'mother and father'. It is as if he has needed this authority figure to tell the truth of his life.

Finally, the Orator himself arrives, a real character (although Ionesco insists that 'If the invisible characters should seem as real as possible, the Orator, conversely, appears unreal'), who signs autographs, but says nothing. The Old Man starts an enormously elaborate speech (all echoed and amplified by his wife) thanking the Orator for coming, and soon thanking everybody for everything:

To the world – or rather to what's left of it! (*broad gesture to the invisible crowd*) To you in other words, dear friends,

the left-overs of humanity – but with left-overs such as
these we can still work miracles in the kitchen.

This sequence reaches an extraordinary climax when the Old
Woman and the Old Man throw themselves out of the windows on either side and fall to their deaths.

The Orator is deaf and dumb, and can only produce gut-
teral sounds. In the last moments, he writes cryptic mes-
sages on the black-board – 'ANGELSWEEP' – and the
half-Greek, anti-religious but apparently Christian inscrip-
tion: 'ΧΡ ΛGOD IS ΛGONE IΣ'. As the play ends, 'human
noises are heard from the invisible crowd; bursts of laughter, muttering, "shush"ing, ironic coughing.' It is as if it
took the deaths of the two old people, and the Orator's message on the blackboard, for life to return, for the sterile
world to be repopulated. Ionesco's grotesque and existential
farce concludes with a gesture of hope, if we care to seek it
out.

> In performance

The Chairs was premièred in an old disused hall in Paris – the
Théâtre Lancry – on 22 April 1952. In a letter to its director
Sylvain Dhomme, Ionesco wrote that the play's subject was:

> not the message, nor the failures of life, nor the moral
> disaster of the two old people, but the chairs themselves;
> that is to say, the absence of people, the absence of the
> emperor, the absence of God, the absence of matter, the
> unreality of the world . . . The theme of the play is *noth-*
> *ingness* . . . the invisible elements must be more and more
> clearly present, more and more real . . . until the point is
> reached – inadmissible, unacceptable to the reasoning
> mind – when the unreal elements speak and move . . .
> and nothingness can be heard, is made concrete.

It was not a critical success, but was supported by a number of
key writers, including Samuel Beckett.

The Chairs received its English première at the Royal Court Theatre on 14 May 1957. It was revived by Theatre de Complicité in 1997, in the West End and on Broadway, in Martin Crimp's fine new translation, with Richard Briers and Geraldine McEwan.

Quotations from Eugene Ionesco, *The Chairs*, tr. Martin Crimp, Faber and Faber, 1997; Martin Esslin, *The Theatre of the Absurd*, Pelican, 1968

Cat on a Hot Tin Roof
Tennessee Williams

1955

> Historical and theatrical context

Tennessee Williams (1914–83) wrote *Cat on a Hot Tin Roof*
during a period of rapid escalation in the Cold War. The
United States's post-war power started to fade once the
Soviet Union developed the atomic bomb. Wherever
Americans looked, Communism seemed to be in the ascen-
dant. At home, the southern states, in the years before the
Civil Rights movement, were opening up to new thinking,
but no resolution to the crisis of race relations was in sight.
Whites hung on to their monopoly of wealth and power
while the blacks lived in abject poverty. Homosexual acts
were still illegal and most gay men and lesbians had to keep
their orientation secret. While political extremism, racial
tension and sexual hypocrisy were not Tennessee Williams's
ostensible subjects, a hot-house of corruption and lies is the
background of his work.

By the time he came to write what is often regarded as his
finest play, Tennessee Williams had already enjoyed two box-
office successes with *The Glass Menagerie* (1944) and *A
Streetcar Named Desire* (1947) and was recognized, with
Arthur Miller, as one of America's greatest dramatists. Both
writers' work was directed by Elia Kazan, one of the founders
of the New York Actor's Studio and a remarkable director of
naturalistic drama, if also a controversial figure because of his
involvement in the anti-Communist hysteria of the 1950s.

Williams's later plays included *The Rose Tattoo* (1951), *Camino
Real* (1953), *Orpheus Descending* (1957), *Suddenly Last Summer*
(1958), *Sweet Bird of Youth* (1959), *The Night of the Iguana* (1961)
and *The Milk Train Doesn't Stop Here Any More* (1963).

> *About the play*

Big Daddy is a fabulously wealthy plantation owner who has terminal cancer. Today is his birthday (Kenneth Tynan called the play 'a birthday party about death') and his family and friends tell him that he has nothing more worrying than a spastic colon. But everyone except his long-suffering wife, Big Mama, knows that death is imminent.

An important part of Williams's notion of 'mendacity' – the lies that run through families and individuals, the lies on which a corrupt and cruel society is built – is the issue of concealed homosexuality. Big Daddy's dissolute son Brick is married to Margaret – the sexually neglected 'Cat on the Hot Tin Roof' of the title – and, to everybody's consternation, they have no children:

> It goes on all the time, along with constant little remarks and innuendoes about the fact that you and I have not produced any children, are totally childless and therefore totally useless!

Since the death of his best friend, Skipper, Brick has become an alcoholic, and in the play's scorching central act Big Daddy confronts him with it:

> Life's important. There's nothing left to hold on to. A man that drinks is throwing his life away. Don't do it, hold on to your life.

Big Daddy boasts of his own rampant heterosexuality ('I'm going to pick me a choice one, I don't care how much she costs, I'll smother her in – minks! Ha ha! I'll strip her naked and smother her in minks and choke her with diamonds! ha ha! I'll strip her naked and choke her with diamonds and smother her with minks and hump her from hell to breakfast.') and confronts Brick with his homosexuality:

> **Brick** You think so, too? You think so, too? You think me an' Skippper did, did, did! – *sodomy!* – together?

Big Daddy Hold – !

Brick That what you –

Big Daddy – ON – a minute!

Brick You think we did dirty things between us, Skipper an' –

Big Daddy Why are you shouting like that? Why are you –

Brick – Me, is that what you think of Skipper, is that –

Big Daddy – so excited? I don't think nothing. I don't know nothing. I'm simply telling you what –

Brick You think that Skipper and me were a pair of dirty old men?

But, of course, Big Daddy is right.

Brick has an older brother, Gooper, a lawyer, whose conventional wife, Mae ('that monster of fertility'), is now pregnant with a sixth child. In the third act, there is a family conference and Big Mama is confronted with the truth of her husband's condition. Gooper announces a plan whereby he can hold the estate in trust after Daddy's death, but Big Mama rejects it, declaring:

> Oh, you know we just got to love each other an' stay together, all of us, just as close as we can, especially now that such a *black* thing has come and moved into this place without invitation.

For her part, Margaret is determined that she, not Mae, should get hold of the estate. To everybody's amazement, she declares that she is pregnant. No one believes her, knowing about her platonic relationship with her husband. But she is determined to make this happen and locks up Brick's liquor cabinet. In the last moments of the play, Big Daddy dies and Margaret seduces her husband, hoping to reform the son and produce the grandchild that Big Daddy always wanted.

In his remarkable introduction to the play, Tennessee

Williams wrote that 'personal lyricism is the outcry of prisoner to prisoner from the cell in solitary where each is confined for the duration of his life'. This empathy for the loner led Williams to describe himself as 'a dramatist of lost souls'. Although Williams himself lamented the personal connection in his introduction ('Of course it is a pity that so much of all creative work is so closely related to the personality of the one who does it'), he himself was a homosexual and his father used to taunt him by calling him 'Miss Nancy'. By modern standards, the allusion to homosexuality in *Cat on a Hot Tin Roof* is oblique, but Williams was writing as one of the 'lost souls' of his time and Margaret's triumph at the end is not something that will necessarily bring joy to Brick.

Cat on a Hot Tin Roof is charged with an extraordinary emotional power which expresses itself in language of astonishing, almost Jacobean, force. It is written with intense theatricality and non-stop dramatic energy: kids keep running in and out in the middle of important discussions, phones ring, the sky changes colour, fireworks go off, snatches of songs are heard and (in the Broadway version at least) a great crackling southern thunderstorm breaks. The play's three acts have no time lapse between them, with each one starting at the exact moment the previous one ended.

Tennessee Williams is very precise in his stage directions, and they merit careful attention. He says:

> The set is the bed-sitting room of a plantation home in the Mississippi Delta. It is along an upstairs gallery which probably runs around the entire house; it has two pairs of very wide doors opening on to the gallery, showing white balustrades against a fair summer sky that fades into dusk and night during the course of the play, which occupies precisely the time of its performance, excepting, of course, the fifteen minutes of intermission.

As in Ibsen, the detail of Williams's stage directions, and the realism, fluency and sparkle of his dialogue, all produce a kind of poetic naturalism which is both symbolic and real, charged and domestic. As a dramatist of genius, Williams knows exactly what effect he is having in everything that he writes.

The result is that *Cat on a Hot Tin Roof* is a great slab of baroque naturalism, thick with atmosphere, heat, sex, booze and death. It is American drama at its scorching best, and one of its most enduring contributions.

> In performance

Cat on a Hot Tin Roof received its world première on 24 March 1955, in a New York production directed by Elia Kazan, about whom Tennessee Williams said 'no living playwright, that I can think of, hasn't something to learn about his own work from a director so highly perceptive as Elia Kazan'. Ben Gazzara played Brick. The play has been seen all over the world ever since. One of the most notable productions was on Broadway with Kathleen Turner in 1990. It was made into a film with Elizabeth Taylor and Paul Newman in 1958.

The play has two different versions of Act Three. The second was written – very readily, it seems – on Kazan's advice. It brings Big Daddy back on stage for the last act and introduces a thunderstorm. In some ways this is a clearer and certainly a more climactic third act than Williams's first draft, but it does lack a certain subtlety, the ambiguity and quicksilver energy of Williams's original conception. An interesting difference is that in the second version the black servants are more present.

Cat on a Hot Tin Roof won Tennessee Williams his second Pulitzer Prize in 1955.

Quotations from Tennessee Williams, *Plays*, Penguin, 1957

The Visit
(*Der Besuch der Alten Dame*)
Friedrich Dürrenmatt

1955, first performed 1956

> Historical and theatrical context

The year in which the Swiss dramatist Friedrich Dürrenmatt's (1921–90) *The Visit* was premièred was one of great upheaval for Central Europe. Austria had been granted its independence as a neutral state in 1955 and in 1956 a popular rebellion in Hungary was put down with Soviet tanks. Switzerland, however, clinging to its neutrality, lived up to its reputation for dullness, so brilliantly caught in Orson Welles's quip in *The Third Man* (1959) that its only claim to fame was the cuckoo clock. Meanwhile, the Suez fiasco challenged what was left of Western European imperial confidence and in Russia the new General Secretary Khrushchev denounced Stalin's crimes.

The Visit (literally 'The Visit of the Old Lady') was very influenced by Brecht (who died the year it was written), but also by expressionism and surrealism. It is a piece of 'disposable' theatre, in which trees are impersonated by actors and high-speed car journeys are made possible by mime. The play demands simple but highly inventive theatricality.

Dürrenmatt's other plays include *Romulus the Great* (1948), *Incident at Twilight* (1959), *The Physicists* (1962), as well as an adaptation of Strindberg's *The Dance of Death*, entitled *Play Strindberg* (1969). His novels include *The Judge and the Hangman* (1950) and essays include *Theatre Problems* (1954).

> About the play

In *The Visit*, Friedrich Dürrenmatt has written a contemporary Greek tragedy, whose catalyst is money and revenge. It is constructed around the proposal that, under certain circumstances, even the finest values are commodities, and that a man's life can be bought and sold. In a Europe reeling from the Second World War and confronted with the bleak realities of the Cold War, its ironies had tremendous resonance.

Guellen is a small railway town, 'a tumbledown wreck', somewhere on one of the main Central European train tracks. None of the express trains stop there any more and the town is bankrupt. Everybody is pinning their hopes on the imminent visit of the fabulously wealthy Claire Zachanassian, who left Guellen when she was a girl.

Having stopped the train by pulling on its emergency brakes, Claire arrives with her retinue: her butler, her seventh husband, a sedan chair (carried by two 'bubblegum chewing brutes' named Roby and Toby), a coffin and two fat, blind eunuchs: Koby and Loby. She is a multi-millionairess, and to the people of Guellen she is their salvation. An old shopkeeper, Mr Ill, who used to be Claire's teenage sweetheart, is thought to be the town's best hope of encouraging her to give them some of her money. They meet, and in the forest, beside a tree where they carved their initials into the bark, they remember their romance. Ill declares that he is just a 'broken-down shopkeeper in a broken-down town' and begs her to assist them.

The Mayor holds a reception for Claire, who offers to give one million pounds to the town, on the extraordinary condition that Ill is killed. Claire's butler declares that when she became pregnant, Ill denied paternity and bribed two young men into swearing that they had slept with her. As a result, she left Guellen in disgrace and became a prostitute. The town is appalled by her proposal and the mayor proclaims: 'we would rather have poverty than blood on our hands'.

By Act Two, however, everybody is behaving as if they were rich already. The two bodyguards are preparing a funeral and Ill says Claire should be arrested because she is inviting people to murder him. But the policeman is not convinced.

Ill demands official protection. The mayor offers bland reassurances, saying that Guellen is 'a city of Humanist traditions. Goethe spent a night here. Brahms composed a quartet here.' Despite all the usual pleasantries, the ground is shifting and Ill is terrified.

Ill confides in the priest. Soon the townspeople are prowling around with hunting rifles. There is a shot, Ill falls, but in fact they are shooting Claire's black panther that has escaped. In despair, Ill goes to the station, but collapses before he can board a train.

Meanwhile, Claire has divorced both her seventh and eighth husbands and married a ninth (a Nobel prizewinner). The schoolmaster and the doctor ask Claire to invest in Guellen unconditionally, arguing that she should let her feeling for humanity prevail. Her reply is:

> The world turned me into a whore. I shall turn the world into a brothel. If you can't fork out when you want to dance, you have to put off dancing.

The press come to visit Ill and blame his wife for marrying him. They caricature the family, take pictures and reduce his life to a soap opera. The schoolmaster makes a drunken prophecy:

> They will kill you . . . The temptation is too great and our poverty is too wretched. But I know something else. I shall take part in it. I can feel myself slowly becoming a murderer. My faith in humanity is powerless to stop it.

The mayor announces a public meeting for that night and says that the decision taken will be final. He suggests Ill should sacrifice himself but Ill insists on a trial.

Ill goes for a drive in his son's smart new car. They drive up into the mountains. Ill is left alone in the woods and comes to terms with what has become inevitable. In a speech of chilling tenderness, Claire says to him:

> I shall take you in your coffin to Capri. I have had a

mausoleum built, in my Palace Park. It is surrounded by
cypress-trees. Overlooking the Mediterranean . . . You
will remain there. A dead man beside a stone idol. Your
love died many years ago. But my love could not die.
Neither could it live. It grew into an evil thing, like me,
like the pallid mushrooms in this wood, and the blind
twisted features of the roots, all overgrown by my golden
millions. Their tentacles sought you out, to take your life,
because your life belonged to me for ever. You are in their
toils now, and you are lost. You will soon be no more than
a dead love in my memory, a gentle ghost haunting the
wreckage of a house.

Everyone assembles at the town hall for the trial. The
schoolmaster declares that Claire just wants to transform the
spirit of the community. None of the relevant authorities
have any questions and everyone votes for 'Justice'. The
Mayor announces that the 'Claire Zachanassian Endowment'
has been accepted and Ill soon disappears into a 'lane of
silent men' and is mysteriously killed. His body is placed in
the coffin. Claire hands the cheque over and leaves. The
town is rich and a chorus proclaims that 'fate' has inter-
vened.

The Visit is a tragicomedy: funny and grotesque, tender and
savage in equal measure. Dürrenmatt creates three fully
rounded characters: the extravagant monster, Claire; the
scared and bewildered victim, Ill; and the inhabitants of
Guellen: hypocritical, greedy, desperate and blind. It is a difficult play to pull off in the theatre. Striking the right stylistic
balance is as hard as working out what the play ultimately
means. Dürrenmatt's own postscript gets the closest:

> I have described people, not marionettes, an action and
> not an allegory . . . I write with an inherent confidence in
> the theatre and its actors . . . I don't account myself a
> member of the contemporary avant-garde . . . Claire
> Zachanassian doesn't represent Justice or the Marshall
> Plan or even the Apocalypse, she's purely and simply what

she is, namely, the richest woman in the world and, thanks to her finances, in a position to act as the Greek tragic heroines acted . . . The Guelleners who swarm round the hero are people like the rest of us. They must not, emphatically not, be portrayed as wicked . . . It's a community slowly yielding to temptation, as in the Schoolmaster's case; but it must be a perceptible yielding. The temptation is too strong, the poverty too wretched. The old lady is a wicked creature, and for precisely that reason mustn't be played wicked, she has to be rendered as human as possible, not with anger but with sorrow and humour, for nothing could harm this comedy with a tragic end more than heavy seriousness.

> *In performance*

The Visit received its première in January 1956 in Zurich. Its English-language première, in a production by Peter Brook, with a good translation by Patrick Bowles and the Lunts (Alfred Lunt and Lynn Fontaine) as Ill and Clare, was a great success on Broadway in 1958 and in London in 1960.

Theatre de Complicite presented a very successful and theatrical version in 1989 at the Almeida and then at the National Theatre. It was also performed in Chichester with Lauren Bacall in 1995. It is often performed in universities but rarely professionally.

Quotations from Friedrich Dürrenmatt, *The Visit* tr. Patrick Bowles, Jonathan Cape, 1962

Look Back in Anger
John Osborne

1956

> Historical and theatrical context

Look Back in Anger was written in the England of the mid-1950s, which John Osborne (1929–94) summed up in the second volume of his autobiography:

> The country was tired, not merely from the sacrifice of two back-breaking wars but from the defeat and misery between them. The bits of red on the map were disappearing as the flags came down and the names we knew on mixed packets of postage stamps were erased. Like so much else, it all happened without people being very aware of it. The leaping hare of the Victorian imagination had begun to imitate the tortoise even before 1914, but in that summer of 1955, it was still easy enough to identify what we regarded as a permanent Establishment.

The play was sent to George Devine in response to an advertisement in *The Stage* seeking new plays for his recently formed English Stage Company. When Devine included the play in his first season, it quickly became a template for the Royal Court's house style: realistic and passionate, and a powerful reaction against what was seen as the polite drama of the fifties, which Arthur Miller described as 'hermetically sealed from reality'.

Osborne's subsequent successes included *The Entertainer* (1957) with Laurence Olivier, *Luther* (1961), *Inadmissible Evidence* (1964) and *A Patriot for Me* (1965), but none could match the strange, uncomfortable and passionate energy which courses through his début. His two volumes of autobiography (*A Better Class of Person*, 1981, and *Almost a*

Gentleman, 1991) were published together in paperback as *Looking Back: Never Explain, Never Apologize* (1999).

> About the play

Looking back on *Look Back in Anger* almost fifty years after its première, several things are striking. One is the play's formal conservatism. Another is the misogyny of Jimmy Porter's tirade. A third is the discrepancy between emotion and cause (which T. S. Eliot said disfigured *Hamlet*). Yet *Look Back in Anger* is driven by such astonishing verbal energy that it still carries real force.

The lower-middle-class, but well-educated, Jimmy Porter lives with his upper-middle-class wife Alison in a one-room flat 'in a large Midland town'. As the curtain rises, Jimmy and his Welsh friend Cliff (who lives in the same house) are reading the Sunday papers, while Alison is doing the ironing. Jimmy holds court, makes them laugh, criticizes the world, is provocative and cracks jokes. He is independent-minded and free-wheeling, politically aware without being either left- or right-wing. His father was badly wounded fighting 'on the losing side' in the Spanish Civil War and as a boy Jimmy watched him die. Stuck in a dead-end job, Jimmy's enemy is complacency and boredom. He is desperate to puncture the calm surface of life and engage with real feeling:

> God how I hate Sundays! It's always so depressing, always the same. We never seem to get any further, do we?
> Always the same ritual. Reading the papers, drinking tea, ironing. A few more hours, and another week gone. Our youth is slipping away.

But Jimmy can also be cruel, and in a brilliant stage metaphor for their marriage, accidentally knocks over the ironing board, burning Alison. She soon confides in the easy-going, friendly Cliff that she is pregnant. Unaware, Jimmy declares:

> Oh, my dear wife, you've got so much to learn. I only

hope you learn it one day. If only something – something would happen to you, and wake you out of your beauty sleep! If you could have a child, and it would die . . . if only I could watch you face that.

This terrible irony brings the curtain down on Act One.

By the start of Act Two, Alison's friend Helena Charles – an actress – has arrived. She has a certain 'matriarchal authority' but is also attractive and well dressed. She is middle-class, effective, everything that Jimmy detests. Their antagonism is instantaneous. She tells Alison that 'I've never seen such hatred in someone's eyes before', and that she must 'fight him. Fight, or get out'. When Helena sets off for church with Alison, Jimmy's tirade is relentless:

You see, I know Helena and her kind so very well . . . They're a romantic lot. They spend their time mostly looking forward to the past. The only place they can see the light is the Dark Ages. She's moved long ago into a lovely little cottage of the soul, cut right off from the ugly problems of the twentieth century altogether . . . She'd rather go down to the ecstatic little shed at the bottom of the garden to relieve her sense of guilt.

It is as if there is a struggle for Alison's soul, which Jimmy, of course, is determined to win. But soon he has to go: his best friend's mother ('a charwoman') has had a stroke, and someone must go and look after her. Alison refuses to go with him.

Meanwhile, Helena has asked Alison's father to come and take her home. Colonel Redfearn cannot understand Jimmy, but his basic decency allows him to recognize his own failings. When Alison and he leave, Helena decides to stay, much to Cliff's annoyance. Jimmy returns and Helena gives him a note from Alison. When he does not flinch when told that Alison is pregnant, Helena slaps him in the face.

At the beginning of Act Three, Helena is doing the ironing. She has replaced Alison in Jimmy's bed and in his heart.

Everyone seems happier. But when Cliff says he is going to leave and find himself a wife, Jimmy is up to his old tricks:

> Why, why, why, why do we let these women bleed us to death? . . . I suppose people of our generation aren't able to die for good causes any longer. We had all that done for us, in the thirties and the forties, when we were still kids. There aren't any good brave causes left. If the big bang does come, and we all get killed off, it won't be in aid of the old-fashioned, grand design. It'll just be for the Brave New-nothing-very-much-thank-you . . . No, there's nothing left for it, me boy, but to let yourself be butchered by the women.

Alison returns, having lost her child. She recognizes what has happened and accepts it. Helena says she is going to leave, despite her love for Jimmy. Jimmy and Alison are left together and Alison exclaims:

> All I wanted was to die. I never knew what it was like . . . I was in pain, and all I could think of was you, and what I'd lost. I thought: if only he could see me now, so stupid, and ugly and ridiculous. This is what he's been longing for me to feel. This is what he wants to splash about in!

Alison's submission has been cited as evidence of John Osborne's misogyny. Certainly, the play *is* weighted against the female characters and in Osborne's delight in Jimmy's tirades, he loses dramatic objectivity. But the ending, with its return to the sickly sweet sentimentality of 'squirrels and bears', can be read more darkly, as full of shared despair.

Jimmy Porter is one of the century's anti-heroes, a devil whose heroism lies in his defiance of morality and decency. His strength is that he can talk, in cascades of scorching rhetoric. It is almost as if Jimmy is speaking for Osborne when he declares:

> One day when I'm no longer running a sweet-stall, I may write a book about us all. It's all here. Written in flames a

mile high. And it won't be recollected in tranquility
either, picking daffodils with Auntie Wordsworth. It'll be
recollected in fire, and blood. My blood.

At times, *Look Back in Anger* feels like Strindberg rewritten by
Webster, and the tension between the realism of the form and
the intense, rhetorical quality of the language can at times
feel abrupt, almost gauche. But the play is bursting apart at
the seams. It is an extraordinary work, by a young writer of
real vision. In a time when anger is unfashionable, and when
the desire for political, social or emotional change is often
dismissed, Osborne's play reads like an explosive time capsule
from a different world.

> In performance

The world première of *Look Back in Anger* took place on 8
May 1956. It was directed by Tony Richardson, who said that
Osborne was 'unique and alone in his ability to put on the
stage the quick of himself, his pain, his squalor, his nobility –
terrifyingly alone'. Jimmy was played by Kenneth Haigh,
Cliff by Alan Bates and Alison by Mary Ure, who was to
become Osborne's second wife.

Most of the initial reviews were poor. However, when
Kenneth Tynan declared in the *Observer* that 'I don't think I
could love anybody who didn't love *Look Back in Anger*', the
play rapidly became a huge hit, both in London and New
York. Perhaps never before – or since – has a piece of dramatic criticism had such an effect, not only on a play's subsequent success but on the culture as a whole. As a result of
the passions that the play provoked, Osborne was labelled (by
a press officer at the Royal Court) one of the 'angry young
men', a group which also included John Arden, Arnold
Wesker and Willis Hall.

Look Back in Anger is revived regularly, both in Europe and
the Unites States. Kenneth Branagh played Jimmy Porter in
the West End in 1989. It was revived by the Royal National

Theatre in 1999, with Michael Sheen as Jimmy Porter in a production which stressed the play's Strindbergian emotional realism. Tony Richardson directed a film version, starring Richard Burton, in 1959.

In 1992 John Osborne wrote a companion piece entitled *Déjà Vu*, in which Jimmy and Cliff are middle-aged. It was not a success.

Quotations from John Osborne, *Look Back in Anger*, Faber and Faber, 1957

A Raisin in the Sun
Lorraine Hansberry

1956–7, first performed 1959

> *Historical and theatrical context*

Lorraine Hansberry's (1930–65) *A Raisin in the Sun* was the first play to show African-American lives realistically on stage. There had been other 'black plays' before – Richard Wright's *Native Son* (1941), Theodore Ward's *Our Lan'* (1946), Louis Peterson's *Take a Giant Step* (1953–4) and Alice Childress's Obie Award-winner, *Trouble in Mind* (1955). But, as the novelist James Baldwin wrote, 'Never before in the entire history of the American theatre had so much of the truth of black people's lives been seen on stage.'

Despite great achievements in sport, and the greatest names in jazz, blues and rock'n roll, African-Americans were still regarded as second-class citizens. Even in the supposedly freer North, 'the promised land' to which so many African-Americans migrated after slavery, discrimination in education and housing was rife.

And in 1956, the Civil Rights victories of the 1960s, and the schism between the integrationist approach of Martin Luther King and the more militant tactics of Malcolm X, had yet to arrive.

Hansberry's family knew all about the ghettoes that sprang up as a result. In 1938, her father, an active campaigner for civil rights, had tried to move his middle-class, well-educated family into a 'white' Chicago neighbourhood and was met by violence (a large piece of concrete smashed a window and hit the eight-year-old Lorraine). This precipitated a famous legal action in which he eventually won the right in the Supreme Court to break Chicago's restricted real-estate 'covenants'. When Lorraine Hansberry died from cancer at the age of thirty-four, the Federal Fair Housing Law of April 1968 was yet to appear. But no less a figure than Martin Luther King, Jr prophecied that 'her creative ability and her profound grasp of the deep social issues confronting the world today will remain an inspiration to generations yet unknown'.

Hansberry's other stage plays include *The Sign in Sidney Brustein's Window* (1964), *To Be Young, Gifted and Black* (1969), *Les Blancs* (1970) – the last two finished posthumously by her husband Robert Nemiroff – and *Where Are the Flowers?*, a post-nuclear play which has never been performed.

> About the play

The title of the play comes from Langston Hughes's poem, 'Harlem':

> What happens to a dream deferred?
> Does it dry up
> Like a raisin in the sun?
> Or fester like a sore –
> And then run?
> Does it stink like rotten meat?
> Or crust and sugar over –
> Like a syrupy sweet?
>
> Maybe it just sags
> Like a heavy load.
>
> *Or does it explode?*

The play depicts a black family living on Chicago's Southside 'sometime between World War II and the present'. It is about family dynamics, marital strife and the fulfillment – or otherwise – of the American dream. It addresses big questions which reach beyond its particular constituency: namely, are there certain values no amount of money can buy, and how are minorities to pursue their dreams?

The Youngers are a three-generation black family living in cramped conditions in a squalid apartment. Despite the tensions of poverty, there is a real sense of a close-knit family: Ruth is continuously trying to juggle everyone else's demands while also working as a maid; her husband Walter Lee is feckless and frustrated and drinks too much ('one thing 'bout [him] he always knows how to have a *good* time'); their ten-year-old son, Travis, is forced to sleep on a camp-bed in the front-room in a place where the sun does not reach (where the 'raisin' of the title cannot be ripened); Walter's sister Bennie is restless and independent-minded, and wants to become a doctor ('I am going to be a doctor and everybody around better understand that!'); and Lena (Walter and Bennie's 'Mama') is an indefatigable God-fearing woman, who rules her adult children with a rod of iron. When Ruth discovers that she is two months pregnant, she is in despair: her marriage is rocky and they cannot afford to move.

The family is eagerly anticipating a $10,000 cheque – the insurance pay-out on the recently deceased Walter Senior's life policy. Walter has set his eyes on using the money to buy his own liquor store – it offers release from the humiliations of working as a chauffeur. Mama's dream is to move to better surroundings ('a little old two-story somewhere, with a yard where Travis could play in the summertime').

Bennie is searching for her 'identity', for a way to 'express' herself, and sees herself as above the realities of money. She even turns down the attentions of a wealthy, young 'assimilationist Negro' (who at one point says: 'Let's face it, baby, your heritage is nothing but a bunch of raggedy-assed spirituals and some grass huts!'). Her other boyfriend, a Nigerian intellectual, turns up with African robes (which she wears with enthusiasm) and a Yoruba nickname. Bennie's witty experimental approach to her 'identity' (at one point she even does a Nigerian dance to 'welcome the men back from the village') points up one of the dilemmas faced by African-Americans in the late 1950s. Walter's failing attempts to submit himself to the dominant white values points up another:

Walter Sometimes it's like I can see the future stretched out in front of me – just plain as day. The future, Mama. Hanging over there at the edge of my days. Just waiting for me – a big, looming, blank space – full of *nothing*. Just waiting for me. But it don't have to be. Sometimes when I'm downtown and I pass them cool, quiet-looking restaurants where them white boys are sitting back and talking 'bout things . . . sitting there turning deals worth millions of dollars . . . sometimes I see guys don't look much older than me –

Mama Son – how come you talk so much 'bout money?

Walter Because it is life, Mama.

By Act Two, Mama has put a deposit down on a small house in Clybourne Park, an exclusively white neighbourhood. Ruth is 'struck senseless with the news, in its various degrees of goodness and trouble' ('goodbye . . . to these goddamned cracking walls'). Walter is devastated: 'So you butchered up a dream of mine – you – who was always talking 'bout your children's dreams.' Furthermore, Walter is about to lose his job because he has not turned up at work for three days. Ruth's worries are confirmed when, amidst the packing and celebration, Karl Lindner, a representative of the Clybourne Park community turns up:

We're not rich and fancy people, just hard-working, honest people . . . And at the moment, the overwhelming majority of our people . . . feel that people get along better . . . when they share a common background.

But Lindner's attempt to buy off the Youngers is rejected. Meanwhile, Mama has given Walter the balance of the money to put down in a bank. At the end of the act news arrives that Walter gave the money to his old drinking pal, Willy Harris, to put down a deposit on the longed-for liquor store. But Harris has disappeared.

In Act Three, Bennie, bitter about lost opportunities,

rejects her previous idealism. Ruth becomes hysterical. Mama tries bravely to put a positive face on it all. Walter enters and, distraught with remorse, reveals that he has called Mr Lindner and told him that they will, after all, accept the buy-off. The family is appalled. 'I come from five generations of people who was slaves and share croppers – but ain't nobody in my family never took no money from nobody that was a way of telling us we wasn't fit to walk the earth,' declares Mama. Walter brazens it out: 'What's the matter with you all! I didn't make this world! It was given to me this way!' But when Lindner returns, Walter changes his mind. They *will* move to Clybourne Park, he declares. It is an electric moment. As Walter Lee salvages his pride, Hansberry returns a sense of faith in humankind to us all.

A Raisin in the Sun is a remarkable work, full of energy, craft, humour and observation. Its sparkling dialogue, shrewd intelligence and great warmth and empathy fully justifies *The Washington Post's* verdict of it as 'one of a handful of great American plays'. Its passionate demand for justice continues to inspire generations of theatregoers beyond Hansberry's own.

> *In performance*

At first, no Broadway management would touch *A Raisin in the Sun*. Audiences, it was thought, would not be interested in the vicissitudes of a black family. It took eighteen months for the money to be raised. But when Lloyd Richards's production opened at the Ethel Barrymore Theater in New York on 11 March 1959 – with a cast that included Sidney Poitier as Walter – Lorraine Hansberry became the first black woman (and, at twenty-nine, the youngest American ever) to have a play on Broadway. The play carried off the New York Drama Critics Best Play of the Year Award. It has been produced in thirty different languages, but was made into a disappointing film, despite Hansberry's own award-winning screenplay.

The first production in Britain was at the Adelphi Theatre in 1959. Yvonne Brewster's Black Theatre Co-operative revived the play in 1985 at the Tricycle Theatre in London, as did Lou Stein at the Watford Palace in 1989. There was a twenty-fifth anniversary production of the play in 1986 at the Kennedy Center in Washington.

Raisin, the musical based on the play, won the Tony Award for Best Musical in 1974. The song 'To Be Young, Gifted and Black' is Nina Simone's tribute to Hansberry.

Quotations from Lorraine Hansberry, *A Raisin in the Sun*, Samuel French, 1987

The Caretaker
Harold Pinter

1960

> Historical and theatrical context

The Caretaker was written at the end of a decade which had
seen a remarkable flowering of world drama. Europe had
started to emerge from the trauma of the Second World War
and was laying the foundations for the boom and upheaval of
the 1960s. *The Sound of Music, Rock Around the Clock* and *Ben
Hur* all appeared in 1960, the year which also saw the election
of President Kennedy (JFK) and the widespread availability
of the contraceptive Pill.

Harold Pinter's (born 1930) early work has been linked
with the 'theatre of the absurd', a term coined to describe a
group of writers whose philosophical base was the 'absurdity'
of the human condition. While Pinter himself acknowledged
his debt to Beckett and there is a Kafkaesque quality about
the writing, it is perhaps more valuable to set him among
those English writers of the 1950s committed to reflecting
the social and emotional nuances of everyday life in colloquial speech and largely dismissive of broader philosophical
questions. Pinter's subject, especially in his early plays, was
the ordinary man and the dispossessed in particular. He used
as raw material his East End background, as well as his days
in near-destitution as a young actor and dramatist. A heady
mixture of intellectual extravagance and down-at-heel realism is the motor of Pinter's early work.

Pinter's many other plays include *The Birthday Party*
(1958), *The Homecoming* (1965), *Old Times* (1971), *No Man's
Land* (1975), *Betrayal* (1978), *Mountain Language* (1988), *A
Kind of Alaska* (1982), *Moonlight* (1993), *Ashes to Ashes* (1996)
and *Celebration* (2000). He has also written a number of

screenplays including *The Go-Between* (1971), *The Servant* (1963) and *The French Lieutenant's Woman* (1981). In 1998, a volume of 'Prose, Poetry and Politics' was published, entitled *Various Voices*.

> *About the play*

Pinter is notoriously reluctant to speak about his working processes, but he has given the reader of *The Caretaker* two remarkable insights. The first is about the way he works:

> I have usually begun a play in quite a simple manner; found a couple of characters in a particular context, thrown them together and listened to what they said, keeping my nose to the ground. The context has always been, for me, concrete and particular, and the characters also. I've never started a play from any kind of abstract idea or theory . . . When a character cannot be comfortably defined or understood in terms of the familiar, the tendency is to perch him on a symbolic shelf, out of harm's way. Once there, he can be talked about but need not be lived with. In this way, it is easy to put up a pretty confident smoke screen, on the part of the critics or the audience, against recognition, against an active and willing participation.

The second insight is into the genesis of *The Caretaker*:

> We were living in this first-floor flat in Chiswick . . . There was a chap who owned the house: a builder, in fact, like Mick who had his own van and whom I hardly ever saw. The only image I had of him was of this swift mover up and down the stairs and of his van going . . . vroom . . . as he arrived and departed. His brother lived in the house. He was a handyman . . . He managed rather more successfully than Aston, but he was very introverted, very secretive, had been in a mental home some years before and had had some kind of electrical shock treatment . . .

Anyway, he did bring a tramp back one night. I call him a tramp, but he was just a homeless old man who stayed three or four weeks . . . I occasionally got glimpses of him in the other fellow's room. He wasn't anywhere near as eloquent as Davies but . . . he didn't seem very content with his lot . . . The image that stayed with me for a long time was of the open door to this room with the two men standing in different parts of the room doing different things . . . the tramp rooting around in a bag and the other man looking out of the window and simply not speaking . . . A kind of moment frozen in time that left a very strong impression.

Pinter's own emphasis on the concrete and the specific, the felt and the heard, is the key to any appreciation of this extraordinary writer's work.

The action of *The Caretaker* centres round the tramp, Davies, who has been thrown out of a café and needs somewhere to live. He is a homeless vagrant who spends his life travelling round London, going from one contact to another, all in search of some repose, some centre. He is taken in by Aston and his brother Mick and made welcome, but is also ridiculed and threatened. Opportunities spring up and are then closed down. Thus, the play is on one level a parable about seemingly random acts of charity and aggression.

Aston is the most mysterious of the three. He reveals that he has received electric shock treatment, but he is capable of simple acts of kindness and provides Davies with a bed, light, a fire and some money. He is patient and slow, and his great ambition is to get a shed built in his garden. He offers Davies a job as a caretaker.

Mick is a haunting presence in the first act, making two short, striking appearances. In Act Two he constantly undermines Davies, making long speeches demonstrating his social mobility, his confident knowledge of London, his easy familiarity with a stylish world of which Davies knows nothing. Mick owns the house and, with a skilful blend of dazzling language, bouts of anger and, later, a feigned friendship, he proceeds to terrorize Davies.

Davies himself exhibits all the characteristics of certain elements of the London working class. He is a strange mixture of arrogant and vulnerable, proud and sentimental, brutal and tender, racist and egalitarian. He is continuously positioning himself on the class ladder – better than blacks, Indians or 'Scotch', but full of deference for his superiors. His language is riddled with cliché, caught within certain constraints and unable to get beyond them. The contrast between the buoyant optimism of his patter and the constraints within which this cliché-ridden language operates is what makes this such a truthful portrait.

Davies finally starts to turn against Aston, complaining about the position of his bed, the lack of a breadknife, an unconnected gas stove, the lack of a clock and so on. The climax is reached when, at a moment of supreme irony, Mick pretends to be shocked at Davies's admission that he is not a 'first class experienced interior decorator' (never having pretended to be one). Mick loses his temper and smashes the statue of Buddha which had sat so calmly on the gas stove, and wisdom, patience and kindness are all smashed with it.

A struggle for territory lies at the heart of *The Caretaker*. The play is not only thick with the geography of modern London, but the house in which it takes place, its maintenance and redecoration, who owns it, who is its caretaker and who lives next door are the constant topics of conversation. In the end, family and property triumph over charity and Davies is thrown out of the house, muttering 'what am I going to do? What shall I do?'

Pinter has stressed that the words in which his characters speak are not a failure of communication so much as an attempt at it by people whose hearts and minds are full to the brim. They love language, even when the words they use are not their own and conceal subterranean depths:

I feel that instead of any inability to communicate there is a deliberate evasion of communication. Communication between people is so frightening that rather than do that there is a continual cross-talk, a continual talking about other things, rather than what is at the root of their relationship.

The Caretaker is written in three acts, with a series of momentary dips in the lighting which indicate a passing of time. It is exquisitely taut and, when well directed, plays with effortless energy in a perfectly dramatic ebb and flow. It is a play which above all demands attention to the detail and texture of its language, for it is written in a vernacular which is so well crafted that it is poetry. Out of the dark heart of London's most unglamorous world, Pinter has fashioned a work of extraordinary beauty and delicacy.

> In performance

The Caretaker received its world première at the Arts Theatre, London, on 27 April 1960, with Donald Pleasance as Davies and Alan Bates as Mick. It was an immediate critical success – in contrast to the brickbats which had greeted the première of *The Birthday Party*. The *Financial Times* carried the most astute notice: 'Mr Pinter's vision begins with the dispossessed and the disconnected. The characters who set him off are those whose connection to the world hangs by a thread'.

The play soon transferred to the larger Duchess Theatre (justifying the producer Michael Codron's risky investment) and was particularly admired by those two stalwarts of the commercial theatre, Noël Coward and Terence Rattigan.

The Caretaker has been revived all over the world, in a wide range of different interpretations. It was staged by the National Theatre in 1980 with Warren Mitchell, Kenneth Cranham and Jonathan Pryce, and revived in 1991 with Donald Pleasance once again playing Davies. Michael

Gambon played Davies in the play's 40th anniversary production, directed by the writer Patrick Marber.

Quotations from Harold Pinter, *The Caretaker*, Faber and Faber, 1960; Harold Pinter, *Various Voices*, Faber and Faber, 1998; Michael Billington, *The Life and Work of Harold Pinter*, Faber and Faber, 1996

Who's Afraid of Virginia Woolf?
Edward Albee

1962

> Historical and theatrical context

1962 was the high point of what came to be called 'Camelot':
the young and glamorous President Kennedy and his wife
Jackie were in the White House and America seemed confident, prosperous and full of vitality. But 1962 was also a time
of real danger, with an escalation of the US–Soviet rivalry and
the construction of the Berlin Wall in August 1961. The US-
sponsored invasion of Cuba had ended in fiasco in April 1961
and the world came close to Armageddon with the missile
crisis of October 1962. What had seemed like effortless
American superiority was revealed to be a terrifying and
apocalyptic responsibility.

This produced a crisis among the intellectual, artistic and
cultural élite. On the one hand, there was a powerful sense of
America as having a new and distinctly modern identity. On
the other, there was a feeling of spiritual emptiness underly-
ing the consumer boom and an intangible sense of impending
catastrophe. All of this was reflected in the work of significant American artists and writers: the highly charged can-
vasses of Abstract Expressionist painters such as Robert
Rauschenberg, William de Kooning and Mark Rothko; the
dazzling poetry of Robert Lowell and Elizabeth Bishop; and
the relentlessly honest early novels of John Updike and
Saul Bellow. Their work echoed their lifestyles: fiercely
intellectual and explosively self-destructive, classical and
alcoholic, suicidal and visionary. The early 1960s was a significant moment in American cultural life, and Edward Albee
(born 1928) stood at its heart.

Albee was an adopted child, whose parents are not known.

He was brought up in a well-established and extremely wealthy theatre family (his adopted grandfather was the theatre impresario of the same name) and educated in Connecticut. His early experimental plays, which show the influence of Beckett and the other 'absurdists', include *The Zoo Story* (1959), *The Death of Bessie Smith* (1960) and *The American Dream* (1960). Following the great success of *Virginia Woolf*, Albee went on to write *A Delicate Balance* (1966), *Seascape* (1975) and *Three Tall Women* (1994). He has been awarded the Pulitzer Prize twice.

> About the play

Who's Afraid of Virginia Woolf? is set in the heartland of WASP (White Anglo-Saxon Protestant) America: a professor's house on the campus of a small college in New England. Its two central characters are named after America's first couple, Martha and George Washington. Its title, with its deliberate echo of 'Who's afraid of the big bad wolf?', brilliantly catches the contradictions of America at the time: behind the witty parlour game lurk the terrors of the nursery. The play is written in three acts, each with its own catchy title, and at a glance the play sets out its deeply American, high-rolling, intellectual stall.

It is two o'clock in the morning and George and Martha have just returned home from a party. He is a 'forty something' History Lecturer, wry and witty, but defeated and feeling his age. She is six years older, the vulgar and noisy daughter of the president of the university. They take pleasure in viciously attacking each other and, fuelled by copious amounts of alcohol ('for the mind's blind eye, the heart's ease, and the liver's craw'), perform a gladiatorial and terrifying *danse macabre*. She has invited a younger couple to come and join them. Honey is twenty-six and plain, Nick twenty-eight and good-looking, a teacher in the biology department. When at one point Honey says 'I didn't know until just a minute ago that you had a *son*', she touches on a raw nerve.

Martha lusts after Honey's 'brilliant' husband and proceeds to humiliate George and Honey. In a breathtakingly theatrical moment (which goes to the heart of the psychological and play-acting violence which runs through the play), George comes in, aims a shotgun at the back of Martha's head and 'a large red and yellow Chinese parasol' pops out at the end. Young Nick knows all about 'chromosomes' and soon George launches into a comical prediction about genetic engineering, defending history and the liberal arts. Meanwhile, Honey has got increasingly drunk and asks when their son is coming home. Martha attacks George, who dismisses any doubt about their son's paternity, and tells Nick that her 'Daddy was looking for someone to take over some time when he was ready to retire', but Daddy came to realize that 'Georgie-boy didn't have the *stuff*', he was a 'a great . . . big . . . fat . . . flop!' The ironically titled first act, 'Fun and Games', ends with Martha reaching a crescendo of disgust with George's failings, while he sings the party song 'Who's afraid of Virginia Woolf?' and Honey rushes off to be sick.

At the start of '*Walpurgisnacht*' (the witches' feast), Nick tells George that he finds Martha's antics embarrassing. He confesses that he married Honey because she had a 'hysteric' (imaginary) pregnancy. The men become increasingly frank with each other and at one point Nick says 'I'd just better get her [Martha] off in a corner and mount her like a goddam dog, eh?' and a primitive struggle between the younger and older man ensues. Honey has now recovered and Martha tells her that when their son was a little boy he also 'used to throw up all the time'. She dances suggestively with Nick and tortures George by reminding him that her father stopped him publishing his novel about a boy who accidentally killed his mother and father, which George had protested was autobiographical. Infuriated, George goes for Martha's throat and says they should play a new game: 'Hump the Hostess' or 'Get the Guests'. He gives a vicious parody of Nick and Honey and her imaginary pregnancy, which makes her sick again. Martha starts to seduce Nick, which, of course,

George witnesses. She says she will make him sorry he made her want to marry him. Honey appears, afraid and ill, and admits that she does not want any children. Meanwhile, Martha and Nick are 'humping' in the kitchen and as the curtain falls George finally says that their 'son is dead'.

The final act, 'The Exorcism', starts with Martha alone. She says:

> We both cry all the time, and then, what we do, we cry, and we take our tears, and we put 'em in the icebox, in the goddam ice trays, until they're all frozen and then . . . we put them . . . in our . . . drinks.

Nick enters, convinced everybody has gone crazy. Martha says that, like George, he is a 'flop'. In an extraordinary passage she speaks of:

> George who is good to me, and whom I revile; who understands me, and whom I push off; who can make me laugh, and I choke it back in my throat; who can hold me at night, so that it's warm, and whom I will bite so there's blood; who keeps learning the games we play as quickly as I can change the rules; who can make me happy, and I do not wish to be happy, and yes I do wish to be happy.
> George and Martha: sad, sad, sad.

George appears, carrying snapdragons, in a bitterly ironic peace gesture, for their 'son's birthday'. But soon he announces: 'we've got one more game to play. And it's called bringing up baby . . . Here we are, on the eve of our boy's home-coming, the eve of his twenty-first birfday' and he and Martha deliver a soaring duologue on the joy of 'the young boy'. Soon they blame each other for their alienation from him. The play reaches an extraordinary, ritualistic, climax as George recites the Latin prayers for the dead, and Martha describes their son as 'the one thing, the one *person* I have tried to protect, to raise above the mire of this vile, crushing marriage'. George then breaks to Martha the devastating news that their son died in a car crash. When Martha demands to see the telegram, he says he ate it. As the curtain falls and George sings 'Who's afraid of Virginia Woolf?', we are left with the dawning realization that the son never existed, that he was invented by the two of them and that game-playing is an essential element in their viciously destructive marriage. Maybe this all-night, alcoholically fuelled feast of hatred has finally exorcized them of their demons.

'Truth and illusion. Who knows the difference, eh, toots? Eh?' asks George at one point, and the depth of Albee's portrayal of the emotional tatters of a hateful marriage lies in its probing of the complex relationship between reality and game play. In the early 1960s America was in a particular kind of crisis – too rich, too powerful, too clever and too foolish – and the marriage of George and Martha, with its rituals and its games, its savagery and its cosiness, is an astonishing metaphor for an entire society in deeper trouble than it knows.

> In performance

Who's Afraid of Virginia Woolf? received its première at the Billy Rose Theater in New York on 13 October 1962, with Uta Hagen as Martha and Arthur Hill as George, in a production by Alan Schneider, a director known above all for his work with Samuel Beckett. It was a considerable success. The acting parts were regarded as so demanding that two casts were required when the play was to be performed twice in the same day. It was first performed in London in 1964, and revived with Diana Rigg and David Suchet in 1996 to great acclaim. A film was made in 1966 with Richard Burton and Elizabeth Taylor, George Segal and Sandy Dennys.

Quotations from Edward Albee, *Who's Afraid of Virginia Woolf?*, Penguin, 1965

Oh What a Lovely War
Theatre Workshop

1963

> Historical and theatrical context

Oh What a Lovely War appeared in a year full of confidence in the possibility of change. The world had survived the Cuban missile crisis in October 1962 and in the last months of his life the young President Kennedy promised to fulfil the hopes of a new generation. Black people were on the move, with Martin Luther King declaring 'I have a dream', while in Britain a weariness with the old way of doing things and a sense that the Conservative Government had run its course resulted in Labour's Harold Wilson coming to power in October 1964, bringing to an end 'thirteen years of Tory misrule'. The old order seemed at last to be fading, but one of the first tasks of the new generation was to understand what had gone wrong.

Theatre Workshop had been set up in 1945 by Joan Littlewood, her partner Gerry Raffles and the singer Ewan McColl, with the aim of touring working-class theatre throughout Wales and the industrial north. In 1953 it took up residence in the dilapidated Theatre Royal Stratford East, and quickly built up an international reputation for classical revivals such as *Arden of Faversham*, *Volpone* and *Edward II*, as well as new plays such as Brendan Behan's *The Quare Fellow* (1956) and *The Hostage* (1958), and Shelagh Delaney's *A Taste of Honey* (1958). This is still a genuinely popular theatre, connected with its local community and producing work of real stature.

Although *Oh What a Lovely War*'s startling theatrical technique seemed highly innovative at the time, it drew its inspiration from experiments in political theatre by Piscator and Brecht in Berlin in the 1920s and 1930s, as well as Meyerhold and others in the early days of the Soviet Union. More importantly, its collaborative and popular nature, under the strict baton of a strong director, had its roots in the best traditions of music-hall and amateur theatre.

> About the play

Oh What a Lovely War has at its centre a number of British soldiers' songs from the First World War. These had been collected by the BBC producer Charles Chilton, whose father had died in the war. On listening to these moving and popular songs – often subversive, sometimes obscene, occasionally breathtakingly beautiful – Littlewood and Raffles asked themselves 'why not let the songs tell the story?' and they wrote the outline of *Oh What a Lovely War* one intense day over a bottle of wine.

Joan Littlewood had been born in 1914. In her autobiography – *Joan's Book* (1994) – she gave a powerful sense of her original inspiration:

> Those songs took me back to childhood – red, white and blue bunting, photos of dead soldiers in silver frames, medals in a forgotten drawer, and that look as family and friends sang the songs of eventide – God, how I loathed those songs – but the pierrot show . . . dirty postcards and ice-cream cornets, sand in your plimsolls and paddling in our knickers.

For its historical analysis, *Oh What a Lovely War* drew on works highly critical of the British General Staff's conduct of the war, in particular Alan Clark's *The Donkeys* (1963).

Oh What a Lovely War is essentially a chronicle of the British experience of the First World War. It opens with a quickfire, cabaret-type summary of the causes of the war. It then gives a vivid sense of the jollity with which Europe went off to slaughter in 1914, the first Christmas in the trenches (the Germans singing 'Heilige Nacht, Stille Nacht') when soldiers on both sides met in No Man's Land, through to the terrible disaster of the Somme in July 1916, the arrival of gas (which blew back into the troops' own trenches when the wind changed), and the battles of attrition of 1917 and 1918 (Passchendaele, Ypres and others). We see the experiences of the common soldiers (who are presented almost entirely uncritically) living in trenches of unspeakable squalor and horror (a leg is used to prop up a wall), obeying insane commands to attack because the alternative is to be shot for cowardice. These are counterpointed with satirical scenes showing the criminal incompetence of the senior officers, squabbling over rank and women, and the vicious greed of the arms manufacturers, worried that peace might break out and their profits be reduced.

Throughout the play, Sir Douglas Haig, the commander of the British forces, is held up to particular ridicule, pressing for his big offensive, forbidding his men to take cover in dugouts, and explaining the policy of attrition:

> We must grind them down. You see, our population is
> greater than theirs and their losses are greater than ours
> . . . In the end they will have five thousand men left and
> we will have ten thousand and we shall have won. In any
> case, I intend to launch one more full-scale offensive, and
> we shall break through and win.

We are also given perspectives from the home front such as women encouraging and shaming the men to go and fight and Emily Pankhust reading from Bernard Shaw and preaching pacifism but being shouted down. In one brilliant scene, we see the way that the newspapers on both sides are full of the same propaganda about the enemy.

The actual dialogue, it has to be said, has neither the sinewy strength of Brecht's *Mother Courage* nor the rhetorical force of Shaw's *Arms and the Man*, nor the poetical power of O'Casey in *The Silver Tassie*. But *Oh What a Lovely War* is a powerful dramatic event whose strangely moving impact lies in the juxtaposition of the deathly white pierrot figures, the ferociously cheerful music-hall patter and the projection of powerful documentary photographs. Perhaps most powerful of all is the rough but deeply felt sound of the songs of the common soldiers who died in such huge numbers in the trenches. The 'newspanel' flashes up facts:

BATTLE OF THE SOMME ENDS . . . TOTAL LOSS . . . 1,332,000 MEN . . . GAIN, NIL.

OCT 12 . . . PASSCHENDAELE . . . BRITISH LOSSES 13,000 MEN IN 3 HOURS . . . GAIN 100 YARDS.

THE WAR TO END WARS . . . KILLED TEN MIL- LION . . . WOUNDED TWENTY-ONE MILLION . . . MISSING SEVEN MILLIONS.

The baldness of these statements makes them almost unbear- able, and at times the songs haunt us like the half-forgotten voices of the dead:

There's a long, long trail a-winding
Into the land of my dreams,
Where the nightingale is singing
And the white moon beams . . .

> In performance

The rehearsals for *Oh What a Lovely War* – which was also the devising period for the piece – are recounted with Joan Littlewood's usual spirit in *Joan's Book*. BBC singers had been engaged, but they quickly withdrew because of different opinions about musical style. One day, Littlewood brought a real drill sergeant into rehearsals who terrified the actors. Together, she and her remarkable company of actors devel- oped a way of telling the story of the Western Front which was popular and serious, funny and heartbreaking, theatrical and true.

Oh What a Lovely War was first performed at the Theatre Royal Stratford East on 19 March 1963 and transferred to the Wyndham's Theatre on 20 June 1963. It was awarded the Grand Prix at the 1963 Paris International Festival of Theatre. The play has been performed all over the world and was revived by the Royal National Theatre in 1999 in a touring circus tent. Richard Attenborourgh made a not entirely successful film of it in 1969, which featured John Gielgud, Ian Holm and Ralph Richardson.

Oh What a Lovely War provided the template for the great boom in cooperative and politically committed theatre companies in Britain in the 1970s and 1980s, such as Joint Stock, 7:84 and many others.

Quotations from Theatre Workshop, *Oh What a Lovely War*, Methuen, 1965; Joan Littlewood, *Joan's Book*, Methuen, 1994

Saved
Edward Bond

1965

> Historical and theatrical context

In October 1964, Harold Wilson's Labour Government was elected on the promise of the 'white heat' of the technological revolution. Early the next year, Winston Churchill died and the Beatles were awarded their MBEs. The post-war consensus was crumbling. Youth culture was on the move, 'the times they were a changin'' and the sixties were about to happen.

Saved was the first of Edward Bond's (born 1934) plays to make a mark. It was commissioned by the Royal Court Theatre in London, after *The Pope's Wedding* had been performed at a 'Sunday night without decor' (a way of trying out new and difficult work at minimum cost). The play gave the new Artistic Director, William Gaskill, his perfect début and helped define the aesthetic principles which dominate the Royal Court to this day. These were summed up by the stage designer Jocelyn Herbert:

> [Devine] wanted to get away from swamping the stage
> with decorative and naturalistic scenery; to let in light and
> air; to take the stage away from the director and designer
> and restore it to the actor and the text.

The Berliner Ensemble's visit to London in 1956 had been influential, but so also was left-wing naturalism, and the essential qualities of the English classical theatre. *Saved* fused these into a new and original vision, one of the purest, and most classical, aesthetic achievements of a decade often criticized for its excess.

Edward Bond's later work includes *Early Morning* (1968), *Narrow Road to the Deep North* (1968), *Lear* (1971), *The Sea*

(1973), *Bingo* (1973), *The Fool* (1975), *The Bundle* (1978), *The Woman* (1978), *Restoration* (1981), *Summer* (1982) and *The War Plays* (1985). Bond increasingly turned to Theatre-in-Education and Young People's Theatre and produced work such as *The Worlds* (1981), *At the Inland Sea* (1995) and *Eleven Vests* (1997). Some feel Bond's emphasis on rationalism has stripped the poetic soul out of his plays, and his work is performed more often in France and Germany than in Britain. Others regard his work as British theatre's greatest twentieth-century achievement.

> About the play

Saved is set on the deprived housing estates of South London. It is a world of young lads in dead-end jobs, of girls getting pregnant to give themselves status, of inarticulacy, casual sex and violence. It is also a world which gets by on laughter and energy, and the attempt, despite it all, to break the patterns that society sets. The play is bleak and to the point, written in a tough, fragmented South-London dialect. But it is also, as Bond himself said, almost 'irresponsibly optimistic'. It is this strange balance between catastrophe and redemption that ultimately makes *Saved* so moving.

Pam has met Len and brought him home to sleep with him, but Pam's father, Harry, is going out on night shift and keeps interrupting them. Len soon becomes a lodger and goes rowing in the park with Pam. They talk about marriage. Four lads are in the park on their lunch break. One of them is going to a funeral for a young boy killed in a traffic accident in which he was involved. They crack jokes about girls and make each other laugh. Pam's mother, Mary, arrives and flirts with the lads.

Pam gives birth to a child which she claims is by her boyfriend Fred and she wants Len to move out. The child's cries are met with complete indifference (people turn up the volume of the telly). Fred arrives to take Pam out on a date. Nobody does anything to help the baby except Len, and even he does not do much. Pam is depressed and Len tries to help her. Len and Fred go fishing as darkness falls. Pam arrives with the pram and Fred shows no interest in her or the baby. They have a row and Pam leaves the baby behind in the park, saying 'An' yer can take yer bloody bastard round yer tart's!' The lads arrive to plan the evening. They start pushing the pram around, joshing and joking, looking for a response from the aspirin-drugged child. Fred throws the first stone and, as the bell rings for the park to close, they stone the baby to death. Len has watched the whole thing and fails to inter- vene. When Pam comes back, she does not even notice that the child is dead.

The second half opens with Fred in a prison cell. Pam is still devoted to him and is waiting for his release. There is growing pressure in the family, and rows between Pam and Len. Meanwhile, Harry and Mary have taken to Len, who has come to replace their son who was killed in the war. When Mary starts to flirt with Len, Harry gets jealous. When Fred is released from prison, he enjoys a new position with his mates. Pam tries to get Len to leave her alone and Fred to come back to her, but fails. Fred storms off. Harry and Mary fight each other, a chair gets broken and Mary smashes a teapot over Harry's head. Pam is in despair:

Why don't 'e go? Why don't 'e go away? All my friends gone. Baby's gone. Nothin' left but rows. Day in, day out.

As with her baby, nobody hears. Len decides to leave but Harry wants him to stay. Harry talks about the war and how he is going to leave Mary one day. In the last scene, Len is accepted into the family and mends the chair. The family is tentatively at peace. As Bond says, they are 'clutching at straws. It's the only realistic thing to do'.

Expressed as bluntly as this, the play can sound desperate- ly pessimistic. But Bond's theatrical technique is exquisitely sophisticated. 'What you have to dramatize is the commen- tary and to show not the structures which the characters impose but those which define them', he says, and it is this powerful sense of society which makes *Saved* such a remarkable work. The behaviour that is shown is not psychopathic but entirely understandable. The analysis is Marxist in its emphasis on violence as 'a function [not] of human nature but of human societies', but the play is full of living, detailed, contradictory human beings.

The quality of the writing is such that its great beauty deliberately clashes with the ugliness being described. As Gaskill says:

> In its delicacy and clarity it reminds me of Chekhov; in its concentration on precise physical actions relentlessly performed it is like a Noh play; in its awareness of imminent violence offstage it is like a Greek tragedy.

Submerged within the drama is an Oedipal story (in which Len flirts with his surrogate mother and fights with his father) carrying its own tragic inevitability. The miraculous fact is that Len rejects this inevitability in favour of moving things on. As Bond says, 'by not playing his traditional role in the tragic Oedipus pattern of the play, Len turns it into what is formally a comedy'. People can be 'saved', even amidst the degradation in which they live. Edward Bond has not only broken all the constricting rules of tragedy; he has written a masterpiece about the possibility of surmounting the terrible alienation of poverty and despair.

> In performance

Saved received its world première on 3 November 1965 at the Royal Court, as part of William Gaskill's first season as Artistic Director (in January 1966, the Court's founding father, George Devine, had died), with a cast that included John Castle (Len), Ronald Pickup (Pete) and Dennis Waterman (Colin). It was almost universally loathed by the critics, who could not see beyond the infamous baby-stoning scene.

Edward Bond had refused the Lord Chamberlain's demands for cuts and a huge row over censorship ensued, which obscured the innate qualities of the play. For its first production, Gaskill decided to turn the theatre into a club (a tactic which had been used earlier for John Osborne's *A Patriot for Me*), but this did not prevent a summons being served in January 1966. Thus *Saved* was both denied a public audience and prosecuted on the grounds that the public had seen it. At the trial, Laurence Olivier, then director of the National Theatre, made a speech defending the play and the Royal Court and Kenneth Tynan set up a forum to discuss the issues. Both Gaskill and the Court were given a conditional discharge but fined fifty guineas costs. A debate was held in the House of Lords and the controversy fuelled the fight against censorship which eventually brought an end to the Lord Chamberlain's powers.

Saved has been revived many times throughout the world. One of the most significant productions was Peter Stein's at the Kammerspiele in Munich in 1967. The Royal Court revived the play in 1984, and there was a particularly well-regarded revival at the Bolton Octagon in 1998. Unfortunately, the play's austere and demanding vision prevent it from being regularly revived.

Quotations from Edward Bond, *Saved*, Methuen, 1966

Rosencrantz and Guildenstern are Dead
Tom Stoppard

1966

> Historical and theatrical context

The mid-1960s were the years of 'swinging London', the Beatles and the Rolling Stones, the mini-skirt and the Pill. England even won the World Cup. But this was also the time of China's catastrophic 'Cultural Revolution', President Johnson's escalation of the American bombing of North Vietnam, the Arab–Israeli Six Day War and a growing sense among many young people that the world needed to change.

Like many others of the post-*Look Back in Anger* generation, Tom Stoppard (born 1937) recognized that 'the theatre was suddenly the place to be'. But he was not interested in sounding the political drum; instead, he went off on a new tack: philosophical, stylish and very un-English. Perhaps his background had something to do with it – born in Czechoslovakia, and a refugee from both Nazi Germany and the war in the Far East, Stoppard came to Britain at the age of nine. His later plays would reflect his engagement with struggles for freedom in his native land, but *Rosencrantz and Guildenstern are Dead* gave us the first sight of the linguistic and theatrical brilliance that has become Stoppard's hallmark, and showed how succesful it could be.

Stoppard's later plays include: *The Real Inspector Hound* (1968), *Jumpers* (1972), *Travesties* (1974), *Every Good Boy Deserves Favour* (1977), *Night and Day* (1978), *The Real Thing* (1982), *Arcadia* (1993), *Indian Ink* (1995) and *The Invention of Love* (1997). He has adapted plays by the Austrian dramatists Schnitzler, Nestroy and Molnar. His radio plays include *If You're Glad I'll Be Frank* (1965), *Albert's Bridge* (1968), *Artist Descending a Staircase* (1973) and *In the Native State* (1991).

TV plays include *Professional Foul* (1977) and *Squaring the Circle* (1984).

> About the play

Stoppard's brilliant début is an extended conceit centred on two peripheral characters in *Hamlet*. In Shakespeare's master-piece, the words of Stoppard's title are spoken by a minor character – the English Ambassador – and Hamlet's treat-ment of them is cursory and brutal. Other writers had been intrigued by the insignificance of such fictional 'bit parts', but the idea of building a whole play around them was decidedly original. The spark came from Stoppard's agent, who had suggested an even more capricious notion: Rosencrantz and Guildenstern arriving with the letter from Claudius to mur-der Hamlet, in an England governed by King Lear.

Stoppard's play-within-a-play-within-a-play explores many of the same questions as its source – the meaning of life and the fact of death, the theatricality of acting and the impossibility of action. As well as Shakespeare, the influence of *Waiting for Godot* is apparent, as is that of T. S. Eliot and the intellectual playfulness of Pirandello, Dada and the Modernists. Behind it all is the philosophical and political pessimism of Stoppard's fellow Czech, Franz Kafka.

The play opens with the slow, unquestioning Rosencrantz and the philosophically sharper Guildenstern – 'two Elizabethan gentlemen' – flipping coins and contemplating the strange law of probability that has brought the coin down eighty-five times in a row as 'heads'. They have no idea why they have arrived at Elsinore. 'We were sent for,' muses Guildenstern (speaking Shakespeare's lines), attempting to anchor himself to something concrete. They chat on, with frequent interferences from *Hamlet*, but no inkling as to their own part in it. A travelling group of players arrives, the cue for a great deal of quick-witted banter on the nature of the-atre, acting and improvisation – in itself a metaphor for the unpredictability and uncertainty of life itself. Guildenstern begs the players to act something, though he cannot afford to pay for it. But he wins a bet and they are just about to start when Hamlet and Ophelia rush in. The two lords find themselves hauled up in front of Claudius and being urged to find out the cause of Hamlet's 'madness'. Thrown into a situation not of their making, they ponder their place in the scheme of things: 'It's a matter of asking the right questions and giving away as little as we can.' It is as if (like Beckett's tramps in *Waiting for Godot*) they are tied to the stage and to their roles in a play they do not understand. Hamlet soon returns with Polonius and the two lords find themselves once more in Shakespeare's play.

In Act Two, Rosencrantz and Guildenstern try to discover the cause of Hamlet's madness. Their dialogue is peppered with a stream of theatre jokes, aphorisms and philosophical musings. Polonius, Claudius and Gertrude enter and the Players rehearse *The Murder of Gonzago*. As the mime continues, the Player King explains that Hamlet has been banished to England and that they have been sent by Claudius to keep an eye on him. Echoing *Hamlet*, the mimed play shows two courtiers being executed. Rosencrantz realizes that the 'actor' courtiers bear uncanny resemblances to himself and Guildenstern, but before they can make more of it, they are swept up into the action of *Hamlet* with Polonius's death, Hamlet's banishment and their departure with him for England.

In Act Three, the scene shifts (with tremendous theatrical flair) to the boat carrying the two of them to England. Guildenstern ruminates on freedom – or their lack of it – and on Claudius's letter to the King of England, asking for Hamlet's death. While they wonder what will happen to them in England, Hamlet (as in Shakespeare) substitutes this letter for another one asking for their deaths instead. The Players are revealed to be aboard, concealed in three barrels. Suddenly the sound of pirates is heard, a general mêlée ensues and Hamlet disappears. Guildenstern is frantic, rips open the letter and discovers all. Bewildered, he stabs the

Player, who falls down dead – only to rise again: it is just one more theatrical joke. But, as Guildenstern reminds us, real death is not the same as a death in the theatre. 'Dying is not romantic, and death is not a game which will soon be over . . .' The play ends with the final scene from Hamlet itself and the last speech is overtaken by darkness, disappearing into the void.

The play's attraction lies in the way that it stretches our minds – our awareness of Shakespeare's masterpiece and our interest in the blanks which are part of its greatness – even as it plays with our emotions. Thus it examines identity and fate in a setting which is already obsessed with it. Just like *Hamlet*, *Rosencrantz and Guildenstern are Dead* is a play concerned with theatricality itself, with illusion, but also with powerlessness and the impossibility of action. 'Words, words, words. They're all we have to go on', says Guildenstern towards the end of Act One. And it is words that Stoppard juggles so brilliantly, both to keep Rosencrantz and Guildenstern occupied in their existential void and audiences dazzled and entertained by his sheer linguistic virtuosity.

> *In performance*

Rosencrantz and Guildenstern are Dead was premièred by an amateur company, the Oxford Theatre Group, on 24 August 1966 as part of the Edinburgh Festival Fringe. The National Theatre's Literary Manager, Kenneth Tynan, read the reviews and sent for a copy of the script. Within a week, he had offered it a slot in the National's repertoire for the following April.

The play received its professional première at the Old Vic Theatre on 11 April 1967, with John Stride and Edward Petherbridge in the title roles. It was an overnight triumph, with the influential critic Harold Hobson calling it 'the most important event in the British professional theatre of the last nine years'. The play has been seen throughout the world and has become a staple of repertory and student companies. In

1990, Tom Stoppard won the Golden Lion award at the Venice Film Festival for the filmed version starring Tim Roth and Gary Oldman, with which he made his directorial début.

Stoppard's award-winning screenplay for *Shakespeare in Love* (1998), which enacts peripheral elements in Shakespeare's life, follows a similar formula to that which made *Rosencrantz and Guildenstern are Dead* such a hit thirty years earlier.

Quotations from Tom Stoppard, *Rosencrantz and Guildenstern are Dead*, Faber and Faber, 1967

What the Butler Saw
Joe Orton

1967

> Historical and theatrical context

The meteoric life and career of Joe Orton (1933–67) epito-
mized the iconoclasm that pervaded so much of British
cultural life in the late 1960s. Openly homosexual when
homosexuality was still criminal (the Sexual Offences Bill was
passed in July 1967), the Leicester-born Orton was a working-class rebel who wanted to '*épater les bourgeois*': 'Get yourself anything you like,' he told his less liberated lover and
mentor, Kenneth Halliwell, 'reject all the values of society.
And enjoy sex.' Orton was battered to death by Halliwell on
10 August 1967.

Largely self-educated, Joe Orton likened himself to the
great Irish stylists – Bernard Shaw, Congreve and Sheridan –
and the *Observer*'s critic, Ronald Bryden, dubbed him 'the
Oscar Wilde of Welfare State gentility'. He was both a sharp-
eyed realist and a master of anarchy, and had been imprisoned
in 1962 for artfully but obscenely defacing library books. He
was an admirer of Ben Travers's Aldwych farces and argued
that 'farce was originally very close to tragedy and differed
only in the treatment of its themes'. His work drew on the
tradition of the British sex comedy, with its smutty innuen-
does and *double entendres*. Wit was Orton's chosen weapon of
attack on the cant and hypocrisy he perceived all around him:
'I write the truth', he declared.

Orton's other plays include *The Ruffian on the Stair*, first
broadcast as a radio play in 1964 together with *The Erpingham
Camp*, produced under the title *Crimes of Passion* (1966/7),
Entertaining Mr Sloane (1964, which Terence Rattigan
declared 'the best first play in thirty years'), *Loot* (1966), *The*

Good and Faithful Servant (televised 1967, staged 1971) and
Funeral Games (televised 1968, staged 1970).

> About the play

Orton completed the first draft of *What the Butler Saw* on 16
July 1967, just three weeks before his death, and expressed
himself well pleased with it. We shall never know how he
might have altered it, although others have tried by tamper-
ing with its highly provocative ending. But the play stands as
an ebullient and theatrical lambasting of a whole range of
authority figures – the medical profession (especially psychi-
atrists), the police, marriage and that untouchable symbol of
'the British spirit', Sir Winston Churchill – with a bravura
that runs from the juvenile to the brilliant.

The play's title may recall a smutty 'McGill' seaside post-
card, but as with all great farce, *What the Butler Saw* is mathe-
matically plotted, with each episode driven by its own internal
logic, culminating in a frenzy of misappropriated identities.
Sex is at its heart – and in its final two-fingers-in-the-air climax
– but Orton's dramatic control throughout is astonishing.

The play is set in a mental asylum and trades stock ideas of
sexual 'normality' (marriage, heterosexuality) and 'abnormality' (homosexuality, transvestitism, incest, rape) and inverts
them. The maddest person on stage is Dr Rance, a senior
government psychiatrist sent to inspect the hospital run by
Dr Prentice. In him we see the designated arbiter of 'normal'
behaviour pushed to the extreme of farce, a sort of psychiatric
Dr Strangelove who sees abnormality at every turn and who
is never happier than when consigning victims to the strait-
jacket. As in the Soviet bloc in the 1960s, a mental hospital is
an instrument of political repression.

The play opens with an attractive young woman,
Geraldine Barclay, coming to see Dr Prentice for an interview as his secretary. In the 'normal' way of things, Dr
Prentice tries to seduce her and an increasingly hysterical
sequence of events is triggered when Prentice's wife walks in.

Miss Barclay, stripped down to panties and bra, hides behind a screen, leaving her clothes lying around in his consulting room. But Mrs Prentice has been enjoying extra-marital excursions of her own, with Nick, a page-boy in the Station Hotel, who has followed her home to blackmail her with photos of their illicit tryst.

In the mêlée that ensues, Miss Barclay's clothes end up on Nick, Nick's on Miss Barclay and Mrs Prentice's on a passing policeman, Sergeant Match. Dr Rance increasingly comes to believe that both Miss Barclay and Dr Prentice are insane and calls for strait-jackets, guns and injections. Mrs Prentice starts to doubt her own sanity and Nick, mistaken for Miss Barclay, is shot. Sergeant Match is drugged and normality is only partially restored by the revelation – *pace* Euripides, Shakespeare and Wilde – that Nick and Geraldine are in fact Mrs Prentice's children, abandoned by her after a wartime rape in a linen cupboard by a stranger who turns out to be Dr Prentice. 'Double incest' salivates Dr Rance, contemplating publication of a book based on recent events, 'even more likely to produce a best-seller than murder'. As the frenzied pace of escaped patients and mistaken identities reaches its climax, Prentice rings the hospital alarm and a grille clangs to the ground. But then a rope ladder descends and the 'prisoners' (of repression? themselves? society?) make their escape, ascending the ladder into 'the blazing light' of freedom.

Orton, however, has one final barb to inflict. On first meeting Dr Prentice, Miss Barclay talks of the loss of her mother under unusual circumstances: blown up by a faulty gas-main together with certain parts of a statue of Sir Winston Churchill. The missing part turns up in the box which Miss Barclay brought in at the beginning and is revealed to be Churchill's phallus. Restored to full complement, 'The Great Man can once more take up his place in the High Street as an example to us all of the spirit that won the Battle of Britain,' enthuses Sergeant Match.

As a gay anarchist, fun at the expense of bourgeois propriety lies at the heart of all Orton's plays. The tone throughout, mischievous and subversive, is almost Wildean: 'What are you doing with that dress?' Mrs Prentice asks of her husband as he attempts to hide it. 'It's an old one of yours,' he replies. 'Have you taken up transvestism?' she barks, 'I'd no idea our marriage teetered on the edge of fashion.' Nowhere did Orton mock the bastions of British institutional life with quite such vitriolic and malevolent glee as in *What the Butler Saw*. Despite its uncomfortable misogyny, the play remains gloriously, tastelessly apt.

> *In performance*

The première of *What the Butler Saw* took place on 5 March 1969, with a stellar cast: Ralph Richardson, Stanley Baxter, Coral Browne and Julia Foster. Despite the abolition of the Lord Chamberlain's Office in 1968, moral squeamishness got the better of the producers and Sir Winston's phallus was replaced by a cigar. The play was still greeted with boos and hisses both on its out-of-town run and at the Queen's Theatre on Shaftesbury Avenue. Cries of 'filth' filled the air. 'They (the audience) really wanted to jump on stage and kill us all,' admitted one of the actors with a guilty sense of exhilaration. The première was reckoned to have been a fiasco. Orton had declared that 'sex is the only way to infuriate them' and *What the Butler Saw* proved him right.

It was not until Lindsay Anderson's 1975 Royal Court revival that the play finally came into its own. Phyllida Lloyd revived it for the National Theatre in 1995, with Richard Wilson as Dr Rance.

Quotations from Joe Orton, *The Complete Works of Joe Orton*, Methuen, 1976

Sizwe Bansi is Dead
Athol Fugard, John Kani and Winston Ntshona

1972

> Historical and theatrical context

Sizwe Bansi is Dead was devised at the height of South Africa's apartheid era, between the crackdown following the Sharpeville massacre of 1960 and the liberalization and collapse of the regime in the 1980s and 1990s. In 1972, as the rest of the world was absorbing the great changes of the 1960s, South Africa seemed stuck in the 1950s. The relative success of South African capitalism produced two different opposition tactics – Marxist–Leninist on the one hand and black nationalist on the other. The African National Congress (ANC) and the liberal opposition was trying to find a way between these two.

As early as the late 1950s, the young white writer Athol Fugard (born 1932) was committed to collaborating with amateur actors from the townships, combining his own understanding of European theatre techniques – particularly Brecht's 'learning plays' – with popular African theatre and story-telling traditions. John Kani had worked in the Ford car plant and Winston Ntshona was a lab assistant before they joined Fugard's Serpent Players in the late 1960s and became the first black professional actors in South Africa.

Athol Fugard's many plays include *Blood Knot* (1961), *Hello and Goodbye* (1965), *Boesman and Lena* (1969), *People Are Living There* (1969), *Statements* (1972), *The Island* (1973), *Dimetos* (1975), *A Lesson from Aloes* (1978), *'Master Harold'* ... *and the Boys* (1982), *The Road to Mecca* (1984), *A Place with the Pigs* (1987), *My Children! My Africa!* (1989) and *Valley Song* (1996). Athol Fugard is one of the key figures, along with novelists Alan Paton, J. M. Coetzee and Nadine Gordimer, in South African anti-apartheid literature.

> About the play

Athol Fugard has always been interested in drama which exploits theatrical potential to the full. His plays tell their stories with the absolute minimum of means and require the simplest settings. Their language is specific and concrete, and charged with a powerful, uniquely South African poetic force. They show in both form and content how invention, energy and wit can surmount the bleakest environment and the cruellest regime.

Sizwe Bansi is Dead is set in Styles's photographic studio in the 'township' of New Brighton, Port Elizabeth. Styles comes on stage with a newspaper and comments on it. ('Ag! American politics. Nixon and all his votes. Means buggerall to us.') In a story which was based directly on John Kani's own experience, Styles describes how when he used to work at the Ford plant, Henry Ford II came on a visit ('Big news for us, man! When a big man like that visited the plant there was usually a few cents more in the pay-packet at the end of the week.') Styles became fed up with the work at Ford and against tremendous odds (including an epic struggle against cockroaches) set up a photographic studio. He describes it as:

> a strong-room of dreams. The dreamers? My people, the simple people, who you never find mentioned in the history books, who never get statues erected to them, or monuments commemorating their great deeds. People who would be forgotten, and their dreams with them, if it wasn't for Styles.

People come to Styles to have their photos taken, mostly poor blacks trying to buy into the capitalist dream of self-improvement. He describes taking a snap of a family of twenty-seven (just before the grandfather died). He talks about his own father who:

fought in France so that this country and all the others
could stay Free. When he came back they stripped him at
the docks – his gun, his uniform, the dignity they'd
allowed him for a few mad years because the world needed men to fight and be ready to sacrifice themselves for
something called Freedom.

Throughout the play, the background is the cruel injustice
and absurd humiliation that the blacks suffered under
apartheid.

A man comes in. He says, somewhat hesitantly, that his
name is Robert Zwelinzima (we find out later, of course, that
his real name is Sizwe Bansi). He wants a picture to send to
his wife who is far away in King William's Town. Styles tries
to teach him how to look happy and optimistic. He gives him
props and provides background pictures of a futuristic city, to
give the illusion of prosperity and comfort. When the camera
finally flashes, we find ourselves looking at a photo which
'comes to life' as he speaks his letter to his wife Noretu.

In his letter, the man says he has 'wonderful news . . . Sizwe
Bansi, in a manner of speaking, is dead'. He says he has been
forced to leave Port Elizabeth and is going to be 'repatriated'.
But he wants to stay in Port Elizabeth because the work is
there. His life is ruled by the all-important passbook and, like
all blacks under Apartheid, he is a victim of the cruel and petty-
minded bureaucracy of tyranny and oppression. He tells his
wife that he has met a man called Buntu and, in a passage that
could be straight out of the *Book of Job*, Buntu tells the story of
the life and death of Outa Jaco:

> The only time we'll find peace is when they dig a hole for
> us and press our face into the earth.

Sizwe Bansi enacts the night he went out drinking in a shebeen. He is walking back and 'needs a piss' and stumbles
across a dead man. He takes the dead man's passbook and
notices it has a work permit. He soon asks the central questions of the play:

I wish I was dead. I wish I was dead because I don't care a damn about anything any more . . . What's happening in this world, good people? Who cares for who in this world? Who wants who? . . . Who wants me friend? What's wrong with me? I'm a man. I've got eyes to see. I've got ears to listen when people talk. I've got a head to think good things. What's wrong with me? . . . Look at me! I'm a man. I've got legs. I can run with a wheelbarrow full of cement! I'm strong! I'm a man.

The photos in the passbook are soon exchanged and Sizwe Bansi becomes Robert Zwelinzima. He can now get a job at the Feltex factory and support his family in King William's Town. In a brilliant sequence, Buntu and he act out his receiving his first pay cheque, buying a suit, memorizing his Native Identity Number, and even enacting his Burial Society registration.

Buntu gives Bansi/Zwelinzima advice, which contains within it the key to survival in a cruel and unjust world.

Shit on names, man! To hell with them if in exchange you can get a piece of bread for your stomach and a blanket in winter. Understand me brother, I'm not saying that pride isn't a way for us. What I'm saying is shit on our pride if we only bluff ourselves that we are men.

What is a man's worth, when he is afforded no value by his society? The only way to survive is to play the game. Switching identity and denying who you are is the best way through.

In *Sizwe Bansi is Dead* Athol Fugard wrote the greatest political drama since Brecht. It brings to a situation of monstrous cruelty a passion for justice, profound humanity, a joyous theatrical spirit and a deeply felt poetic sensibility. It is to the play's credit, and to that of the anti-apartheid movement in the arts as a whole, that the system that the writers despised has finally fallen.

> *In performance*

Athol Fugard described the squalid rehearsal conditions for *Sizwe Bansi* in his Notebook:

> A Group Areas ruling had closed down the school so Johnny, Winston and I were able to rent a classroom to rehearse. Appalling and depressing contrast with the building of five years ago when we rehearsed *Antigone* . . . Then it had been well-kept and clean and bustling with activity. This time we encountered total dereliction – classroom floors strewn with abandoned textbooks, maps, etc., the last lessons fading away on blackboards, windows and doors smashed, and on everything a thick layer of the ugly grey-blue dust of Korsten.

The play had its première on 8 October 1972 at the recently established Space Theatre in Cape Town in a production directed by Athol Fugard and performed by his co-writers John Kani and Winston Ntshona. It was seen at the Royal Court in London in 1973 and was part of the influential South African Season there in 1974 when it was set alongside *The Island*, the same writers' great play about Robben Island, the prison where Nelson Mandela, and other ANC leaders were held. The plays were premièred in New York in 1974. *Sizwe Bansi is Dead* was hailed by liberal audiences but criticized as being anti-South African by apologists for the regime.

The play's success led to the foundation, with the director Barney Simon, of the Market Theatre in Johannesburg: a beacon of tolerance in a racist society. In 1963, forty-five British writers had signed a declaration refusing South African performing rights for their work. Others soon followed and no new European or American plays were performed in South Africa until the downfall of apartheid. In the early 1970s it was left to the Market Theatre, and Athol Fugard in particular, to provide an indigenous opposition voice.

Quotations from Athol Fugard, *Notebooks*, Faber and Faber, 1983

Absurd Person Singular
Alan Ayckbourn

1972

> *Historical and theatrical context*

The early 1970s was a time of increasing social polarization in Britain. The youthful optimism of the late 1960s had given way to a darker mood. Edward Heath's Conservative government (1970–4) was battling to contain union might, the 1960s economic boom was fading fast and Ulster was suffering its worst crisis since 1921.

The early 1970s also saw an enormous growth in subsidized theatres in Britain – a moment of expansion and investment before the financial crises of the mid-1970s and the cultural retrenchment of the 1980s. The dominant spirit in the theatre was one of radicalism and the early 1970s saw writers and directors emerging who regarded their craft primarily as a tool for social change.

To Alan Ayckbourn (born 1939), however, drama was something far more pragmatic – popular entertainment. He had worked in the theatre since he was seventeen and started writing in 1965, as a radio drama producer in Leeds. Stephen Joseph at Scarborough asked him for a play that would 'make people laugh when their seaside summer holidays were spoiled by the rain' and *Relatively Speaking* was the result. Ayckbourn was still declaring in 1999: 'I want to make it as fun as possible for the audience'.

Ayckbourn was the most commercially successful British playwright of the twentieth century. His work sits squarely between the classic farces of Pinero, Feydeau and Labiche and popular British sex comedies. Ayckbourn introduces a fresh and sharp social commentary into farce, and *Absurd Person Singular* gave the first hint, Joe Orton apart, of something significant emerging from a field that had been consistently derided. As he said, 'fun doesn't have to mean mindless fun'.

Ayckbourn's more than fifty other stage plays include: *Relatively Speaking* (1965), *How the Other Half Loves* (1970), *Family Circles* (1970), *The Norman Conquests* (1974), *Absent Friends* (1974), *Bedroom Farce* (1977), *Just Between Ourselves* (1977), *Joking Apart* (1978), *Way Upstream* (1982), *A Chorus of Disapproval* (1985), *Woman in Mind* (1985), *A Small Family Business* (1987), *Mr A's Amazing Maze Plays* (1988 – for children), *Communicating Doors* (1994), *The Things We Do for Love* (1998), *Comic Potential* (1998) and *House* and *Garden* (1999).

Alan Ayckbourn has been Artistic Director of the Stephen Joseph Theatre in Scarborough since 1971. He usually directs the premières of his own plays there, and many of them have transferred to London and Broadway.

> *About the play*

Ayckbourn had already proved with *Relatively Speaking* that he was a natural *farceur* with an uncommon flair for comic invention. But in *Absurd Person Singular* he harnessed this to a brilliant and serious social metaphor and started to explore themes which were to preoccupy him for many years: English insensitivity and casual cruelty; male oppression and female neurosis; the sterility of English middle-class family life and the festive rituals that are such a gruesome part of it. Desperation cowering just beneath the surface of socialized behaviour is the stuff of Ayckbourn's acutely observed social comedy.

Formally, *Absurd Person Singular* introduced the multi-perspective device that became one of Ayckbourn's trademarks, allowing for repeated incidents seen through the eyes of various couples, in different time spans and locations. The play also exploits the 'dramatic possibilities of offstage action', used brilliantly to explore social mobility and 'relative values'. It is, as he says, the 'first of [his] offstage action plays'.

Absurd Person Singular opens in Sidney and Jane Hopcroft's spotlessly kept, gadget-filled kitchen, 'Last Christmas'. Sidney is an upwardly mobile builder/property developer, a dab hand at DIY, and Jane is his willing and put-upon wife. They are holding a small drinks party to which they have invited local friends and it is clear to Sidney that they will be useful to him: Ronald, a bank manager, and his gushing wife Marion, along with a local architect called Geoffrey and his pill-popping, neglected wife, Eva.

The characters are sketched in with Ayckbourn's usual speed and precision. Jane is obsessive about cleaning and Sidney is the kind of husband who undermines his wife at every turn; Ronald is vague and Marion is a tippler; Geoffrey is a compulsive womanizer and Eva is desperate. Lower-middle-class pretensions are ruthlessly lampooned, not least when Jane, having forgotten to buy enough soft drinks, is forced by sheer social terror (and Sidney) to rush through her own lounge in gumboots, raincoat and hat as if she were a delivery boy from the local off-license. Meanwhile, offstage and unseen, are two further guests, Dick and Lottie ('monstrously overwhelming, hearty and ultimately very boring, and far better heard occasionally but not seen'); with great comic skill, Ayckbourn has his characters talk to them offstage and suddenly change as soon as they are out of earshot.

The play's *tour de force* is its second act, set 'This Christmas', in Geoffrey and Eva's perfect middle-class kitchen. Eva's distress has deepened into suicidal despair. The off-stage hilarity now focuses on Geoffrey and Eva's large dog, whose intimidating growls prevent the guests from leaving the kitchen. In a series of remarkable sequences, both funny and disturbing, Eva tries to commit suicide in a variety of ways, all unsuccessfully. Her guests, oblivious to her true state, mistake each attempt as a request for more practical help in the kitchen. Blackly comic in its depiction of human selfishness, Ayckbourn's skill is at a pitch of ferocity seldom surpassed, even by his own prodigious standards.

Act Three takes place 'Next Christmas', in the run-down

home of Ronald and Marion. As Ayckbourn says, the tone of the writing 'darkens considerably' and the scene is one of unmitigated domestic collapse. There is no heating and Ronald is camping in his own home. Marion's drinking has turned into outright alcoholism and she has become a recluse, shut up in her bedroom. When Geoffrey and Eva appear, their marriage seems to have changed too: Geoffrey's career is on the skids due to his involvement in a failed shopping development, while Eva has recovered and is now in charge.

With grim inevitability, Sidney and Jane also turn up uninvited and give the reluctant host and guests wildly inappropriate Christmas presents. Sidney is now riding high as a property developer and he bullies his unfortunate host and friends into playing a game of Musical Forfeits. The roles are firmly reversed and the humiliation of the former professionals – bank manager and architect – is complete. They must all now dance to a different tune: 'Dance. Come on. Dance. Come on. Dance. Dance. Keep dancing,' exhorts the triumphant Sidney.

Absurd Person Singular shows Ayckbourn at a fascinating point in his development, revealing himself as both comic virtuoso and astute social commentator. The play's exploration of the middle classes discovering an aggressive and entrepreneurial streak foretold the social changes that were to overtake England in the decade that followed. It would be hard to think of a play that caught this seismic moment with greater hilarity or pain than *Absurd Person Singular*.

> *In performance*

Absurd Person Singular opened at the Library Theatre in Scarborough in 1972, before moving to the Criterion Theatre in London the following year in a production directed by Eric Thompson, with Richard Briers as Sidney.

Ayckbourn's work is performed all over the world, especially in Germany where he is valued for his 'critique' of class and bourgeois behaviour.

In 1997, Ayckbourn became the first playwright to be knighted since Terence Rattigan.

Quotations from Alan Ayckbourn, *Three Plays*, Penguin Books, 1979

American Buffalo
David Mamet

1975

> Historical and theatrical context

By 1975, the United States faced a crisis of confidence. Two years earlier, fourfold oil price rises had challenged America's confidence in the supremacy of its economy. In August 1974, President Nixon had finally resigned, to avoid the impeachment to which the Watergate scandal was heading, leaving his successor Gerald Ford to declare – somewhat optimistically – that the country's 'long nightmare' had come to an end. In April 1975, the North Vietnamese Communists took Saigon, leaving America divided about this most traumatic of wars. Meanwhile, the emergence of the 'new right', both in the US and in Britain, was being built on a widespread perception of the economic, moral and cultural and failure of 1960s liberalism.

One of the great strengths of the Chicago-born David Mamet (born 1947) is that he is first and foremost a man of the theatre. He was a founding member and Artistic Director of the St Nicholas Theater Company in Chicago and in 1978 was appointed Associate Artistic Director of the Goodman Theatre, also in Chicago, where many of his plays were premièred. He has become increasingly involved in the British theatre, directing work by other writers as well as having some of his plays first performed in London.

Mamet's plays include *Duck Variations* (1972), *Sexual Perversity in Chicago* (1976), *The Water Engine* (1977), *Prairie du Chien* (1979), *Glengarry Glen Ross* (1983), *Edmond* (1982), *Speed-the-Plow* (1988), *Oleanna* (1993), *The Cryptogram* (1994) and *A Boston Marriage* (2001). He is also the author of several volumes of essays, three novels, half a dozen screenplays and a first-class translation of Chekhov's *The Cherry Orchard*.

He has published a provocative book about acting entitled *True and False* (1998).

> About the play

American Buffalo is prefaced by two lines from an old American folk-tune:

> Mine eyes have seen the glory of the coming of the Lord,
> He is peeling down the alley in a black and yellow Ford.

The tone of this verse exactly matches the play's jaunty, comic American flavour, with its yoking together of the deepest strands of American myth ('The Battle Hymn of the Republic') with the colourful detritus of America's consumerist scrapyard. The play is set in a junkshop and an essential part of Mamet's purpose is the image of a small American business, morally bankrupt, industrially deserted and trading on the junk of the past. In this parable of late-twentieth century America, it is as if all the old ideals of thrift, hard work and creativity of America's founding fathers have been broken up and left to rot.

The play has three characters: Don Dubrow, in his late forties and the owner of Don's Resale Shop; his friend Walter Cole (always known as Teach); and young Bob, Don's gopher, who is desperate for money. The men are tough-talking and weak-willed, some of Mamet's most acute portrayals of male bluster.

It is morning. Bob has let Don down, because he has not kept his look-out for 'the guy'. Don tells him 'that this isn't good enough. If you want to do business . . . if we got a business deal, it isn't good enough' and talks in almost moralistic terms about the way business works. He praises his friend Fletcher, who won 'four hundred bucks' in last night's poker game:

> You take him [Fletcher] and you put him down in some strange town with just a nickel in his pocket, and by night-fall he'll have that town by the balls. This is not talk, Bob, this is action . . . And this is why I'm telling you to stand

up. It's no different with you than with anyone else. Everything that I or Fletcher know we picked up on the street. That's all business is . . . common sense, experience, and talent.

Then he starts lecturing Bob about the importance of a proper breakfast. When Teach turns up, he is in a filthy mood: not only did he also lose money at poker, but the girl (Ruthie) who did win money last night won't even buy him breakfast ('Southern bulldyke asshole of a vicious nowhere cunt').

Teach is appalled at the price of the junk in the shop ('If I kept the stuff I threw out . . . I would be a wealthy man today. I would be cruising on some European yacht.') Bob has good news: he saw 'the guy' putting a suitcase in his car and leaving the house in travelling clothes. Don tells Teach of his plan to steal 'the guy's' coin collection and sell it to a specialist, saying that 'the guy' came into the shop and much to Don's surprise ('I didn't even know it's there') offered him fifty dollars for 'a buffalo-head nickel [five-cent piece] from nineteen something', which cleverly, Don sold to him for ninety. Teach is interested in the plan, but warns Don not to 'send the kid in', suggesting he should do the robbery himself ('I'll go in and gut this motherfucker'). His fifty per cent cut would be 'better than the ninety per cent of some broken toaster that you're gonna have, you send the kid in'.

Bob returns with 'a piece of pie and a Pepsi'. He wants his money up front, but Don will only offer him 'twenty [dollars] for spotting the guy'. Don is reluctant to let him in on the burglary. Disappointed, Bob leaves, but with fifty dollars (partly loaned) in his hand. Meanwhile, Teach is desperate to get going and he and Don talk about the burglary like two businessmen speculating on the market ('Wake up. Don, let's plan this out. The *spirit* of the thing? . . . Let's not be loose on this. People are *loose*, people pay the price'). But underneath is anxiety: how will they find the coins in the 'guy's house' and how will they know which ones to take when some are valuable and others are worth only 'twenty fucking cents'? Don wants Fletch to join them, to put 'some depth on the team', and Teach finally agrees, declaring grandiloquently that it will give them 'safety in numbers . . . a division of labour'. They 'lay the shot out' (they will meet that night at eleven o'clock) and go out on their own.

It is 11.15 at night. Don is on the phone. Fletcher has not shown up. Bob arrives, wanting to sell Don a buffalo-head nickel that he has found, hoping that Don will offer him 'ninety bucks'. Teach turns up late because his watch broke. Teach and Don are desperately nervous, squabbling with each other, arguing and worrying, trying to work out how to do the burglary, terrified that too many people know, confused about why Fletch has not turned up and anxious about how they are going to crack the safe (if he has got a safe). Running through all this is a strange philosophical meandering:

> Free enterprise [is]. . .the freedom . . . Of the *Individual*
> . . . To Embark on any Fucking Course that he sees fit . . .
> In order to secure his honest chance to make a profit. Am
> I so out of line on this? . . . Does this make me a Commie?
> . . . The country's *founded* on this Don. You know this.

Things come to a head when Teach makes the connection between Fletch's non-appearance and 'the kid' coming in with 'a certain coin'. Teach draws a gun (for 'protection, deterrence'). When Bob arrives, he says Fletch is in hospital, but when Don rings the hopital he finds that Fletcher is not there. Don and Teach beat Bob up, but it soon transpires that Fletcher *is* in hospital, but not the one they thought (Columbus Hospital, significantly named). Don and Teach are about to take Bob there (they will say that Bob fell down the stairs) when they find out that Bob bought the nickel for fifty dollars. When Bob also says that he did not see 'the guy with the suitcase that morning', Teach has an hysterical, rhetorically charged outburst:

> He's saying he didn't see the guy?
> When he came out, I was in here. *Then* you saw him.

When he had the suitcase.
Then.
You saw him *then*.
My Whole Cocksucking Life.
The Whole Entire World.
There Is No Law.
There Is No Right And Wrong.
The World Is Lies.
There Is No Friendship.
Every Fucking Thing.

At the centre of the play is the image of the extinct American buffalo on the old nickel, a perfect metaphor for the adventure of American capitalism as well as the moral corruption that undermines it. The dramatic tension is extraordinarily well constructed, thrilling to watch, like a battlefield. It examines with humour and energy the powerful connection between business and crime which is so often evident in Mamet's work. But the play is also about language itself. With its vernacular thickness and inarticulate masculine poetry, *American Buffalo* stands at the heart of the great American dramatic tradition.

> In performance

American Buffalo was premièred on 23 November 1975 at the Goodman Theatre in Chicago, in a production directed by Mamet's long-time associate Gregory Mosher. Its first British production was at the Cottesloe Theatre in June 1978, directed by Bill Bryden. The film actors Robert Duvall and Al Pacino have both played the part of Teach, in New York and London respectively, and the play has been revived all over the world. The 1997 film version starring Dustin Hoffman was directed by Michael Corrente.

American Buffalo won an Obie award in 1977.

Quotations from David Mamet, *American Buffalo*, Methuen, 1978

Plenty
David Hare

1978

> *Historical and theatrical context*

Britain in 1978 was a society with an identity crisis. The post-war consensus of universal welfare funded by progressive taxation had broken down. Britain's economy was declining, relative to its competitors, and the Trade Unions were increasingly regarded as 'bloody-minded'. A political philosophy emerged, led by the Conservative Party's new leader, Margaret Thatcher, that insisted that the failures of a series of British governments and the excesses of the 1960s had created a society in which personal responsibility was shirked and business could not thrive. The 'winter of discontent' (1978–9), in which rubbish was not collected and the dead lay unburied, seemed emblematic of a once great nation in terminal decline.

Britain's theatre was similarly divided. The 1970s had seen a huge growth in the 'fringe' and radical, alternative theatre companies were springing up everywhere. But the recently opened National Theatre on the South Bank in London seemed to be soaking up resources while the regional and repertory theatres were beginning to feel the chill wind of recession.

David Hare (born 1947) had helped set up the anarchist, or situationist, Portable Theatre group, which was interested in dramatizing the 1960s view that a complete breakdown of society was imminent. In 1978, he publicly attacked the crudities of some Marxist theatre, and argued for genuinely inquiring plays which asked difficult questions, rather than simply coming up with ready-made answers.

David Hare's other stage plays include *Slag* (1970), *Lay-by* (1971, written collaboratively with five others), *Brassneck* (1973, with Howard Brenton), *Knuckle* (1974), *Fanshen* and *Teeth 'n' Smiles* (1975), *Licking Hitler* (1978, for television), *A Map of the World* (1983), *Pravda* (1985, with Howard Brenton), *The Secret Rapture* (1988), a trilogy for the National Theatre – *Racing Demon* (1990), *Murmuring Judges* (1991), and *The Absence of War* (1993), *Skylight* (1995), *Amy's View* (1997), *Via Dolorosa* (1998), *The Judas Kiss* (1998) and *My Zinc Bed* (2000), as well as adaptations of Brecht, Chekhov and Schnitzler.

> About the play

Plenty opens with the 'middle thirties' Susan Traherne sitting on a packing case in an overcoat, rolling herself a cigarette. It is London's Knightsbridge in 1962. Her husband is lying naked at her feet: he has taken 'a couple of Nembutal and twelve fingers of Scotch'. The room is cleared of all furniture and Susan is about to leave. She is with her friend Alice: 'Tell him I left with nothing that was his. I just walked out on him.'

Suddenly the play flashes back nineteen years to November 1943, to occupied France, where Susan – a courier in the French Resistance – is meeting an English fighter, code-named 'Lazar', who has just arrived by parachute. She is sharp and effective:

A friend who was here used to say, never kill a German, always shoot him in the leg. That way he goes to hospital where he has to be looked after, where he'll use up enemy resources. But a dead soldier is forgotten and replaced.

The next scene is set in the British Embassy in Brussels in 1947, where Susan strikes up an unlikely but sharp-witted liaison with the upright and kindly Third Secretary Raymond Brock, who is bored of Brussels.

A few months later they are married, but Brock still lives in Brussels while Susan shares her drab Pimlico flat with the foul-mouthed Alice ('I thought my clitoris was like a torch battery, you know, use it too much and it runs out'). Susan's restlessness is palpable: 'I'd like to change everything but I don't know how'. The fact is that she misses the excitement of the war and her marriage is in trouble.

In 1951, Susan is working for the Festival of Britain. She asks the working-class Mick, a man she hardly knows, to father her child. She is becoming increasingly independent in her thinking:

> I'm afraid I'm rather strong-minded, as you know, and so with them [men] I usually feel I'm holding myself in for fear of blowing them out of the room. They are kind, they are able, but I don't see . . . why I should have to compromise, why I should have to make some sad and decorous marriage just to have a child. I don't see why any woman should have to do that.

By 1952, Susan has become an artist. Mick turns up, now in love with her. But Susan is still not pregnant and wants to stop sleeping with him. When Mick calls her 'cruel and dangerous' and 'actually mad' she appears with a pistol and shoots over his head three times.

Susan's behaviour becomes increasingly eccentric. At an official dinner party at the height of the Suez crisis she finally loses all attempts at decorum. It is an acutely satirical and strangely poignant scene which catches the hypocrisy and deviousness of the British establishment with merciless accuracy:

> **Brock** I see, I see, so what you're saying is, the British may do anything, doesn't matter how murderous, doesn't matter how silly, just so long as we do it in good faith.

> **Darwin** Yes, I would have defended it, I wouldn't have minded how damned stupid it was. I would have defended it had it been honestly done. But this time we are cowboys and when the English are cowboys, then in truth I fear for the future of the globe.

Having insulted the Burmese Ambassador's wife, Susan declares:

> Even for myself I do like to make a point of sleeping with men I don't know. I do find once you get to know them you usually don't want to sleep with them any more.

In 1961 – moments after Darwin's funeral – Susan helps the 'stupid' seventeen-year-old Dorcas with money for an abortion ('Kill a child. That's easy. No problem at all.'). But Brock's career is in trouble, and Susan goes to see Sir Andrew Charleson, the Head of Personnel at the Foreign Office, to plead for him. She challenges him:

> **Susan** What you are saying is that nobody may speak, nobody may question . . .
>
> **Sir Andrew Charleson** Certainly tact is valued very high . . . that is the nature of the service, Mrs Brock. It is called diplomacy. And in its practise the British lead the world . . . [but] as our power declines, the fight among us for access to that power becomes a little more urgent, a little uglier perhaps. As our influence wanes, as our empire collapses, there is little to believe in. Behaviour is all.

When Susan has got nowhere, she declares:

> If Brock is not promoted in the next six days, I am intending to shoot myself.

But this fails and by 1962, the time of the first scene of the play, Brock is out of work and increasingly convinced that Susan is insane. When she breaks an expensive ornament on purpose he denounces her:

> Your life is selfish, self-interested gain. That's the most charitable interpretation to hand. You claim to be protecting some personal ideal always at a cost of almost infinite pain to everyone around you. You are selfish, brutish, unkind. Jealous of other people's happiness as

well, determined to destroy other ways of happiness they find.

But he still loves her and wants to talk it through. However, at the end of the scene she 'pours out a spectacularly large Scotch [and] pushes it across the table to Brock'.

Susan's final flight into illusion signals a profound disappointment with the values of a world that failed to produce the changes so longed for. 'There will be days and days and days like this' she enthuses in her final hallucination of how it was, in a French field full of golden corn in 1942 – transformed miraculously from the 'filthy' Blackpool hotel where she meets up with 'Lazar' again in 1962 within months of leaving her husband.

Hare has said that 'people go clinically mad if what they believe bears no relation to how they live' and Susan's 'madness' is a protest against the lies and deceptions forced upon her by English conformity: 'The clearest way I can describe *Plenty*', Hare has said, 'is as a play about the cost of spending your whole life in dissent'. But Hare has another, less austere intention:

> I write love stories. Most of my plays are that. Over and over again I have written about romantic love because it never goes away. And the view of the world it provides, the dislocation it offers, is the most intense experience that many people know on earth.

Sometimes sentimental, sometimes arch, always theatrical, and often sharply satirical, the play is both an extended eulogy for a moment of romantic bliss felt by so many in war-time but never repeated in times of 'plenty', and a powerful portrait of a country trapped by the myths of its past.

> In performance

Hare has spoken of how women have influenced his plays and *Plenty* was no exception. When first staged at the National

Theatre in 1978, Susan was played by the Canadian actress Kate Nelligan, to whom he paid tribute: 'Kate had not just a faultless ear for my lines, but a very extraordinary tension in her physicality as well.'

In retrospect, *Plenty* was Hare's stepping-stone to mainstream popularity and he has hardly looked back. The play went to Broadway and was made into a film with Meryl Streep, Charles Dance and John Gielgud in 1985. In April 1999, its revival by the Almeida Theatre in the West End starred Australia's charismatic Cate Blanchett as Susan Traherne.

Quotations from David Hare, *Plenty*, Faber and Faber, 1978

Translations
Brian Friel

1981

> Historical and theatrical context

Translations was written against the background of Northern Ireland's escalating violence, the collapse of the power-sharing experiment in Stormont and despair at the hardening of attitudes in both the Protestant and Catholic communities. Lord Mountbatten, a close friend of the Royal Family, was assassinated by the IRA in 1979 and in 1981 IRA man Bobby Sands starved himself to death on hunger strike in the Maze Prison. The election of centre-right governments in Britain and the United States simply strengthened the mood of uncompromising confrontation.

In the face of this, there emerged throughout Ireland a growing belief in cultural politics as the best way of bringing about political and social change. The economic boom in the Republic (Eire) helped bring about a revival of interest in Irish traditions: folk music, traditional dancing and the Gaelic language, all of which had previously been in decline.

Brian Friel (born 1929) is a Northern Irish Catholic from Omagh. When he was ten, his family moved to the depressed and predominantly Catholic Derry, where he grew up in the time of 'triumphalist Unionism'. His father was a schoolmaster and Friel learned Gaelic as a boy. Though sympathetic to the Nationalist cause, Friel has never been an explicitly political writer. He moved to County Donegal, in the Republic, in the 1960s.

Friel's many other plays include *Philadelphia, Here I Come!* (1964), *The Freedom of the City* (1973), *Volunteers* (1975), *Aristocrats* (1979), *Faith Healer* (1980), *The Communication Cord* (1983), *Making History* (1988), *Dancing at Lughnasa*

(1990), *Wonderful Tennessee* (1993), *Molly Sweeney* (1994) and *Give Me Your Answer, Do!* (1997), as well as adaptations of Chekhov and Turgenev. A volume of Friel's *Essays, Diaries, Interviews: 1964–1999* was published in 1999.

> About the play

Translations is set in the fictional community of Baile Beag (or BallyBeg) in the wilds of County Donegal in 1833, only a decade before the potato famine would change Ireland for ever. It is a Gaelic-speaking, materially deprived, inward-looking community. The play takes place in a 'hedge school' – one of the many informal, outdoor schools that were common throughout Ireland in the early nineteenth century. It captures the moment when Gaelic education was being replaced by the imposed English Language National Schools.

Friel has revealed that he had been thinking of writing a play:

> about the nineteenth century, somewhere between the Act of Union and the Great Famine, a play about Daniel O'Connell and Catholic emancipation; a play about colonialism; and the one constant – a play about the death of the Irish language and the acquisition of English and the profound effect that that change-over would have on a people.

One of Friel's sources, John Andrews's *A Paper Landscape*, was published in 1975 just as Friel discovered that his great-great-grandfather, who had been a travelling scholar who educated the rural poor, had settled in Donegal. Friel was also reading George Steiner's *After Babel* for its exploration of the difficulties of translation, of locating private meanings and of understanding the nature of individual truth. Suddenly, Friel had his theatrical and philosophical metaphor – the standardization of Ireland through the mapping of its countryside to bring it into line with the rest of the United Kingdom.

Like Chekhov, *Translations* is constructed out of contradictions: the old and the new, Irish and English temperaments, men and women. Too quizzical to be overtly political, Friel's aim is to shift attitudes by gently mocking the old Ireland with its backward-looking attachment to the past and suggesting that, however tragically, that attachment must give way to change.

Act One sets the scene and introduces a brilliant theatrical conceit. Friel's locals are for the most part Gaelic-speakers, but Friel contrives it that we understand they are non-English speakers while they are speaking English (and sometimes Latin and Greek). We meet Hugh O'Donnell, the drunken but classically knowledgeable hedge-school master, and his students; Hugh's patient, gammy-legged son, Manus; the silent and speech-impeded Sarah; Maire, a bright local girl who sees English as a way to realize her dream and move to the USA; Jimmy Jack, in whom the gods and goddesses of Classical texts live more vividly than everyday reality; and Doalty and Bridget, typical village gossips, weasely and unpredictable in their affiliations and loyalties.

Into this closed community come two English engineers, sent to carry out an official Ordnance Survey of the area: the upright imperial servant, Captain Lancey, and his subordinate, the romantic Lieutenant Yolland. With them is their interpreter, Hugh's other son, Owen, who has 'escaped' but is now returning home from Dublin. With the ambivalent Owen (whose 'interpreting' is a crucial part of the colonizing process) and his developing relationship with Yolland, Friel draws out cultural, tribal and linguistic differences in unexpected ways. Perhaps surprisingly, it is the Englishman, Yolland, who first realizes that 'something is being eroded' in the process of renaming. And it is Yolland who, finding in Baile Beag 'a consciousness that wasn't striving nor agitated but at its ease and with its own conviction and assurance', exchanges love tokens with the Gaelic-speaking Maire in Act Two. Neither speaks the other's language, but they manage to

communicate their mutual attraction and in them Friel sym-
bolizes the movement of old Ireland into its future.

This romance is the last moment of joy in a play that hurries
towards a desolate end. Sarah has seen the lovers embrace. She
manages to tell Manus, who had hoped to marry Maire and
take her with him to a job he has been offered as a hedge-
master in the south. Devastated, Manus decides to move
away. Yolland, meanwhile, has gone missing after walking
Maire home. Friel implies that these events are about to
bring about a change of heart in Owen, who learns from
Bridget and Doalty that Yolland may have been murdered by
local rebels. In reprisal, Lancey threatens to lay waste the
entire area if news of Yolland's fate is not revealed.

The play ends in despair, the earlier scenes of rural simpli-
city replaced by uncertainty and an even greater polarization
between the Irish and their English colonizers. It is left to
Hugh to speak the final words, in a classical allusion that
harks back to an earlier struggle for civil rights:

> an ancient city which t'is said, Juno loved above all the
> lands . . . Yet in truth she discovered that a race was
> springing from Trojan blood to overthrow some day these
> Tyrian towers.

But this speech carries an ironic twist. Earlier Hugh had said
of the new anglicized place names 'we must learn to make
them our own'. By the end, his powers of memory and the
oral tradition that had been the key to his people's identity is
failing. The past, it seems, is already disappearing.

In writing *Translations*, Friel drew on historical fact, particularly in relation to the English characters, but then recast
them for his own purposes. This brought him considerable
criticism and he was accused of historical distortion. But
there is no doubt about Friel's artistic achievement with
Translations, which stands as one of the most powerful and
eloquent plays about national identity, cultural memory and
linguistic colonialism. In the tragedy of one small community, Friel found a metaphor for an entire troubled island.

> *In performance*

Translations was the first play produced by the young, Derry-based Field Day Theatre Company founded by Brian Friel in 1980 with the actor Stephen Rea, musician David Hammond and poets Seamus Deane, Seamus Heaney and Tom Paulin.

The play was premièred in Derry in September 1980 with Stephen Rea, Ray McAnally and Liam Neeson in the cast. The *Irish Press* described 'a unique occasion with loyalists and nationalists, Unionists and SDLP, Northerners and Southerners laying aside their differences to join in applauding a play by a fellow Derryman, and one with a theme that is uniquely Irish'. The play soon transferred to London's Hampstead Theatre Club, the Royal National Theatre and the Manhattan Theater Club in New York – all within the same year. By the time it was revived thirteen years later at London's Donmar Warehouse, it had become recognized as a modern classic.

By all accounts, the first performance was an emotional affair. Coming at a time of increased sectarian tensions in the province, in a building (the Guildhall) that still bore the scars of sectarian violence, the bringing together of Catholic and Protestant was a poignant endorsement of Field Day's desire to change attitudes through works of the imagination.

Quotations from Brian Friel, *Translations*, Faber and Faber, 1981

Top Girls
Caryl Churchill

1982

> Historical and theatrical context

The most significant political event behind *Top Girls* was the
election of a Conservative Government in Britain in May
1979, with a mandate to roll back the welfare state, deregu-
late the market and encourage the private sector and 'enter-
prise culture'. This was one of the turning-points in twentieth-
century British history and Margaret Thatcher went on to
become the dominant force in political life for over a decade,
defeating the Argentinians in war and the coal-miners at
home, and radically restructuring life in Britain in the
process.

The election of the first female Prime Minister divided
feminist opinion. On the one hand, she provided a role model
for ambitious women. On the other hand, to use the termi-
nology of the time, her agenda seemed entirely 'masculine'.
To many women, it seemed that now it was not just a question
of how to get to the top, but of what you would do when you
got there.

Top Girls was Caryl Churchill's (born 1938) twenty-eighth
play. She started by writing radio plays (as the best way of
combining writing with motherhood), and by the end of the
1970s had almost as many radio as stage plays produced. But
it was a series of theatre pieces that established her as the
most significant female playwright of her day. Feminist theatre was at its most pronounced in the early 1980s but
Churchill has always resisted the label. She consistently
breaks the rules and reinvents herself for every play – the only
constant is the excellence of her writing.

Top Girls – with its cast of seven actresses playing sixteen roles – reflects Churchill's commitment to the collective approach popular in the theatre during the late 1970s and early 1980s. Many of her plays were created through workshops with cooperative companies such as Joint Stock Theatre Group and Monstrous Regiment, and also at the Royal Court, whose Artistic Director, Max Stafford-Clark, was to direct the first productions of many of Churchill's plays.

Churchill's plays include *Owners* (1972), *Objections to Sex and Violence* (1975), *Light Shining in Buckinghamshire* (1976), *Vinegar Tom* (1976), *Cloud Nine* (1979), *Fen* (1983), *Softcops* (1984), *A Mouthful of Birds* (1986, with David Lan), *Serious Money* (1987), *Ice Cream/Hot Fudge* (1989), *Mad Forest* (1990), *The Skriker* (1994), *Blue Heart* (1997), *Far Away* (2000) and a translation of Seneca's *Thyestes* (1994).

> *About the play*

Caryl Churchill broke all kinds of rules in *Top Girls*. Adventurous in its structure, the play jumps styles, switches times and continuously challenges its audience's preconceptions. At its heart is an examination of the crucial question facing women in the eighties: career or motherhood? Some have described the play as classically Brechtian in that 'it suggests that what we need is a new way of seeing if we are to understand and confront the pressures the characters fail to understand'. Others detected a tacit endorsement of 'bourgeois feminism', which supports the *status quo* but demands a larger slice. Churchill herself described the play as simply 'a celebration of the extraordinary achievements of women'.

It opens with one of the most arresting scenes in modern drama. The career-oriented high-flyer Marlene, recently appointed managing director of the Top Girls Appointment Agency, is hosting a dinner party for five assorted 'heroines': Pope Joan, the first and only female pope, stoned to death when she gave birth and was revealed to be a woman; Isabella Bird, a nineteenth-century Scot who might have succumbed to 'nerves' had she not escaped her claustrophobic Victorian mould and become an intrepid traveller at the age of forty; Lady Nijo, a thirteenth-century concubine who became a Buddhist nun; Griselda, a model of the patient woman whose self-sacrificing role of loyal wife is mentioned in Petrarch, Boccaccio and Chaucer; and finally Dull Gret, a peasant character immortalized by Brueghel and usually regarded as a symbol of female covetousness. The women get drunk and tell stories about their lives and their often painful domestic situations. The overlapping dialogue catches the vigour of their conversations. This brilliant *tour de force* shows women overcoming the various obstacles of birth and cultural stereotyping and sets up parallels with the entirely modern scenes that follow.

Much of the action of the rest of the play takes place in the Top Girls Appointment Agency and focuses on Marlene and her two subordinates, Nell and Win. Marlene's dim-witted niece, Angie, idolizes her high-flying aunt and, fantasizing that Marlene might be her real mother, runs away from home and arrives in London. Monosyllabic and truculent, and not unlike Dull Gret, Angie's future in a highly competitive world looks bleak. As Marlene says, 'she's not going to make it'. Churchill exposes in a series of satirical (if slightly sketchy) scenes in the agency the bargain women strike when they try to become 'top girls'.

The point of the play is an examination of the moral basis of Marlene's material success. For it emerges that Angie is in fact Marlene's child, brought up by Marlene's sister, the patient, maternal Joyce, who has done the 'traditional thing', stayed at home to keep an eye on her ageing parents and cared for Angie as her own. Marlene's 'success', Churchill seems to suggest, is based on betrayal, on turning her back on her past, on her working-class roots and her underachieving daughter.

The tremendous final scene (which in real time takes place a year before Angie's arrival in London) is a perfect example of how the 'personal is political'. Set in East Anglia, in Joyce's home, it stages a powerful confrontation between the two sisters. Long-held guilt and resentment come bursting out, and two very different value systems collide:

Marlene . . . I think the eighties are going to be stupendous.

Joyce Who for?

Marlene For me. / I think I'm going up up up.

Joyce Oh for you. Yes, I'm sure they will.

Marlene And for the country, come to that. Get the economy back on its feet and whoosh. She's a tough lady, Maggie. I'd give her a job. / She just needs to hang in there. This country

Joyce You voted for them, did you?

Marlene needs to stop whining. / Monetarism is not stupid.

Joyce Drink your tea and shut up, pet.

Marlene It takes time, determination. No more slop. / And

Joyce Well I think they're filthy bastards

Marlene who's got to drive it on? First woman prime minister. Terrifico. Aces. Right on. / You must admit. Certainly gets my vote.

Joyce What good's first woman if it's her? I suppose you'd have liked Hitler if he was a woman. Ms Hitler. Got a lot done, Hitlerina. / Great adventures.

Marlene Bosses still walking on the workers' faces? Still Dadda's little parrot? Haven't you learned to think for yourself? I believe in the individual. Look at me.

Joyce I am looking at you.

Marlene Come on, Joyce, we're not going to quarrel over politics.

Joyce We are though.

Marlene Forget I mentioned it. Not a word about the slimy unions will cross my lips.

'I didn't really mean all that,' says Marlene finally. 'I did,' says Joyce. She has seen Marlene's individualism for what it is, and an unbridgeable gulf has opened up between the two.

Top Girls arrived with perfect timing and prescient insight, exploring as it did the clash between the 'have-it-all, get-up-and-can-do' new women of the 1980s, with an older more communitarian form of feminism. The balance of opinion ultimately falls Joyce's way and some women have felt that the play's conclusion – with its endorsement of Joyce's maternalism – was in some sense reactionary and anti-feminist. But like much of Churchill's work, *Top Girls* is open to many interpretations. Crucially, the play pointed up a major contradiction for feminists in the 1980s: in all the striving for success, the desire to be a 'top girl', what was going to happen to the Angies of this world? Mrs Thatcher declared that there was 'no such thing as society'; *Top Girls* examined the fatal consequences of that idea.

> In performance

Top Girls was premièred at the Royal Court Theatre, London in August, 1982 in a production directed by Max Stafford-Clark, with a cast that included Lindsay Duncan, Deborah Findlay, Lesley Manville, Gwen Taylor, Carole Hayman, Selina Cadell and Lou Wakefield. This transferred to the Public Theatre in New York and returned to the Royal Court in 1983. The play was revived ten years later by the Royal Court, when its prophecy of the impact of career feminism was seen retrospectively and shown to have had stinging accuracy.

The play has been performed throughout the world and by a wide range of companies. It has become a staple on campuses, where its exploration of female ambition continues to strike powerful chords. It was filmed for television in 1991 with Deborah Findlay repeating her role of Joyce, Lesley Manville as Marlene and Lesley Sharp as Angie.

Quotations from Caryl Churchill, *Top Girls*, Methuen, 1982

Fool for Love
Sam Shepard

1982

> Historical and theatrical context

The early 1980s saw the high point of the 'new right' in the United States, with President Reagan describing the Soviet Union as 'the focus of evil in the modern world', and launching his over-ambitious but devastating 'Star Wars' Strategic Defence Initiative. US marines were in Beirut, the CIA was bankrolling anti-government forces in Nicaragua and Britain won the 1982 Falklands War.

Many writers and artists, often of the left, felt eclipsed by this and confused as to how to respond. Although some tried to devise an explicitly political, oppositional aesthetic, many of the more successful ones discovered a more introspective tone and examined private life and the imagination with much greater intensity. This was also the time of an increased interest in Latin American 'magic realism', including the novels of Gabriel Garcia Marquez, Mario Vargas Llosa and Jorge Luis Borges, whose shifting narratives, complex structures and self-reflexive playfulness seemed to provide a way forward.

Although Sam Shepard (born 1943) spent some time in London in the 1970s, he was brought up in Northern California and the disjointed, surreal quality of Californian life is the dominant characteristic of his work. It is revealing that many of his plays were premièred in San Francisco, the home of the Beat Poets, the Summer of Love and Apple Computers, and for a while the capital of alternative lifestyles, and 'out there' thinking.

Sam Shepard's many other plays include *Icarus's Mother* (1965), *The Tooth of Crime* (1972), *Action* (1974), *Killer's Head*

(1975), *The Curse of the Starving Class* (1977), *Savage/Love* (1981), *Buried Child* (1978), *True West* (1980), *A Lie of the Mind* (1985) and *Simpatico* (1994). He is also a successful film actor, and writer of novels and short stories.

> *About the play*

The opening stage direction for *Fool for Love* states that the play 'is to be performed relentlessly without a break' and violent passion is the overwhelming atmosphere of the play. The setting is a 'stark, low-rent motel room on the edge of the Mojave desert'. Shepard's stage directions are both filmic in their detail and theatrical in their effect; he even insists that the doors should be amplified so that every time they are slammed, they 'boom'. This is a play about love and passion, jealousy and desire, and Shepard asks the two main protagonists to throw themselves at each other, against the walls and through the doors with terrifying physicality: 'fools for love' indeed.

Eddie is a cowboy in his late thirties: macho and tough. He says that he has travelled 'two thousand, four hundred and eighty miles' to be with May. She is a bit younger: sexy, passionate, emotional and has been living in a trailer waiting for him to return ('What do you think it's like sittin' in a tin trailer for weeks on end with the wind ripping through it? Waitin' around for the Butane to arrive. Hiking down to the laundromat in the rain. Do you think that's thrilling or somethin'?'). She is convinced that he is having an affair (she can smell 'pussy' on his hands). One stage direction says:

> She looks him straight in the eyes, then suddenly knees him in the groin with tremendous force.

This is a couple in the grip of an obsession ('you're like a disease to me.'). They adore and hate each other in equal measure. At one point May says:

> I don't understand my feelings. I really don't. I don't

understand how I could hate you so much after so much time. How, no matter how much I'd like not to hate you, I hate you even more. It grows. I can't even see you now. All I see is a picture of you. You and her.

But he does not leave and she does not want him to.

Off to one side of the stage, in a separate space from the motel room, is an Old Man sitting in a rocking chair, wearing a Stetson hat. It slowly emerges that he is the father of both of them. Like a figure from a classical chorus, he comments on the action, but soon gets increasingly involved. He talks about when May was a baby, crying uncontrollably on a car journey ('through Southern Utah . . . in that old Plymouth we once had'). He remembers stopping the car, taking her out into the dark and sensing the enormous black shapes of cattle in the darkness; this silenced her crying, and telling the story silences her now.

While Eddie is cleaning his shotgun and drinking tequila, May announces that a 'man' is coming to see her. Eddie teases her for using the word 'man', saying that he cannot be a 'guy', and practises his lassooing, showing off his physical prowess, one minute saying she has invented 'the man', the next saying he is going to 'nail his ass'.

A big, black, 'extra-long' Mercedes Benz draws up outside, apparently driven by a woman. Suddenly a pistol explodes, glass breaks, headlights arc through the room, the horn blares and Eddie pulls May down on to the floor. Neither of them know who it is. May presumes it is 'the countess'. Eddie sees that she has 'blown the windshield outa' my truck'. May keeps switching the light on, and Eddie says 'we either have to get outa' here now or you have to keep the fuckin' light off'. But when the Old Man says that the two of them are 'totally unrecognizable [to him] . . . could be anybody's. Probably are', Eddie declares:

> I'm not leavin'. I'm stayin' right here. I don't care if a hundred 'dates' walk through that door – I'll take every one of 'em on. I don't care if you hate my guts. I don't

care if you can't stand the sight of me or the sound of me or the smell of me. I'm never leavin'. You'll never get rid of me.

May refuses to believe it ('you've been jerking me off like this for fifteen years') and tells him that she does not love him.

The headlights flash across the room again, and suddenly, to their amazement, Martin – May's 'man' – enters. Eddie taunts him:

We were actually in the middle of a big huge argument about you. It got so heated up we had to turn the lights off . . . It was about whether or not you're actually a man or not. Ya' know? Whether you're a 'man' or just a 'guy'.

The two of them fight each other, until Martin tries to escape by climbing through a window. Finally, in a moment that could be straight from a Greek tragedy, Eddie admits that May is his 'half sister', and that they had 'fooled around' at high school. Martin cannot understand how that could have happened, and when Eddie starts to explain, the Old Man says 'now don't be too hard on me boy. It can happen to the best of us.' In the most beautiful and lyrical speech in the play, Eddie recalls the Old Man taking him as a boy for a long walk in the dark, buying a bottle of liquor and sharing it with him:

It was a hot, desert breeze and the air smelled like new cut alfalfa. We walked right up to the front porch and he rang the bell and I remember getting real nervous because I wasn't expecting to visit anybody. I thought we were just out for a walk. And then this woman comes to the door. This real pretty woman with red hair. And she throws herself into his arms. And he starts crying. He just breaks down right there in front of me. And she's kissing him all over the face and holding him real tight and he's just crying like a baby. And then through the doorway, behind them both, I see this girl.

May denies all this (even though Eddie says 'there's not a

movie in this town can match the story I'm going to tell') and gives her own account: her mother was obsessed by the Old Man, tracked him down and found him with Eddie and Eddie's mother, and Eddie's mother 'blew her brains out' as a result. The Old Man challenges this account, and is desperate that Eddie and May should not be close. When they kiss, the headlights arc across the room again, there is an explosion, horses gallop wildly past, a gasoline fire blazes, Martin says 'the truck with the horse trailer is on fire' and all the horses are loose. Eddie leaves, for good.

At the end, the Old Man points to an empty space:

Ya see that picture over there? Ya' see that? Ya'know who that is? That's the woman of my dreams. That's who that is. And she's mine. She's all mine. Forever.

Fool for Love is an extraordinarily original work: tragic, lyrical and mysterious. With its intense focus on the secrets of the family and its Wild-West feel, the play is both specifically American and profoundly classical. Its atmosphere is both timeless and particular, and with it Sam Shepard has written one of the significant works of modern American drama.

> In performance

Fool for Love was premièred at the Magic Theatre in San Francisco on 8 February 1983 in a production directed by Shepard himself. The British première took place in the autumn of 1984 at the National Theatre in a production directed by Peter Gill, with Julie Walters and Ian Charleson as May and Eddie.

Robert Altman made a fine film of the play in 1985, with Shepard as Eddie, Kim Basinger as May, and Harry Dean Stanton as the Old Man.

Quotations from Sam Shepard, *Fool for Love*, Faber and Faber, 1984

Observe the Sons of Ulster Marching Towards the Somme
Frank McGuinness

1985

> Historical and theatrical context

The causes of Northern Ireland's sectarian violence go back
more than four hundred years. In the sixteenth and seventeenth century, a large number of English and Scottish
Protestants were 'settled' in Ireland as a way of subduing the
independent-minded Catholic Irish. Oliver Cromwell pursued a particularly brutal kind of 'pacification' in Drogheda
in 1649. In 1690, the newly crowned King William III (of
Orange) defeated a French and Irish Catholic army (led by
the deposed King James II) at the Battle of the Boyne. The
repression of the independence movements of the 1790s and
the potato famine of the 1840s all created powerful anti-
English feelings. The creation of the six counties in 1921 as a
separate entity loyal to Britain was devised to give Northern
Ireland's Protestant majority a homeland and resolve
Ireland's tragic divisions, but since 1969, 'the Troubles' flared
constantly. By the 1980s, paramilitaries on both sides ensured
that sectarian violence had become an everyday occurrence
affecting all parts of the community.

Despite – or maybe because of – the ferocity of the
Troubles, the 1980s saw a ferment of theatrical activity in the
province, much of it coming from the Nationalist and
Catholic community. Frank McGuinness (born 1953), a specialist in medieval studies and lecturer in drama and linguistics, started writing in 1980. A chance meeting with the director Patrick Mason, while attending a writing workshop in
Galway, led to their friendship; five years later, Mason directed McGuinness's masterpiece.

McGuinness's many stage plays include *The Factory Girls* (1982), *Baglady* (1985), *Carthaginians* (1988), *Mary and Lizzie* (1989), *The Bread Man* (1991), *Someone Who'll Watch Over Me* (1992), *The Bird Sanctuary* (1994), *Mutabilitie* (1997) and *Dolly West's Kitchen* (1999). He has also produced fine adaptations of Lorca, Ibsen, Chekhov, Brecht, Sophocles, Strindberg and Valle-Inclán.

> About the play

Observe the Sons of Ulster Marching Towards the Somme was inspired by memorials to the six thousand mostly Protestant soldiers of the 36th Ulster Division who died in July 1916 at the Battle of the Somme. Seeing the names of the dead, McGuinness was moved to imagine 'their lives back into existence "as friends, sons and lovers"'.

Part memorial, part eulogy and part critique of Loyalism and its traditions, the play is stylistically ambitious, constructed in four sections. The first, 'Remembrance', features old Kenneth Pyper, the mad, caustic, sole survivor of a group of eight Ulster volunteers all killed on the Somme. He is lying in bed, cursing his inner voices (and an unfeeling God) for making him remember the horror of the battle and the guilt of having survived:

Again. As always, again. Why does this persist? What more have we to tell each other? I remember nothing today. Absolutely nothing.

But the ghosts insist, forcing from him the central, overriding question: 'Answer me why we did it. Why we let ourselves be led to extermination?' And in almost the same breath, they supply the answer: 'In the end, we were not led, we led ourselves'. The unspoken implication is that 'we did it for Ulster'.

In the second part – 'Initiation' – his dead comrades take fleshly shape. First, there is Pyper as his younger self, a cynical upper-class sculptor; then there is David Craig, a blacksmith's son from Enniskellen; next are two volunteers from Coleraine, William Moore and John Millen. And then comes Christopher Roulston, a lapsed and tortured preacher, followed by the football-mad Martin Crawford from Derry Town, and finally, two workers from the Belfast shipyards, George Anderson and Nat McIlwaine. The eight men meet each other in an army barrack-room after their initial call-up; they are independent and bloody-minded, but the atmosphere is tinged with homo-eroticism as they jostle for position and test out each other's vulnerabilities. The language is spare and naturalistic as friendships are forged.

But the tone changes in 'Pairings'. The soldiers are back in Ireland on leave and are seen as four distinct couples (or pairings) in four different locales. McGuinness's technique allows for an overlapping, surreal commentary. The ties that bind these men to Ulster is eloquently framed in the scene on the rope bridge in County Antrim: Moore, shell-shocked, is stuck; he can neither cross nor go back. But Millen, by turns cajoling, supporting and summoning up the Loyalist spirit, finally gets him to the other side. Meanwhile, in the churchyard where he used to preach, Roulston and Crawford, a Protestant and a half-Catholic, talk about religion. Crawford does not believe in Christ; his loyalty, he says, is simply to the men beside him. Roulston, the fire-and-brimstone preacher once convinced of his mission as one of God's 'chosen', ends brokenly by admitting he is just a man like any other.

Elsewhere, in a field in Edenderry, McIlwaine and Anderson re-enact the rituals of the glorious Twelfth of July – the lambeg drum, the march, the inherited hatred of the Fenian – with a savagery that is almost an exorcism. Meanwhile, on Boa Island in County Fermanagh, Pyper talks of his rejection of the all-demanding Protestant gods, of his desire to create rather than destroy. The two men express their love for each other, but Craig tells Pyper of his belief that one of them, Pyper, will survive (Craig has already saved Pyper's life in battle by giving him the kiss of life). Each of these situations constitutes a form of 'homecoming', an absolution before death.

Finally, in 'Bonding', McGuinness returns us to the Somme on the eve of the battle, as the men await their final, suicidal sacrifice for 'king, country and Ulster'. There is a strange smell in the air, identified as fear. But in a brilliant final twist, McGuinness replaces France with Ulster in the men's minds by having them recite a litany of place names and rivers from home and perform a crazy re-enactment of the Battle of the Boyne. Pyper, playing King Billy's horse, fatefully sabotages the game when he trips up and falls. The men go through a final ritual of hymn-singing and an exchange of orange sashes. A powerful, elegiac sense of resignation emerges and old and young Pyper are left to eulogize on Ulster, its tragic pride and stubborn allegiance to the doctrine of 'No Surrender':

Let this day at the Somme be as glorious in the memory of Ulster as that day at the Boyne, when you scattered our enemies. Lead us back from this exile. To Derry, to the Foyle. To Belfast and the Lagan. To Armagh. To Tyrone. To the Bann and its banks. To Erne and its islands. Protect them. Protect us. Protect me. Let us fight bravely. Let us win gloriously. Lord, look down on us. Spare us. I love – Observe the sons of Ulster marching towards the Somme. I love their lives. I love my own life. I love my home. I love my Ulster. Ulster. Ulster. Ulster. Ulster. Ulster. Ulster. Ulster. Ulster.

It is ironic that one of the great plays about the Loyalist tradition should have been written by a Catholic from Donegal. In writing it, McGuinness said, he had to confront his own bigotry: 'It was an eye-opener for a Catholic Republican, as I am, to have to examine the complexity, diversity, disturbance and integrity of the other side, the Protestant people.' So well did he succeed that, after seeing the play, many thought him a Protestant, and not for nothing has *Observe the Sons of Ulster* been called the greatest anti-war play since Sean O'Casey's *The Silver Tassie*.

With great formal daring, McGuinness's tale of eight young soldiers bravely and brilliantly suggested a bridge to the future by an expiation of the ghosts tethering Northern Ireland to its past.

> *In performance*

Observe the Sons of Ulster Marching Towards the Somme was first staged by Patrick Mason at the Peacock Theatre, Dublin, in February 1985. It was immediately recognized as a towering achievement, in subsequent months winning many awards, from the *Evening Standard*'s Most Promising Playwright to the Rooney Prize for Irish Literature. A year after the play's Dublin première, it was restaged at London's Hampstead Theatre in July 1986, in a production directed by Michael Attenborough.

A decade later, Mason's Abbey Theatre revival for the Edinburgh Festival in the wake of the 1995 Northern Irish ceasefire showed that the play, this time with a more sculptural quality and stronger homosexual emphasis, fully deserved its title of a modern-day classic.

Quotations from Frank McGuinness, *Observe the Sons of Ulster Marching Towards the Somme*, Faber and Faber, 1986

Fences
August Wilson

1985

> Historical and theatrical context

August Wilson (born 1945) is one of the finest writers to have emerged from the American theatre of the 1980s. Growing up in the industrial city of Pittsburgh during the 1950s and 1960s as the only black child in a school of 1,500, Wilson experienced racism at first hand. He dropped out of school at sixteen and received his education in the local library, on street corners and in the emerging Black Power movement. In 1968, he helped set up the Black Horizons Theater in Pittsburgh.

Fences is the fourth play in Wilson's historical cycle of the African-American experience in the twentieth century, each play representing a decade. This sequence covers a period of immense upheaval in the US, starting in September 1957 when Federal troops were brought in to desegregate a school in Little Rock, Arkansas, continuing with Lyndon B. Johnson's civil rights reforms in 1964 and culminating in the assassinations of Malcolm X in 1965, and Martin Luther King in 1968. The plays examine the persistence of racial divisions in the United States, despite legislation.

Wilson's other stage plays include *Ma Rainey's Black Bottom* (1984), *Joe Turner's Come and Gone* (1988), *The Piano Lesson* (1990), *Two Trains Running* (1990) and *Seven Guitars* (1995).

> About the play

For August Wilson, history is important: 'The theme I keep coming back to is the need to re-connect yourself . . . the sense of standing in your grandfather's shoes . . . Having shared a common past, we have a common past and a common future.' The history of African-Americans, from the catastrophe of slavery to the humiliation of 'Jim Crow' (the post-slavery segregation) to the poverty and violence of the modern ghettoes, is a history that Wilson insists must be understood, no matter how painful, if African-Americans are to go forward.

In *Fences*, past, present and future are brought together in the character of Troy Maxson, a retired baseball player who now works as a garbage man. Set in the urban sprawl of 1957 America, the play charts Troy's decline as the legacies of a poisoned inheritance take their toll. As with Arthur Miller's *Death of a Salesman*, Wilson's skill lies in giving dignity and status to an ordinary man humilated and driven to despair by circumstances.

The play opens with Troy talking to his drinking buddy, Bono, in the partially fenced yard of his home. It is Friday: payday. Despite being ill-educated and embittered by the loss of his dreams, Troy cuts an impressive figure. But he is all too full of human frailties: he fantasizes, has a wandering eye and browbeats Rose, the wife he says he adores. But he also has a highly developed sense of family responsibility.

Troy questions why all the easier driving jobs have been given to whites but Bono is worried that this questioning will cost him his job. Meanwhile, Rose is trying to persuade Troy to let Cory, their son, join the local college baseball team. But Troy insists he must continue with his part-time job at the local store. Rose argues that times have changed, and that since the integration of baseball leagues in 1947 there is now a future for black baseball players. Troy, as if to reinforce his own pride and belief in himself (with the help of a drink or two), launches into a powerful account of a fever-induced confrontation with Death. Troy may not have much learning, but Wilson gives him a rich, poetic form of self-expression:

At the end of the third night we done weakened each other to where we can't hardly move. Death stood up,

throwed on his robe . . . and went off to look for his sick-
le. Say, 'I'll be back'. Just like that . . . I wasn't no fool. I
wasn't going looking for him. Death ain't nothing to play
with. And I know he's gonna get me . . . But as long as I
keep my strength and see him coming.

Troy's relationship with his thirty-four-year-old son Lyons is
not much better than that with Cory. When he asks for a ten
dollar loan, Troy refuses because he is suspicious of Lyons's
desire to become a musician. With his rigid, self-made work
ethic, Troy finds it impossible to accept other ways of doing
things.

Troy has a younger brother, Gabriel, whom war service has
left with severe mental disability. 'Gabe' believes himself to
be the Archangel Gabriel. Troy watches over him with anx-
iously, full of guilt that he has used Gabriel's discharge money
for his own purposes. Without it, he muses bitterly, they
would not have a home to call their own.

Troy's difficulties begin to multiply. Cory asks Troy for
confirmation of his love, but Troy's cruel, sad answer is that
there is no room left for love in him, only the practicalities of
making sure that his son is fed, clothed and housed. By the
end of the act, Troy has finally been promoted to driver and
harmony reigns. But when Cory enters, furious with his
father for refusing to sign the papers for his baseball recruit-
ment, an irreconcilable rift opens up between them.

By Act Two, Troy's relations with his family have wors-
ened. Bono warns Troy he may lose Rose if he carries on this
way. Troy tells him that he has been having an affair and is
going to become a father again. Troy bails out Gabriel, who
has been arrested for causing a disturbance. But in an act of
ambiguous motivation (there is money involved), he allows
Gabriel to be recommitted to hospital.

Troy admits his infidelity to Rose, saying he needed a
respite from the continuous responsibility of providing for
others. But Rose has had to make sacrifices too: 'I been standing with you! I been right here with you, Troy. I got a life too

. . . Don't you think I ever wanted other things? Don't you think I had hopes and dreams?' Things are never the same between them after this. She cuts herself off from him and turns to the church. But when Troy's girlfriend dies in childbirth, Rose, with enormous generosity, agrees to bring the child up as her own. Relations between Troy and Bono cool and Cory finally stands up to Troy physically. But the fence – both literal and metaphorical – that Troy has failed to fix is finally mended.

· The play jumps forward seven years. Troy has died of a heart attack and it is the day of his funeral. His young daughter, Raynelle, is planting a small garden in the yard. Cory, now an enlisted marine, turns up. At first he refuses to attend the funeral, citing the destructive shadow Troy cast over him in life. But Rose berates him: 'That shadow wasn't nothing but you growing into yourself. You either got to grow into it or cut it down to fit you. But that's all you got to make life with.'

Raynelle appears and she and Cory sing Troy's favourite song. In a dramatic turnaround, Cory agrees to go to the funeral. Gabriel arrives, allowed out for the day, and tries to blow the golden horn he always carries. He blows and he blows but no sound is made. Undeterred – in a gesture that reaches deep into the soul of African-American life – he dances out the journey of Troy's soul up to heaven. Wilson transforms defeated, broken lives with a single stroke of inspirational theatre.

One of August Wilson's great strengths is his refusal to indulge in polemics. His dramatic structure and form may be conventional, but his emotional honesty and ability to present huge issues through the vocabulary and actions of the everyday make his work deeply impressive, providing African-Americans with a uniquely powerful dramatic voice.

> In performance

Fences opened on 26 March 1987 at the 46th Street Theater on Broadway. As with all Wilson's work, the production was directed by Lloyd Richards (who had directed the triumphant première of *A Raisin in the Sun* in 1959, and to whom Wilson dedicated *Fences*: '[he] adds to whatever he touches'). It was a transfer from the Yale Repertory Theater, where it had originally been staged in April 1985 with James Earl Jones playing Troy. A year earlier, in 1986, Wilson became the first black writer to have two plays running on Broadway at the same time.

Fences' British première was presented by Bill Kenwright at the Garrick Theatre in London in September 1990 with the Hollywood actor Yaphet Kotto as Troy and Adrian Lester as Cory.

Quotations from August Wilson, *Fences and Other Plays*, Penguin, 1988

Our Country's Good
Timberlake Wertenbaker

1988

> Historical and theatrical context

The late 1980s saw the triumphant phase of the Anglo-American New Right, with the election of George Bush in the US and Margaret Thatcher's third (and final) term in Britain. One of the key themes of both governments was a hard line on crime and punishment, with a resulting growth in prison populations. It was also a time when the value of the liberal arts was being forcefully challenged by the doctrines of economic liberalism and reactionary social policies.

The French-born Timberlake Wertenbaker was commissioned by the Royal Court, whose Artistic Director, Max Stafford-Clark, had been a key figure in developing an oppositional aesthetic. He stressed the kind of ensemble work which he had been developing with Joint Stock, the cooperative theatre company he had run with William Gaskill in the 1970s. He was also committed to women writers and Andrea Dunbar, Caryl Churchill and Sarah Daniels all enjoyed considerable successes at the Royal Court.

Timberlake Wertenbaker's other plays include *The Grace of Mary Traverse* (1985), *The Love of the Nightingale* (1988), *Three Birds Alighting on a Field* (1991), *The Break of Day* (1995), *After Darwin* (1998) and *Credible Witness* (2000) as well as numerous translations from French and Greek.

> About the play

Our Country's Good is inspired by two books: Thomas Keneally's novel *The Playmaker* (1987), which tells the story of the first performance of a play in Australia, and Robert Hughes's *The Fatal Shore* (1987), a history of the Australian penal colony. The play benefited from a two-week workshop with actors, which included interviews with both inmates and prison oficers as well as work on historical sources. Wertenbaker has said that going to Wormwood Scrubs to see a play performed by the prisoners was essential to her conception.

The play is set in Sydney in 1789, shortly after the arrival of the First Fleet, amidst the cruelty and degradation of the prison colony, where human life was cheap, dignity impossible, prostitution widespread and brutality and prejudice the norm. The play's title derives from the notion that the convicts were exiled from England for their country's good. It also carries a more positive overtone, for by the end of the play there is a chance that their new country *is* good.

The characters fall into two distinct groups. The naval officers and marines exhibit widely different attitudes towards their charges. The Governor-in-Chief is Captain Arthur Phillip, who has a belief in the fundamental humanity of his charges and is opposed to casual brutality. It is his idea that the convicts should put on a play, George Farquhar's *The Recruiting Officer* (1707), and this provides the central action:

> The theatre is an expression of civilisation. We belong to a great country which has spawned great playwrights . . . The convicts will be speaking a refined, literate language and expressing sentiments of a delicacy they are not used to. It will remind them that there is more to life than crime, punishment.

Major Ross, by contrast, is utterly brutal, driven by hatred of the convicts, convinced that the play is a dangerous project, and is an all-too-familiar kind of prison officer. Lieutenant Ralph Clark is a young man struggling with his sexuality, idolizing his wife Betsey Alicia in England but plagued by the attraction of the female convicts. He is ambitious and sees his staging of the play as a way of gaining favour with the Governor. His growing love for a young convict, Mary Brenham, provides the play with its powerful romantic motor.

The old midshipman Harry Brewer is tormented by visions of the dead, of the men he has hanged. He is acutely jealous of the much younger Duckling, whom he loves. In addition, there is a series of brilliantly drawn minor figures: such as Ross's acolyte, Captain Campbell, who speaks in a kind of bastardized language, invented by Wertenbaker, which encapsulates an almost comic brutality; or Dawes, who is only interested in his telescope; or the fiercely intelligent and legalistic Collins.

The other group is the convicts, and one of Wertenbaker's achievements is to give them voice and individuality. They are bound together in suffering and are much more than dispossessed, anti-social delinquents. Mary Brenham is shy, industrious and deeply unhappy about the sexual compromise she made on the ship. It is her conformity, as much as anything else, that leads her to fall in love with Ralph Clark. Her friend Dabby Byant is forward, gipsy-like and adventurous. She proffers an uncomplicated but incisive criticism of Farquhar's comedy of manners. At the end she speaks of her plan to escape and sail back to Devon.

Duckling is one of the most delicately drawn portraits: a young girl involved in a relationship with old Harry Brewer, who is devastated when he dies. Lizzy Morden is the hard case: bitter, recalcitrant, difficult. She cannot read and learns her lines by rote. She is wrongly condemned to death for stealing food and refuses to speak at her trial because she does not trust the court. The rehearsals encourage her to tell the truth, and when she is reprieved she announces:

> Your excellency, I will endeavour to speak Mr Farquhar's lines with the elegance and clarity their own worth commands.

The male convicts are equally well drawn. Ketch Freeman is an Irish hangman, despised by the others for his collaboration with the authorities. There is a rich and poetical quality to his language and a touching loneliness. In a brilliant scene, he has to measure Lizzy Morden for the gallows. Later, he tells her that he would have refused to hang her and is reconciled with the others in the joint endeavour.

Sideway is a flamboyant pickpocket, full of grotesque confidence in his own theatrical knowledge and his humiliation is one of the most disturbing moments in the play. For all his peacocking, Sideway shows real heroism in the face of Major Ross's brutality and he is an essential part of the ensemble. John Wisehammer is an intellectual Jew. He values language and is adamant in rehearsals that Farquhar's text should be accurately followed. He falls in love with Mary, who is already committed to the young lieutenant. Arscott is a hardened criminal: despite an appalling whipping, his commitment to the play remains and he gets to play Kite, the tough recruiting sergeant who is so central a part in Farquhar's play. The black convict Caesar just wants to return to Madagascar to die with his ancestors. The play also includes an Aborigine who comments on what he witnesses and interprets the events according to Aboriginal mythology. He is not a central figure, but his presence places the whites within a much broader context.

Our Country's Good has an epic, Brechtian structure. The scenes each have a subtitle, and shift from story to story and place to place. This builds up the pattern of contradiction which gives the play its dialectical richness. It has a cumulative effect in the theatre, with many different stories all coming together, interweaving and building up to the final scene, just before the performance of *The Recruiting Officer*, where the circle of energy essential to any creative act is made visible.

The play has its weaknesses: an almost salacious interest in sexual commerce, an over-optimistic view of the power of art and a tendency to rely on the goodwill and humanity of Captain Phillip, whose benevolence is perhaps overstated. Yet *Our Country's Good* is a powerfully humane affirmation of the value of art amid cruelty. The play does not present a revolutionary critique of the appalling cruelty of the British penal colony, but it does give us, in gripping dramatic form, a vision of the redemptive and unifying power of art and the collaborative process of the theatre itself.

> *In performance*

In 1988, under extreme financial pressure, the Royal Court was looking to stage a popular classic. George Farquhar's *The Recruiting Officer* was an ideal and obvious choice and the two plays were conceived to run in tandem, sharing the same cast, on a flexible set and playing in repertoire. Stafford-Clark turned economy of means into a virtue and in both plays the large cast of characters was played by ten actors.

Following its première at the Royal Court on 10 September 1988, Stafford-Clark's production of *Our Country's Good* was an astonishing success, with the *Guardian* calling it a 'moving and affirmative tribute to the transforming power of theatre'. It has been performed throughout the world, and the process came full circle when it was staged by prisoners at Wormwood Scrubs.

Our Country's Good won the Olivier Awards Play of the Year (1988) and the New York Drama Critics' Circle Award for Best Foreign Play (1990).

Quotations from Timberlake Wertenbaker, *Plays: One*, Faber and Faber, 1996

Angels in America
Part One: Millennium Approaches
Part Two: Perestroika
Tony Kushner

1989–91, first performed in repertoire in 1993

> Historical and theatrical context

Tony Kushner (born 1956) wrote the two parts of *Angels in America* in the late 1980s and early 1990s at the peak of the US AIDS epidemic. AIDS had been identified in 1981. By 1984, over 4,000 cases had been diagnosed in the US and the deaths of Rock Hudson in 1985 and Liberace in 1987 both raised public awareness. Ronald Reagan was re-elected President in 1984 and George Bush won the Republicans a third term in 1988. In the Soviet Union, Mikhail Gorbachev came to power in 1985 and the Chernobyl nuclear power station exploded in 1986. The Berlin Wall fell in 1989. The *zeitgeist* seemed to indicate that although some of the biggest monoliths might be movable, catastrophe and the millennium loomed.

Millennium Approaches and *Perestroika* are written with great theatrical flair, mixing documentary realism with informal – and camp – throwaway. The feeling is of a huge American epic, focussing on a group of central characters but ranging across racial, sexual, linguistic, religious and political divides. Kushner says the plays benefit from a 'pared down style of presentation', but they are a challenge for any theatre to produce. They are connected, but as in Shakespeare's *Henry IV, Parts One* and *Two*, the second play is more discursive, harder to achieve in the theatre, more far-ranging and ultimately more satisfying. Together, they add up to one of the most impressive dramatic achievements of the late twentieth century.

Tony Kushner's other work includes *A Bright Room Called Day* and *Slavs!* (1993) as well as translations of Corneille, Goethe, and Brecht. His collection of essays, poems and reflections on his work, called *Thinking About the Longstanding Problems of Virtue and Happiness* was published in 1995.

> About the play

With *Angels in America*, Tony Kushner emerged as America's most talented young dramatist and as one its most important contemporary chroniclers. The two plays together are subtitled 'A Gay Fantasia on National Themes' and they give a powerful insight into the complexities of a specific moment in America's national life. Realistic events are interspersed with fantastical and camp scenes, set both on earth and in heaven (with San Francisco, of course, being the ultimate gay heaven) and the plays are peppered with Kushner's New York Jewish, camp wit and intelligence.

Angels in America offers a more than usually useful definition of the notion that the 'personal is political'. Instead of simply showing how personal acts have political consequences, Kushner demonstrates that thinking politically, talking politically and acting politically can be in direct contradiction with one's own private behaviour, particularly one's sexuality. Kushner's characters exist in a world where political consciousness is a central part of identity, be it Jewishness, blackness, homosexuality, Republicanism, the new right or whatever. These identities are not mutually exclusive or all-defining, nor are they stuck on by Kushner as an extra. His real people live public lives, as well as having often contradictory private lives.

At the heart of the two plays is the extraordinary Roy Cohn, an extreme right-wing New York lawyer who was involved in the McCarthy trials of the 1950s. For the liberal characters, Cohn is the devil himself ('the polestar of human evil, he's like the worst human being who ever lived'), and Kushner enjoys his monstrosity. But he also shows that the contradiction between his gay-bashing republicanism and his own homosexuality is more than mere hypocrisy. It is almost tragic in its complexity and death-defying energy. Not only does Cohn refuse to accept that he is gay, he also refuses to accept that he has AIDS ('Roy Cohn is not a homosexual, Roy Cohn is a heterosexual man, Henry, who fucks around with guys . . . AIDS is what homosexuals have. I have liver cancer.'). He gets hold of a huge stack of AZT pills and, in a Shakespearian touch, is visited on his deathbed by the ghost of Ethel Rosenberg, for whose execution he was partly responsible.

Joe Pitt is the Chief Clerk of Court and Cohn offers him a job in Washington with the new Reagan administration. Joe is attracted by the prospect, but is soon fighting his Mormon wife, Harper, both about the move and his own homosexuality. He dreams about 'wrestling with the angel' of his own gayness. Meanwhile Harper, who is taking too much valium, is hallucinating and goes on an extraordinary interior journey, dreaming of the Antarctic, recalling her Mormon roots and worrying about the hole in the ozone layer. She is devastated and desperate for him to return.

Louis works as a 'lowly' word processor in the Court. His boyfriend Prior discovers that he is dying of AIDS ('One dies at thirty, robbed of decades of majesty'). An angel visits him and Prior dreams of his ancestors. Meanwhile Louis, having spoken to the Rabbi at his grandmother's funeral, decides to leave Prior: he cannot deal with his illness. He meets Joe and they get together. But Prior still loves Louis and feels utterly abandoned.

The former drag queen Belize is now a registered nurse. He looks after his ex-lover Prior and makes him laugh. And in a reversal of role and status, Belize finds himself looking after Cohn too. In bringing Jewishness and blackness up against each other, Kushner is entering the most explosive area of racial conflict in American culture (the 1980s had seen race riots between Jews and Blacks in Brooklyn Heights). It is part of Kushner's genius that he will enter an area as fraught as this and come up with something as human, funny, and true to life as Roy's speech:

> Jews and Coloureds, historical liberal coalition, right? My people being the first to sell retail to your people, your people being the first people my people could afford to hire to sweep out the store Saturday mornings, and then we all held hands and rode the bus to Selma. Not me of course, I don't ride buses, I take cabs. But the thing about The American Negro is, he never went Communist. Loser Jews did. But you people had Jesus so the reds never got to you. I admire that.

The angels of the title appear several times, once in an extraordinary scene in heaven in which they discuss the implications of the Chernobyl accident. The angels are not comforting. They have been abandoned by God (who 'should be sued', Prior jokes) and the implication is that human beings can and should wrestle with them. Kushner's prayer for AIDS concludes with a direct admonition to the heavenly powers – whoever they might be – 'be thou more sheltering God. Pay more attention'. This is often expressed in a kind of camp, tongue-in-cheek tone but is nevertheless passionately felt.

The last scene of *Perestroika* provides a powerful emotional coda to this extraordinary American epic. Belize and Louis are engaged in their usual witty sparring, this time about the fall of the Berlin Wall and Gorbachev. The world seems to be changeable. But Roy is dead and Prior is very ill. He says that the Bethesda fountain in Central Park (and Jerusalem) will flow again when the millennium comes. But even when talking about the fountain's stone angels, Louis and Belize are still talking politics ('I mean we don't want this to have sort of Zionist implications'). Prior says he is going to 'turn the volume down', and turns to the audience:

> The fountain's not flowing now, they turn it off in the winter, ice in the pipes. But in the summer it's a sight to see. I want to be around to see it. I plan to be. I hope to be.

This disease will be the end of many of us, but not nearly all, and the dead will be commemorated and will struggle on with the living, and we are not going away. We won't die secret deaths anymore. The world only spins forward. We will be citizens. The time has come.

Bye now.

You are fabulous creatures, each and every one.

And I bless you: *More Life*.

The Great Work Begins.

> *In performance*

The two parts of *Angels in America* were commissioned by the Eureka Theater in San Francisco. They were workshopped and performed in a variety of different versions, and with different casts, by the Eureka and the Mark Taper Forum in Los Angeles. They were staged in repertoire at the Walter Kerr Theatre in New York in November 1993.

Millennium Approaches received its British première at the National Theatre on 17 January 1992 and *Perestroika* joined it in repertoire on 12 November 1993, both in productions directed by Declan Donnellan.

Angels in America was a tremendous success in New York and London, and Tony Kushner was awarded the Pulitzer Prize and the Evening Standard Play of the Year Award in 1993. The plays have been staged all over the world and have had an enormous influence.

Quotations from Tony Kushner, *Angels in America*, *Part One* (1992) and *Two* (1994), Nick Hern Books and Royal National Theatre

Blasted
Sarah Kane

1995

> Historical and theatrical context

Following the fall of the Berlin Wall in 1989 and the collapse of the Soviet Union, a new kind of international politics replaced the old certainties of the Cold War. In 1991 Iraq invaded Kuwait, and the combined forces of the UN recaptured it. This vividly demonstrated the West's extraordinary military and technological superiority, while also raising valid questions about means and ends. President George Bush spoke of a 'new world order', but the break-up of the former Yugoslavia and the appearance of 'ethnic cleansing', paramilitary terror and rape being deployed as weapons of war brought images of horror that Europe thought it had banished.

One of the striking factors was the speed and intensity with which these wars were presented on television. CNN reporters commented on US air raids from the roof of a Baghdad hotel and Bosnia's horrors were relayed nightly on colour television. War came to dominate Sarah Kane's (1971–99) thinking: 'For me, there isn't anything else to write about. It's the most pressing thing to confront.'

Sarah Kane committed suicide in February 1999, aged twenty-eight. Her work – and *Blasted* in particular – came to be identified with the arrival of the wave of 'in-yer-face' young British dramatists: writers whose work adopted a tone of nihilistic, drug-fuelled, hard-edged, sexually explicit bravado in an attempt to reflect the new realities. This work lay at the heart of Stephen Daldry's successful directorship of the Royal Court Theatre.

Planned as the first in an uncompleted trilogy of plays about war, *Blasted* was followed by an adaptation of Seneca's *Phaedra* called *Phaedra's Love* (1996), *Cleansed* (1998), *Crave* (1998) and *4.48 Psychosis* (1999, staged posthumously in 2000).

> About the play

Blasted takes place in 'a very expensive hotel bedroom in Leeds'. Ian, a middle-aged tabloid journalist, enters with Cate, a young woman, planning to spend the night together. They are an unlikely couple. Ian, a typical 'tabloid hack', is flabby and unhealthy. It emerges that he only has one lung and is dying, largely thanks to years of cigarette and alcohol abuse. He is also astonishingly sexist, racist and homophobic ('Tip that wog when he brings up the sandwiches' and 'Hate this city. Stinks. Wogs and Pakis taking over') – and he carries a gun. Cate, by contrast, is mentally vulnerable, sucks her thumb like a child and stutters when under stress.

A strange, almost romantic bond appears to bind the two together, a sexual relationship which goes back a long time, but about which Cate now feels ambivalent. Fuelled by a steady diet of gin, champagne, room-service sandwiches and full English breakfast (though Cate, a vegetarian, will have none of it), the first two scenes of the play explore this odd romance in a naturalistic fashion. At one point, Cate appears to faint ('I just go. Feels like I'm away for minutes or months sometime, then I come back just where I was'). Ian tries to persuade Cate to have sex and is only partly successful. None the less, a variety of sexual acts – masturbation, fellatio, dry humping – uncomfortably chart the sometimes blurred boundaries between collusion and abuse:

> Don't pity me, Cate. You don't have to fuck me 'cause I'm dying, but don't push your cunt in my face then take it away 'cause I stick my tongue out.

The dialogue is terse, and the circumstances squalid and unpredictable. One moment Cate is recoiling from Ian, the next she is kissing his neck; love and cruelty seem interchangeable, although she draws the line at 'making love'. At one point she even bites Ian's penis after she has masturbated him. Ian is obsessed by his own dirt and constantly takes showers.

At the end of Scene Two, a new element is introduced. Ian has been consistently edgy and it transpires that in the recent past he has been involved as an undercover agent for a right-wing nationalist group. A knock at the door announces the arrival of a soldier. Armed and menacing, the soldier gobbles up the breakfast, passes salacious comments about the missing Cate (who has disappeared into the bathroom) and tells Ian the town is now in their hands.

Scene Three starts with a blinding flash which reveals that the hotel has been hit by a mortar; the naturalism of the first part is exploded as surely as the hotel. The soldier (we never know his name) continues to taunt Ian, recounting the sexual atrocities he has committed and giving the impression that he is seeking revenge for the mutilation of his girlfriend by other soldiers:

> Went to a house just outside town. All gone. Apart from a small boy hiding in the corner. One of the others took him outside. Lay him on the ground and shot him through the legs. Heard crying in the basement. Went down. Three men and four women. Called the others. They held the men while I fucked the women. Youngest was twelve. Didn't cry, just lay there. Turned her over and – Then she cried. Made her lick me clean. Closed my eyes and thought of – Shot her father in the mouth. Brothers shouted. Hung them from the ceiling by their testicles.

He insists that Ian can help him by telling his story. But Ian maintains that nobody would be interested:

> I'm a home journalist . . . I do other stuff. Shootings and rapes and kids getting fiddled by queer priests and school-teachers. Not soldiers screwing each other for a patch of land.

The soldier's stories grow even darker:

Saw thousands of people packing into trucks like pigs trying to leave town. Women threw their babies on board
hoping someone would look after them. Crushing each
other to death. Insides of people's heads came out of their
eyes. Saw a child most of his face blown off, young girl I
fucked hand up inside her trying to claw my liquid out,
starving man eating his dead wife's leg.

And then, astonishingly, the soldier turns on Ian, rapes him,
sucks his eyes out and eats them before killing himself. Cate
returns from the bathroom, with a baby in her arms. Ian asks
her to stay. His attitude is more tender now, but he has also
become suicidal. In a bleakly comic exchange, Cate castigates
him for his despair. 'God wouldn't like it, I've got blind
friends, you can't give up.' When he finally puts the gun to his
mouth, the barrel is empty. Cate's baby has died, too.

Scene Five starts with Cate burying the baby beneath the
floorboards. She decides to go off and scavenge for food.
When she has gone, Ian makes a nightmarish descent into
degradation, culminating with him starting to eat the dead
baby. Finally, he climbs into the hole beside the baby, with his
head sticking out of the ground. It seems as if he is going to
die. When Cate returns, she is bleeding between her legs but
has got hold of some bread and sausages, which she eats, and
a bottle of gin. She sits down beside Ian and feeds him, and in
a rare moment of humanity he thanks her.

Blasted drives through in five short, powerful scenes. Like a
classical tragedy by Seneca, it has one setting (albeit an
extraordinary one) and is punctuated only by the sound of
increasing rain. Kane outlined her aesthetic beliefs:

All good art is subversive, either in form or content. And
the best art is subversive in form *and* content. And often,
the element that most enrages those who seek to impose
censorship is form . . . I suspect that if *Blasted* had been a
piece of social realism it wouldn't have been so harshly
received.'

The play, she said, was 'about the destruction of naturalism' and in its strange, awkward way it is extraordinarily successful. Not since Shakespeare's *Titus Andronicus* has a play indulged quite so spectacularly in graphic displays of human degradation and cruelty, while extracting such barbed humour and psychological insight. Kane argued that the violence was not so much a shock tactic to gain attention as a device to re-awaken our desensitized consciousness to the unspeakable horrors enacted on our doorstep. For the play is a full-frontal attack on the cynicism and moral relativism of the media and the way that it helps make modern society immune to military violence.

Given its excesses, it is perhaps not surprising that the immediate response to *Blasted* was vociferous. But as the dust settles, Kane's extraordinary début begins to take on the shape of a finely crafted modern parable. Whether her explicitness proved counter-productive is a moot point. But few doubt the power of her moral outrage, or the integrity of her sardonic and at times almost tender assault on the values of the world around her.

> *In performance*

Blasted had its première at the Royal Court Theatre Upstairs in London on 12 January 1995, in a production directed by James MacDonald. Not since Edward Bond's *Saved* has a play in London provoked such critical hostility, with the *Daily Mail* saying: 'Until last night I [thought I] was immune from shock in any theatre. I am not.' The *Evening Standard* denounced it as 'sheer unadulterated brutalism'. Despite, or perhaps because of its critical reception, *Blasted* was very influential and both Harold Pinter and Edward Bond publicly admired the play.

Blasted was revived by the Royal Court in 2001 as part of a Sarah Kane retrospective and has met with worldwide critical acclaim.

Quotations from Sarah Kane, *Blasted*, Methuen, 1995

The Weir
Conor McPherson

1997

> Historical and theatrical context

One of the most remarkable successes of the 1990s was the transformation of the Republic of Ireland from an 'economic basket case' in the mid 1980s into the 'celtic tiger' by the turn of the millennium. This was partly the result of European Community aid to a depressed region, but also because of shrewd political leadership and a well-educated work-force. It was accompanied by the rapid secularization of a society which had been dominated by the Catholic Church for centuries. These changes took political form with the election of the remarkable President Mary Robinson.

The great tradition of Irish playwriting goes back to the seventeenth and eighteenth centuries, with George Farquhar and Richard Brinsley Sheridan. Modern drama is unthinkable without such figures as Oscar Wilde, W. B. Yeats, J. M. Synge, Sean O'Casey and Samuel Beckett. The 1970s and 1980s saw a further flourishing of Irish drama, with important plays by Brian Friel, Frank McGuinness, Anne Devlin and others, while the generation of playwrights that came into their own in the 1990s include such diverse talents as Billy Roche, Garry Mitchell, Sebastian Barry, Martin McDonagh, Lin Coghlan and the Dublin-born and educated Conor McPherson (born 1971).

McPherson's other plays include *Rum and Vodka* (1992), *The Good Thief* (1994), *This Lime Tree Bower* (1995), *St Nicholas* (1997), *Dublin Carol* and *Port Authority* (2001).

> *About the play*

The Weir is set in a small pub in 'northwest Leitrim or Sligo' in the heart of rural Ireland. We are a long way from Dublin, both culturally and physically: superstitious, sexually charged and suspicious about everywhere else. In its form, the play is a ghost drama: a group of people gather together and tell each other – and the audience – increasingly frightening but perfectly formed tales of the supernatural. It has a powerful atmosphere and is compelling to watch. It is a beautifully observed piece of dramatic naturalism, full of colloquial detail, and written with an astonishingly sharp ear.

Jack runs a garage in Knock. He meets Brendan, who owns the pub (this is a small community where everybody knows each other: Jack can help himself to a pint before Brendan arrives). Jack thinks Brendan should get married. Jim lives alone in a remote house with his elderly mother and wants to sell up. There is much talk about a girl ('very nice looking') who has come down from Dublin and is living in the area. She has bought an old house from Finbar – a local bigshot – and they have been seen together – 'like a courting couple or something' – despite the fact that he's married.

Finbar arrives with Valerie and introduces her. The men are awkwardly on their best behaviour. There is a delicious comic moment when she asks for a glass of white wine (unheard of in a rural Irish pub) and there is much talk about Jack's betting on the horses. After another round ('three small ones'), Finbar shows Valerie some old black-and-white photos on the pub wall of a local weir which had been opened in the 1950s and 'the view of Carrick from our top field up there'.

Finbar starts to talk about the 'fairies' that are supposed to haunt the old fort – 'an area steeped in old folk-lore' – and Jack tells the story of the 'fairy road'. The woman, Maura, who has sold Valerie her house, heard fairies knocking on the doors when she was a child:

Well Maura said her mother never told the others, and
one day when it was only the two of them there, a priest
came and blessed the doors and windows. And then there
was no more knocking. And it was only years later that
Maura heard from one of the older people in the area that
the house had been built on what they call a road . . . But
Maura never heard the knocking again except on one time
in the fifties when the weir was going up.

They have another drink and Finbar talks about a house he
used to live next door to. He was in his early twenties and the
young girl who lived there started 'doing the Ouija board'
and went mad – she had seen a 'woman on the stairs'. The
house was exorcized but the girl's brother saw a dead neighbour of theirs 'standing out in the garden, looking at the
house'. The young Finbar was so terrified that he could not
leave the fire and go upstairs to bed. And soon after, he
moved out of the house and went to live down in the town.
    They talk about their lives, and at one point Jack says:

Me and Brendan are the fellows on our own. Jack has the
mammy to look after, but we're, you know, you can come
in here in the evenings. During the day you'd be working.
You know, there's company around. Bit of a community
all spread around the place, like.

Valerie says she's moved up there to get some 'peace and
quiet'. Jim buys a few drinks. There's a wedding planned next
day at Finbar's hotel: young Nuala Donnelly's. Jim starts to
talk about the day her father Declan hired him to dig a grave
in a churchyard in the rain. When the body was finally
buried, a 'fella' appeared, saying that he had dug the wrong
grave, and pointed to 'a white one with a picture of a little girl
on it'. Jim went down with a bad case of the 'flu, but when he
recovered he looked at the obituaries in the paper and saw a
picture 'the spit of your man I'd met in the graveyard'.
    This upsets Valerie, who goes off to the Ladies (although
the Ladies is 'busted' and she has to go into the house). The

men realize they've scared her and blame each other. Finbar senses that 'there's something obviously going on . . . in her life', and they get more drinks in: 'we might tell a few jokes when she comes back'. But Valerie wants to tell her own story, about her daughter, Niamh, who couldn't sleep: 'she was afraid of the dark . . . there were people at the window, there were people in the attic, there was someone coming up the stairs. There was children, knocking.' One day, Niamh went swimming with her school, hit her head and drowned: 'And I gave her a little hug. She was freezing cold. And I told her Mammy loved her very much. She just looked asleep but her lips were gone blue and she was dead.' Then, months later, the phone rang and it was Niamh's voice saying she was at her friend Nana's. The men are shocked by the reality of it all and come up with theories about the call ('a wrong number or something wrong with the phone'). They all express their sympathy for Valerie and feel it is time to go. But Jack wants to know if 'you ever get over something like that' and they decide to stay and have 'a last one'.

Valerie asks Jack if he ever got married. Jack talks of a 'lovely girl [he had] back then'. She went to live in Dublin and he didn't join her and he behaved badly to her and she married someone else. At the wedding, she 'just looked at me like I was another guest at the wedding. And that was that. And the future was all ahead of me. Years and years of it. I could feel it coming. All those things you've got to face on your own.' He talks of how he went into a bar and the barman made him a sandwich:

> And I took this sandwich up and I could hardly swallow it,
> because of the lump in my throat. But I ate it all down
> because someone I didn't know had done this for me.
> Such a small thing. But a huge thing. In my condition.

As they are leaving, Jack holds out Valerie's jacket for her. She comments: 'Oh now. Very nice', and Jack responds: 'These are the touches, ha, Brendan?' As they leave, Valerie is able to joke, saying that she will come back, even if the place is full of tourists: 'I might even pick up some German'. It is a sense of community, McPherson seems to be saying, that binds the living together – the pub, the jokes, the stories, the drinks, the shared history – even in the face of loneliness, fear and a child's death.

The main criticism levelled at *The Weir* is that it is formally conservative and that its reliance on monologues prevents it from being truly dramatic. The other – possibly more penetrating – point is that the play presents a vision of rural Ireland which is out of date, when Ireland's rural economy was expanding at an astonishing rate and such stereotypes were fading fast. What these criticisms fail to take into account is the extraordinary quality of McPherson's writing: beautifully heard, sensitively poised, sometimes chilling, often witty, luminous and touching in equal measure. Conor McPherson inherited the hefty mantle of the great Irish dramatic tradition at a very young age, but did it with grace and ease, and wrote a play of quite exceptional literary quality.

> *In performance*

The Weir was commissioned by the Royal Court Theatre in London. Ian Rickson's production was a popular success when it opened at the Ambassadors Theatre in the West End and became a major commercial hit when it transferred to the Duke of York's Theatre in the West End. When the reopening of the refurbished Royal Court Theatre in Sloane Square was delayed, *The Weir* was instrumental in keeping the Royal Court going while 'in exile'.

Quotations from Conor McPherson, *The Weir*, Nick Hern Books, 1997

Closer
Patrick Marber

1997

> *Historical and theatrical context*

Just three weeks before the première of Patrick Marber's (born 1964) *Closer*, Tony Blair's New Labour Government was elected with a crushing majority, bringing to an end eighteen years of Conservative rule. This landmark political event seemed to reflect a decisive break with the past and the embrace of a powerful sense of the new. New Labour's appeal lay in its bringing together the most successful elements of Thatcherism within a more communitarian moral imperative. On 1 May 1997, old-style socialism seemed dead and buried and New Labour's constituents were interested in education, health, economic prosperity and personal fulfilment.

A central element in this project of modernization was the progress made in micro-technology. By 1997, access to the internet and e-mail was widespread and Britain was leading the way (in Europe) in the ownership of personal computers. In a symbolic act, one of Blair's early visitors to Downing Street was Bill Gates, the richest man on earth and head of the gigantic Microsoft Corporation.

Patrick Marber was part of a new generation of British dramatists (mostly male), steeped in alternative comedy, at home with film and television, frank about sexuality, tough, urban and sassy, interested in the intimacies of modern life and in moving beyond the explicitly political (and often feminist) agenda of the 1970s and 1980s. Marber's earlier plays include *Dealer's Choice* (1995) and the television play *After Miss Julie* (1995).

> About the play

Closer has only four characters (two men, two women) and Marber carefully defines them by age and background: Dan, the obituarist who fails as a novelist ('from the suburbs. Thirties'); Larry, the dermatologist struggling with the NHS ('from the city. Late thirties/early forties'); Alice, the waif, waitress and stripper ('from the town. Early twenties'); and Anna, the successful photographer ('from the country. Mid thirties'). Marber also indicates a specific sense of time and place: twelve days between 1993 and 1997 in different locations throughout London.

Alice is in a hospital waiting-room with Dan, having been knocked over by a car driven by him. Larry treats her and notices a scar on her leg. When asked, she reveals that she used to work as a stripper ('Men want a girl who looks like a boy. They want to protect her but she must be a survivor. And she must come . . . like a train . . . but with elegance'). She persuades Dan to take a day off work and phones through to his office on his behalf. Eighteen months later, Dan is living with Alice and has written a book about her ('About sex. About love'). Anna is taking promotional photographs of Dan when Alice arrives unannounced, wanting to have her picture taken.

By chance, the two men find themselves writing to each other on their computers in a 'chat-room', using all the codes and in-jokes of internet language. In a brilliant comic twist, Dan pretends to be 'Anna', a woman looking for a sexual partner. We read the increasingly pornographic dialogue on the screen while, simultaneously, Larry's phone rings and he gives out instant medical diagnoses. Larry is desperate to meet 'Anna' and they make a plan to meet at the aquarium. The next day, to his acute embarrassment, Larry discovers his mistake and meets Alice instead.

By June 1995, Anna is exhibiting her photographs, including a large print of Alice ('Young woman. London'). Alice is worried that Dan is going to leave her, but he insists that he is in love with her. Although Larry and Anna have been

together for four months, Larry chats up Alice while Dan
tries to persuade Anna to leave Larry for him:

Dan I cannot live without you.

Anna You can, you do.

Dan This is not me, I don't do this. Don't you see? All
the language is old, there are no new words . . . I love you,
I 'fucking' love you. I need you. I can't think, I can't work,
I can't breathe. We are going to die. Please. Save me.
Look at me. Tell me you're not in love with me.

She looks at him.

Anna I'm not in love with you.

Pause.

Dan You just lied. See me next week. Please, Anna. I'm
begging you . . . I'm your stranger . . . jump . . .

A year later, in a brilliantly counterpointed scene, the two
couples split up. On one side of the stage, Dan tells Alice he
is in love with Anna and Alice is furious. On the other side,
Larry, who is by now married to Anna, announces that he
'fucked someone [a prostitute] in New York'. In return, Anna
reveals that she is in love with Dan and the act ends in a
whirlwind of jealousy, betrayal and vivid sexual imagining,
sending a powerful charge of recognition through a modern
'thirty-something' audience.

By the start of Act Two, Alice is 'entertaining' Larry in the
lapdancing club where she works. Her professional name is
Jane, but Larry wants her to admit to her real name. Larry is
desperate to get 'closer' to her, asking at one point: 'What do
you have to do to get a bit of intimacy round here?' He avenges
himself by ordering her to 'turn round very slowly and bend
over and touch the fucking floor for my viewing pleasure'.

Anna and Dan meet for a concert. Although she is now
with Dan and has divorced Larry, she admits to Dan that she
'fucked' Larry that afternoon. Dan is terribly jealous, but

wonders what the meaning of sex is anyway. A month later, it is Larry's birthday. Dan has left Anna to go to Alice and when Anna turns up the two women compare notes about men:

> This is what we're dealing with; we arrive with our baggage and for a while they're brilliant, they're baggage handlers. We say 'Where's your baggage?' They deny all knowledge of it, they're in love, they have none. Then, just as you're relaxing, a great big juggernaut arrives . . . with their baggage.

Scene Ten takes place in Larry's surgery. Dan wants Anna back and challenges him:

> **Dan** If you love her, you'll let her go so she can be happy.

> **Larry** She doesn't want to be happy.

> **Dan** Everyone wants to be happy.

> **Larry** Depressives don't. They want to be unhappy to confirm they're depressed.

When Dan asks Larry if he thinks Anna enjoyed being with him, he replies: 'I didn't fuck her to give her a nice time. I fucked her to fuck you up.' Later in the scene, Larry says:

> We're the old people, Dan; old men shaking our fists over these women, like some ancient ritual. We should go back to the aquarium and evolve. From Big Bang to weary shag, the history of the world. And if women saw one minute of our home movies, the shit that slops through our minds every day . . . they'd string us up by our balls, they really would.

Larry later admits that he 'fucked' Alice and the scene ends with a terrifying tension between the two men.

Dan and Alice are together in a hotel bedroom. She is going to take him to New York to celebrate having been together for four years. Dan wants Alice to admit to what he already knows – that she 'fucked' Larry. Alice tells him that she doesn't love him any more ('I'm bored of loving a piece of shit'), they struggle and he hits her.

In the last scene of the play, Larry and Anna are separated but amicable. Alice has died, in New York. Her real name was Jane Jones. Dan appears to lay flowers at the memorial to the Victorian girl heroine after whom she named herself. All four are alone, in solitude, and it seems that closeness is impossible.

Closer's power lies in its mixture of quick-fire, sharp-witted, brilliantly heard, ribald dialogue and its finely sensed, moving exploration of love and longing, desire and heartbreak. With its portrait of four very real young people, alone in the anonymity of the modern city and desperately wishing to be 'closer' to someone else, Patrick Marber has written one of the defining works of British *fin de siècle* modernity.

> *In performance*

Patrick Marber developed *Closer* at The Studio, the Royal National Theatre's 'research and development' laboratory. His own production of the play opened in the National's Cottesloe Theatre on 29 May 1997, to very positive reviews ('the most assured sense for dramatic rhythm, of any English playwright to have emerged since Pinter'). It transferred to the larger Lyttelton Theatre on 16 October of the same year, and moved into the West End the following year. It opened on Broadway (with Anna Friel) on 25 March 1999.

In 1997, *Closer* received both the Evening Standard Award for Best Comedy and the Time Out Award for Best New Play. True to its spirit, *Closer* was probably the first play in Britain to have had its own website: www.closer.co.uk.

Quotations from Patrick Marber, *Closer*, Methuen, 1997

Copenhagen
Michael Frayn

1998

> Historical and Theatrical Context

In 1959, the novelist C. P. Snow described the widening disparity between science and art as the 'two cultures'. By the late 1990s, in Britain at least, he would have been surprised to learn how much the gap had closed. Electronic media, global communications and the popularization of science by figures such as Stephen Hawking, Richard Dawkin and Stephen Jay Gould all helped to revolutionize public interest. Genetics, nuclear physics, quantum mechanics and biotechnology, once the knowledge of a few, came within reach of the many. Worrying scientific developments – the devastation reaped by AIDS in sub-Saharan Africa, the great advances in biotechnology and genetic engineering, and nuclear proliferation on the Indian subcontinent – all posed difficult questions about where mankind's knowledge was leading us as the new millennium dawned.

As a genre, the 'scientific' play had its precedents: T. P. Leivick's *The Golem* (1921), Bertolt Brecht's *The Life of Galileo* (1943–5) and Friedrich Dürrenmatt's *The Physicists* (1962). More recently, Terry Johnson's *Insignificance* (1982), Tom Stoppard's *Arcadia* (1993), Stephen Poliakoff's *Blinded by the Sun* (1996) and Shelagh Stephenson's *An Experiment with an Air Pump* (1998) all tried, with varying degrees of success, to make potent drama from the inevitable conflict between scientific advance and morality.

When Michael Frayn (born 1933) wrote *Copenhagen*, he was still best known for his farces, particularly the magnificent *Noises Off* (1982). But philosophy had been an abiding passion and in an interview in 1999 he declared that 'all my plays are informed by my reading of philosophy'. They include *Alphabetical Order* (1975), *Clouds* (1976), *Donkey's Years* (1976), *Make and Break* (1980) and *Benefactors* (1984). He has also written fluent translations of Chekhov's four great plays and an original adaptation, *Wild Honey* (1984), of Chekhov's early play *Platonov*. He is the author of a number of novels, including *A Very Private Life* (1968) and *Headlong* (1999).

> About the play

According to Frayn, the idea for *Copenhagen* came after he read *Heisenberg's War*, Thomas Powers's biography of the German Nobel prizewinner and nuclear physicist, Werner Heisenberg, creator of the Uncertainty Principle.

From this, Frayn created a philosophical, psychological and scientific thriller based on the real-life meeting in 1941 in occupied Copenhagen between Heisenberg and his half-Jewish Danish mentor (and fellow Nobel prizewinner) Niels Bohr – a meeting which has continued to be the subject of heated debate ever since. The question is: did Heisenberg go to Copenhagen to discover how far the Allies had gone in their plans to make an atomic bomb, or was it to warn Bohr of German nuclear advances and thus prevent a German victory? Was Heisenberg a hero or a Nazi collaborator? As Heisenberg declares at the beginning of the play:

> There are only two things the world remembers about me. One is the Uncertainty Principle, and the other is my mysterious visit to Niels Bohr in Copenhagen in 1941. Everyone understands uncertainty. Or thinks he does. No one understands my trip to Copenhagen.

The tone throughout is cool and ironical. With great technical virtuosity, Frayn draws out the themes of memory, scientific discovery, professional competitiveness, father-and-son relationships and the differing male and female perspectives on life. As if testing a scientific hypothesis, he presents the meeting from various perspectives – those of Bohr, his wife

Margrethe and Heisenberg himself, each reliving it for clues as to what actually happened. But just as Heisenberg's Uncertainty Principle holds that the more accurately you know the position of a given particle, the less accurately you know its velocity, Heisenberg's motivation becomes almost impossible to establish and he is the person least likely to know himself.

This investigation is presented as a vortex of interlinked issues that expound the intricacies of quantum physics, the splitting of the atom and its associated discoveries, and set them alongside the personal reactions of Heisenberg, Bohr and Margrethe, all within a dramatic structure that itself cunningly replicates scientific behaviour. Round and round they encircle each other, like so many particles around a nucleus, and Frayn's control of these concentric circles is breathtaking.

Though discursive in style (some have dismissed *Copenhagen* as 'a radio play'), there is no lack of dramatic tension. Rather, there is exhilaration in the intellectual thrust and counterthrust, as Bohr and Margrethe recall the first time Heisenberg appeared in their midst. 'So quick, and eager' says Bohr; 'Too quick. Too eager' returns Margrethe. And Bohr muses: 'The more I look back on it, the more I think Heisenberg was the greatest of them all'.

At the centre of these concentric circles, then, is Heisenberg at the door to Bohr's house in September 1941, recalling his visit to Copenhagen to give a lecture on astrophysics, but in his head rehearsing another, more private text. Bohr argues for Heisenberg's benevolent motives, since he is taking a risk in coming because of his host's association with 'Jewish physics'. To Bohr, Heisenberg is first and foremost a friend; to Margrethe, he is always a German. (One of the historical ironies Frayn exposes is that had the Nazis not persecuted their Jewish physicists, the outcome of the war might have been different).

Round and round they go, Heisenberg analysing his motivations, Margrethe wondering if it could be something to do with the making of an atom bomb; Bohr denying the possibility. Yet this is exactly the suspicion aroused in Bohr when Heisenberg asks him, on a fateful walk, whether, as physicists, they have the 'moral right to work on the practical exploitation of atomic energy'. Bohr is furious, cuts him off and returns to the house. The mystery deepens: what did Bohr understand – or misunderstand – by the question?

Frayn sets his riddle against the contrasting characteristics of the two men – Bohr slow and cautious, Heisenberg always going too fast for his own good. Frayn also draws on the surrogate father–son relationship that grew out of Bohr's loss of one of his own sons in a sailing accident, for which he feels continual guilt. Indeed, the fact that the paternal Bohr was not available to stop Heisenberg making a crucial error in his calculations in the making of the atom bomb is yet one more irony in Frayn's demonstration of how the course of history is subject to the infinitely personal and the random.

Underlining the point, Frayn constantly shifts time sequences, making Bohr and Heisenberg confront each other in the present whilst Margrethe brings their rarefied scientific discourses down to earth from a different perspective of time and gender:

> I'm sorry but you want to make everything seem heroically abstract and logical. And when you tell the story, yes, it all falls into place . . . But I was there and when I remember what it was like . . . what I see isn't a story! It's confusion and rage and jealousy and tears and no one knowing what things mean or which way they're going to go.

Using a theatrical technique not unlike Brecht's *Verfremdungseffekt* (alienation effect) Frayn gives us the possibility of what occurred from three very different standpoints. And he heightens the moral relativism that exists in any judgement when he shows Heisenberg – the German who loved his country, who felt torn by the implications of the creation of the atom bomb and who may have come to Copenhagen to seek absolution from the man they all regarded as 'the Pope'

– speaking with Bohr – the 'good man' who, by his involvement at the American nuclear weapons plant at Los Alamos, must share the responsibility for more than a hundred thousand deaths.

Frayn's ending is an epiphany to random chance – the tiny actions which, like a chain reaction, go on multiplying, affecting the course of public and private lives. This uncertainty, Frayn seems to suggest, might just be the grit that saves humanity from itself as it enters a new millennium. *Copenhagen*, with its fusion of humanity and intellectual brilliance, brings that possibility into closer focus.

> *In performance*

Peter J. Davison's white, circular setting provided a perfect university lecture theatre atmosphere for the première of Michael Blakemore's *Copenhagen* in the Royal National Theatre's Cottesloe Theatre in May 1998. It starred David Burke as Bohr, Sara Kestelman as Margrethe and Matthew Marsh as Heisenberg. Nine months later, the production transferred to the Duchess Theatre, and two years later to Broadway. *Copenhagen*'s success took even its author by surprise: 'I didn't think anyone would produce it. It was written entirely for my own benefit and I thought I might just get it on to radio. I am still baffled by how much it has caught people's fancy.'

Quotations from Michael Frayn, *Copenhagen*, Methuen, 1998

A Chronology of a Thousand Plays of the Twentieth Century

1900
David Belasco, *Madam Butterfly*
Romain Rolland, *Danton*
Arthur Schnitzler, La Ronde
George Bernard Shaw, *Captain Brassbound's Conversion*
August Strindberg, The Dance of Death, Parts 1 and 2
August Strindberg, *Easter*

1901
Anton Chekhov, *Three Sisters*
Maxim Gorky, *The Philistines*
Harley Granville Barker, *The Marrying of Ann Leete*
George Bernard Shaw, *Caesar and Cleopatra*
August Strindberg, *To Damascus, Part III*
J. M. Synge, *When the Moon has Set*

1902
J. M. Barrie, *The Admirable Crichton*
J. M. Barrie, *Quality Street*
Maxim Gorky, *The Lower Depths*
Lady Gregory and W. B. Yeats, *Cathleen ni Houlihan*
Lady Gregory and W. B. Yeats, *The Pot of Broth*
Romain Rolland, *14th July*
August Strindberg, *A Dream Play*

1903
Somerset Maugham, *A Man of Honour*
J. M. Synge, *In the Shadow of the Glen*

1904
J. M. Barrie, *Peter Pan*
Anton Chekhov, The Cherry Orchard
Maxim Gorky, *Summerfolk*
Lady Gregory, *Spreading the News*

Arthur Schnitzler, *The Lonely Road*
George Bernard Shaw, *John Bull's Other Island*
J. M. Synge, *Riders to the Sea*
W. B. Yeats, *On Baile's Strand*
W. B. Yeats, *The King's Threshold*

1905
David Belasco, *The Girl of the Golden West*
Maxim Gorky, *Children of the Sun*
Harley Granville Barker, *The Voysey Inheritance*
George Bernard Shaw, *Major Barbara*
George Bernard Shaw, *Man and Superman*
J. M. Synge, *The Well of the Saints*

1906
John Galsworthy, *The Silver Box*
Maxim Gorky, *Barbarians*
Maxim Gorky, *Enemies*
Arthur Wing Pinero, *His House in Order*
Arthur Schnitzler, *The Call of Life*
George Bernard Shaw, *The Doctor's Dilemma*

1907
Georges Feydeau, *A Flea in her Ear*
Harley Granville Barker, *Waste*
Lady Gregory, *The Rising of the Moon*
August Strindberg, *The Burnt House*
August Strindberg, *The Ghost Sonata*
August Strindberg, *The Great Highway*
August Strindberg, *The Pelican*
August Strindberg, *Storm*
J. M. Synge, *The Playboy of the Western World*
W. B. Yeats, *Deirdre*

1908
J. M. Barrie, *What Every Woman Knows*
J. M. Synge, *The Tinker's Wedding*
W. B. Yeats, *The Unicorn from the Stars*

1909

Georges Feydeau, *Look After Lulu*
John Galsworthy, *Strife*
D. H. Lawrence, *A Collier's Friday Night*
Maurice Maeterlinck, *The Blue Bird*
Ferenč Molnár, *Liliom*
Arthur Wing Pinero, *Mid-Channel*
Carl Sternheim, *The Knickers*

1910

John Galsworthy, *Justice*
Maxim Gorky, *Vassa Shelesnova*
Harley Granville Barker, *The Madras House*
Ferenč Molnár, *The Guardsman*
Edmond Rostand, *Chantecler*
Rabindranath Tagore, *The King of the Dark Chamber*

1911

Hugo von Hofmannsthal, *Everyman*
D. H. Lawrence, *The Widowing of Mrs Holroyd*
Arthur Schnitzler, *Undiscovered Country*
Carl Sternheim, *The Money Box*

1912

Stanley Houghton, *Hindle Wakes*
D. H. Lawrence, *The Daughter-in-Law*
Arthur Schnitzler, *Professor Bernhardi*
Githa Sowerby, *Rutherford and Son*
Carl Sternheim, *Burger Schippel*

1913

Georg Kaiser, *The Burghers of Calais*
George Bernard Shaw, *Pygmalion*

1914

James Joyce, *Exiles*
Carl Sternheim, *The Snob*

1915
Carl Sternheim, *The Candidate*

1916
Solomon Ansky, *The Dybbuk*
Harold Brighouse, *Hobson's Choice*
Georg Kaiser, *From Morning till Midnight*

1917
J. M. Barrie, *Dear Brutus*
Luigi Pirandello, *Right You Are – If You Think So*

1918
Bertolt Brecht, *Baal*
Georg Kaiser, *Gas I*
Luigi Pirandello, *The Rules of the Game*

1919
Susan Glaspell, *Bernice*
Karl Kraus, *The Last Days of Mankind*

1920
J. M. Barrie, *Mary Rose*
John Galsworthy, *The Skin Game*
Georg Kaiser, *Gas II*
Eugene O'Neill, *Beyond the Horizon*
Eugene O'Neill, *The Emperor Jones*
George Bernard Shaw, *Heartbreak House*
Ernst Toller, *Man and the Masses*

1921
Karel Čapek, *R.U.R.*
Clemence Dane (Winifred Ashton), *A Bill of Divorcement*
Susan Glaspell, *Inheritors*
Susan Glaspell, *The Verge*
T. P. Lievick, *The Golem*
Somerset Maugham, *The Circle*
Eugene O'Neill, *Anna Christie*
Luigi Pirandello, *Six Characters in Search of an Author*

1922
Jean-Jacques Bernard, *Martine*
Bertolt Brecht, *Drums in the Night*
Karel and Josef Čapek, *The Insect Play*
John Galsworthy, *Loyalties*
Eugene O'Neill, *The Hairy Ape*
Luigi Pirandello, *Henry IV*
George Bernard Shaw, *Back to Methuselah*
Ernst Toller, *The Machine Wreckers*

1923
Frederick Lonsdale, *Aren't We All?*
Sean O'Casey, *The Shadow of a Gunman*
Elmer Rice, *The Adding Machine*
George Bernard Shaw, *Saint Joan*

1924
Jean Cocteau, *Orphée*
Noël Coward, *The Vortex*
Sean O'Casey, *Juno and the Paycock*
Eugene O'Neill, *All God's Chillun Got Wings*
Eugene O'Neill, *Desire Under the Elms*
Luigi Pirandello, *Each in his Own Way*

1925
J. R. Ackerley, *The Prisoners of War*
Noël Coward, *Hay Fever*
Ben Travers, *A Cuckoo in the Nest*

1926
Mikhail Bulgakov, *The White Guard*
Paul Green, *In Abraham's Bosom*
Frederick Lonsdale, *On Approval*
Somerset Maugham, *The Constant Wife*
Sean O'Casey, *The Plough and the Stars*
Ben Travers, *Rookery Nook*
Sergei Tretyakov, *Roar, China!*

1927

Marieluise Fleisser, *Pioneers in Ingolstadt*
Vladimir Mayakovsky, *Mystery-Bouffe*
Ernst Toller, *Hoppla, We're Alive!*
Ben Travers, *Thark*

1928

Mikhail Bulgakov, *Flight*
Paul Green, *The House of Connelly*
Ben Hecht and Charles MacArthur, *The Front Page*
Eugene O'Neill, *Strange Interlude*
R. C. Sherriff, *Journey's End*
Ben Travers, *Plunder*
Sophie Treadwell, *Machinal*

1929

Patrick Hamilton, *Rope*
Vladimir Mayakovsky, *The Bed-Bug*
Sean O'Casey, *The Silver Tassie*
Luigi Pirandello, *Tonight We Improvise*
Luigi Pirandello, *Lazarus*
Elmer Rice, *Street Scene*
George Bernard Shaw, *The Apple Cart*

1930

Joe Corrie, *In Time o' Strife*
Noël Coward, *Private Lives*
Susan Glaspell, *Alison's House*
George S. Kaufman and Moss Hart, *Once in a Lifetime*
Vladimir Mayakovsky, *The Bath House*
Luigi Pirandello, *As You Want Me*
Miguel de Unamuno, *Dream Shadows*

1931

James Bridie, *The Anatomist*
Noël Coward, *Cavalcade*
Ödön von Horváth, *Tales from the Vienna Woods*
Eugene O'Neill, *Mourning Becomes Electra*
Ben Travers, *Turkey Time*

Carl Zuckmayer, *The Captain from Köpenick*

1932
Bertolt Brecht, *St Joan of the Stockyards*
Ödön von Horváth, *Casimir and Caroline*
Somerset Maugham, *For Services Rendered*
J. B. Priestley, *Dangerous Corner*

1933
Mikhail Bulgakov, *Bliss*
Noël Coward, *Design for Living*
Gordon Daviot (Elizabeth Mackintosh), *Richard of Bordeaux*
Jack Kirkland, *Tobacco Road*
Federico García Lorca, *Blood Wedding*
J. B. Priestley, *Laburnum Grove*

1934
Jean Cocteau, *The Infernal Machine*
Ronald Gow and Walter Greenwood, *Love on the Dole*
Lillian Hellman, *The Children's Hour*
Federico García Lorca, *Yerma*
Sean O'Casey, *Within the Gates*
J. B. Priestley, *Eden End*
Vsevelod Vishnevsky, *The Optimistic Tragedy*

1935
George Abbott, *Three Men on a Horse*
Antonin Artaud, *The Cenci*
W. H. Auden and Christopher Isherwood, *The Dog Beneath the Skin*
T. S. Eliot, *Murder in the Cathedral*
Federico García Lorca, *The House of Bernarda Alba*
Jean Giraudoux, *The Trojan War Will Not Take Place*
Witold Gombrowicz, *Princess Ivona*
Clifford Odets, *Awake and Sing*
Clifford Odets, *Paradise Lost*
Clifford Odets, *Waiting for Lefty*
Emlyn Williams, *Night Must Fall*

1936

Rodney Ackland, *After October*
W. H. Auden and Christopher Isherwood, *The Ascent of F6*
Mikhail Bulgakov, *Molière*
Clare Booth Luce, *The Women*
Terence Rattigan, *French Without Tears*
Montague Slater, *Stay Down Miner*

1937

Ödön von Horváth, *Don Juan Comes Back from the War*
Ödön von Horváth, *Figaro Gets a Divorce*
Clifford Odets, *Golden Boy*
J. B. Priestley, *I Have Been Here Before*
J. B. Priestley, *Time and the Conways*

1938

Karel Čapek, *The Mother*
Jean Cocteau, *The Terrible Parents*
Patrick Hamilton, *Gaslight*
George S. Kaufmann and Moss Hart, *You Can't Take It With You*
Clifford Odets, *Rocket to the Moon*
J. B. Priestley, *When We Are Married*
Dodie Smith, *Dear Octopus*
Thornton Wilder, *Our Town*
Emlyn Williams, *The Corn is Green*

1939

Alexei Arbuzov, *Tanya*
Robert Ardrey, *Thunder Rock*
Philip Barry, *The Philadelphia Story*
Noël Coward, *This Happy Breed*
T. S. Eliot, *The Family Reunion*
Jean Giraudoux, *Ondine*
Lillian Hellman, *The Little Foxes*
George S. Kaufman and Moss Hart, *The Man Who Came to Dinner*
Eugene O'Neill, *The Iceman Cometh*

William Saroyan, *The Time of Your Life*
Alexei Tolstoy, *The Road to Victory*
Carl Zuckmayer, *The Devil's General*

1940
Bertolt Brecht, *The Good Person of Setzuan*
Eugene O'Neill, *Long Day's Journey into Night*

1941
Bertolt Brecht, *Mother Courage and her Children*
Bertolt Brecht, *Mr Puntila and His Man Matti*
Bertolt Brecht, *The Resistible Rise of Arturo Ui*
Noël Coward, *Blithe Spirit*
Lillian Hellman, *Watch on the Rhine*

1942
Rodney Ackland, *Strange Orchestra*
Terence Rattigan, *Flare Path*
Jean-Paul Sartre, *The Flies*
Thornton Wilder, *The Skin of Our Teeth*

1943
Bertolt Brecht, *The Caucasian Chalk Circle*
Bertolt Brecht, *The Life of Galileo*
Bertolt Brecht, *Schweyk in the Second World War*
Paul Claudel, *The Satin Slipper*
Noël Coward, *Present Laughter*
Eugene O'Neill, *A Moon for the Misbegotten*

1944
Jean Anouilh, *Antigone*
Albert Camus, *The Misunderstanding*
Jean-Paul Sartre, *In Camera*

1945
Albert Camus, *Caligula*
Eduardo De Filippo, *Napoli milionaria!*
Jean Giraudoux, *The Madwoman of Chaillot*
J. B. Priestley, *An Inspector Calls*
Tennessee Williams, *The Glass Menagerie*

1946
Eduardo De Filippo, *Filumena*
Christopher Fry, *A Phoenix Too Frequent*
Lillian Hellman, *Another Part of the Forest*
Garson Kanin, *Born Yesterday*
Terence Rattigan, *The Winslow Boy*
Jean-Paul Sartre, *The Respectable Prostitute*
Theodore Ward, *Our Lan'*

1947
Jean Anouilh, *Ring Round the Moon*
Wolfgang Borchert, *Outside the Door*
Jean Genet, *The Maids*
William Douglas Home, *The Chiltern Hundreds*
Arthur Miller, *All My Sons*
Sean O'Casey, *Cock-a-Doodle Dandy*
Ena Lamont Stewart, *Men Should Weep*
Tennessee Williams, *A Streetcar Named Desire*

1948
Eduardo De Filippo, *Grand Magic*
Eduardo De Filippo, *Inner Voices*
Christopher Fry, *The Lady's Not For Burning*
Eugene Ionesco, *The Bald Primadonna*
Pär Lagerkvist, *The Philosopher's Stone*
Robert MacLeish, *The Gorbals Story*
Terence Rattigan, *The Browning Version*
Terence Rattigan, *Harlequinade*
Jean-Paul Sartre, *Dirty Hands*

1949
Ugo Betti, *Corruption in the Palace of Justice*
Albert Camus, *The Just*
Friedrich Dürrenmatt, *Romulus the Great*
T. S. Eliot, *The Cocktail Party*
Jean Genet, *Deathwatch*
Arthur Miller, *Death of a Salesman*

1950

Jean Anouilh, *The Rehearsal*

Christopher Fry, *Venus Observed*

William Inge, *Come Back Little Sheba*

Eugene Ionesco, *The Lesson*

Heiner Müller, *The Scab*

1951

Peter Ustinov, *The Love of the Colonels*

John Whiting, *A Penny for a Song*

John Whiting, *Saint's Day*

Tennessee Williams, *The Rose Tattoo*

1952

Rodney Ackland, *The Pink Room (Absolute Hell)*

Jean Anouillh, *The Waltz of the Toreadors*

John Chapman, *Dry Rot*

Agatha Christie, *The Mousetrap*

Max Frisch, *Don Juan*

Eugene Ionesco, *The Chairs*

John Osborne and Anthony Creighton, *Epitaph for George
  Dillon*

Terence Rattigan, *The Deep Blue Sea*

1953

Arthur Adamov, *Professor Taranne*

Jean Anouilh, *The Lark*

Samuel Beckett, *Waiting for Godot*

Horton Foote, *The Trip to Bountiful*

T. S. Eliot, *The Confidential Clerk*

Graham Greene, *The Living Room*

William Inge, *Picnic*

Arthur Miller, *The Crucible*

1954

Brendan Behan, *The Quare Fellow*

Eugene Ionesco, *Amédée*

Louis Peterson, *Take a Giant Step*

Terence Rattigan, *Separate Tables*

Dylan Thomas, *Under Milk Wood*
John Whiting, *Marching Song*

1955
Arthur Adamov, *Ping-Pong*
Enid Bagnold, *The Chalk Garden*
Alice Childress, *Trouble in Mind*
William Inge, *Bus Stop*
Ray Lawler, *Summer of the Seventeenth Doll*
Arthur Miller, *A View from the Bridge*
Jean-Paul Sartre, *Nekrassov*
Tennessee Williams, *Cat on a Hot Tin Roof*

1956
Friedrich Dürrenmatt, *The Visit*
Jean Genet, *The Balcony*
Errol John, *Moon on a Rainbow Shawl*
John Osborne, *Look Back in Anger*
Peter Ustinov, *Romanoff and Juliet*

1957
Arthur Adamov, *Paolo Pauli*
Samuel Beckett, *All That Fall*
Samuel Beckett, *Endgame*
Günter Grass, *Flood*
Graham Greene, *The Potting Shed*
Bernard Kops, *The Hamlet of Stepney Green*
John Osborne, *The Entertainer*
N. F. Simpson, *A Resounding Tinkle*
Wole Soyinka, *The Lion and the Jewel*
Tennessee Williams, *Baby Doll*
Tennessee Williams, *Orpheus Descending*

1958
John Arden, *Live Like Pigs*
Samuel Beckett, *Krapp's Last Tape*
Brendan Behan, *The Hostage*
Shelagh Delaney, *A Taste of Honey*
T. S. Eliot, *The Elder Statesman*

Max Frisch, *The Fire Raisers*
Günter Grass, *Mister, Mister*
Anne Jellicoe, *The Sport of My Mad Mother*
John Mortimer, *The Dock Brief*
Harold Pinter, *The Birthday Party*
Reginald Rose, *Twelve Angry Men*
Peter Shaffer, *Five Finger Exercise*
Arnold Wesker, *Chicken Soup with Barley*
Tennessee Williams, *Suddenly Last Summer*

1959
Edward Albee, *The Zoo Story*
Alexei Arbuzov, *It Happened in Irkutsk*
Jean Anouilh, *Becket*
John Arden, *Serjeant Musgrave's Dance*
Eduardo De Filippo, *Saturday, Sunday, Monday*
Jack Gelber, *The Connection*
Jean Genet, *The Blacks*
Günter Grass, *Only Ten Minutes to Buffalo*
Graham Greene, *The Complaisant Lover*
Willis Hall, *The Long and the Short and the Tall*
Lorraine Hansberry, *A Raisin in the Sun*
Jean-Paul Sartre, *Altona*
N. F. Simpson, *One Way Pendulum*
Arnold Wesker, *The Kitchen*
Arnold Wesker, *Roots*
Tennessee Williams, *Sweet Bird of Youth*

1960
Edward Albee, *The Death of Bessie Smith*
John Arden, *The Happy Haven*
Robert Bolt, *A Man for All Seasons*
Shelagh Delaney, *The Lion in Love*
Willis Hall and Keith Waterhouse, *Billy Liar*
Eugene Ionesco, *Rhinoceros*
Arthur Kopit, *Oh Dad, Poor Dad, Mamma's Hung You in the Closet and I'm Feelin' So Sad*
Harold Pinter, *The Caretaker*

Harold Pinter, *The Dumb Waiter*
David Rudkin, *Afore Night Come*
Wole Soyinka, *The Dance of the Forests*
Arnold Wesker, *I'm Talking About Jerusalem*

1961

Edward Albee, *The American Dream*
Samuel Beckett, *Happy Days*
Max Frisch, *Andorra*
Athol Fugard, *The Blood Knot*
Jean Genet, *The Screens*
Ann Jellicoe, *The Knack*
Tom Murphy, *A Whistle in the Dark*
John Osborne, *Luther*
John Whiting, *The Devils*
Tennessee Williams, *The Night of the Iguana*

1962

Edward Albee, *Who's Afraid of Virginia Woolf?*
Edward Bond, *The Pope's Wedding*
Friedrich Dürrenmatt, *The Physicists*
Charles Dyer, *Rattle of a Simple Man*
Günter Grass, *The Wicked Cooks*
Eugene Ionesco, *Exit the King*
Henry Livings, *Nil Carborundum*
Roger Planchon, *La Remise*
Peter Shaffer, *The Private Ear*
Peter Shaffer, *The Public Eye*
Arnold Wesker, *Chips with Everything*

1963

John Arden, *The Workhouse Donkey*
Rolf Hochhüth, *The Representative*
Bill Naughton, *Alfie*
Neil Simon, *Barefoot in the Park*
Theatre Workshop, *Oh What a Lovely War*

1964

John Arden, *Armstrong's Last Goodnight*
James Baldwin, *Blues for Mr Charlie*
Brian Friel, *Philadelphia, Here I Come!*
Witold Gombrowicz, *The Marriage*
Leroi Jones (Amiri Baraka), *Dutchman*
Heinar Kipphardt, *In the Matter of J. Robert Oppenheimer*
Slawomir Mrozek, *Tango*
Joe Orton, *Entertaining Mr Sloane*
John Osborne, *Inadmissible Evidence*
Peter Shaffer, *The Royal Hunt of the Sun*
Peter Weiss, *Marat/Sade*

1965

Edward Albee, *Tiny Alice*
Alexei Arbuzov, *The Promise*
James Baldwin, *The Amen Corner*
Edward Bond, *Saved*
Athol Fugard, *Hello and Goodbye*
Günter Grass, *The Plebeians Rehearse the Uprising*
David Halliwell, *Little Malcolm and His Struggle Against the
    Eunuchs*
Václav Havel, *The Memorandum*
David Mercer, *Ride a Cock Horse*
John Osborne, *A Patriot for Me*
Harold Pinter, *The Homecoming*
Peter Shaffer, *Black Comedy*
Neil Simon, *The Odd Couple*
Wole Soyinka, *The Road*
Michel Tremblay, *The Sisters-in-Law*
Peter Weiss, *The Investigation*

1966

Edward Albee, *A Delicate Balance*
Samuel Beckett, *Come and Go*
Marguerite Duras, *La Musica*
Peter Handke, *Offending the Audience*
John B. Keane, *The Field*

Frank Marcus, *The Killing of Sister George*
John McGrath, *Events while Guarding the Bofors Gun*
David Mercer, *Belcher's Luck*
Joe Orton, *Loot*
Wole Soyinka, *Kongi's Harvest*
Tom Stoppard, *Rosencrantz and Guildenstern are Dead*
David Storey, *The Restoration of Arthur Middleton*
Jean-Claude Van Itallie, *America Hurrah!*

1967
Fernando Arrabal, *The Architect and the Emperor of Assyria*
Alan Ayckbourn, *Relatively Speaking*
Amiri Baraka (Leroi Jones) *Slaveship*
Samuel Beckett, *Eh Joe*
Rolf Hochhüth, *Soldiers*
Peter Luke, *Hadrian the Seventh*
Peter Nichols, *A Day in the Death of Joe Egg*
Joe Orton, *What the Butler Saw*
Peter Terson, *Zigger Zagger*
Charles Wood, *Dingo*

1968
Peter Barnes, *The Ruling Class*
Alan Bennett, *Forty Years On*
Ed Bullins, *The Electronic Nigger*
Tankred Dorst, *Toller*
Christopher Hampton, *Total Eclipse*
Peter Handke, *Kaspar*
Arthur Kopit, *Indians*
Arthur Miller, *The Price*
Tom Murphy, *Famine*
Neil Simon, *Plaza Suite*
Tom Stoppard, *The Real Inspector Hound*
Michel Tremblay, *The Duchess of Langeais*
Peter Weiss, *Vietnam Discourse*

1969

Amiri Baraka (Leroi Jones), *The Death of Malcolm X*

Peter Barnes, *Leonardo's Last Supper*

Lonne Elder, *Ceremonies in Dark Old Men*

Dario Fo, *Mistero Buffo*

Athol Fugard, *Boesman and Lena*

Charles Gordone, *No Place to Be Somebody*

Peter Nichols, *The National Health*

Neil Simon, *The Last of the Red Hot Lovers*

David Storey, *In Celebration*

David Storey, *The Contractor*

Kenneth Tynan, *Oh! Calcutta!*

Charles Wood, *H*

1970

Robert Bolt, *Vivat! Vivat Regina!*

Dario Fo, *Accidental Death of an Anarchist*

Trevor Griffiths, *Occupations*

John Guare, *The House of Blue Leaves*

A. R. Gurney, Jr, *Scenes from American Life*

Christopher Hampton, *The Philanthropist*

Mike Leigh, *Bleak Moments*

David Mercer, *After Haggerty*

Trevor Rhone, *Smile Orange*

Anthony Shaffer, *Sleuth*

Wole Soyinka, *Madmen and Specialists*

David Storey, *Home*

Peter Terson, *The 1861 Whitby Lifeboat Disaster*

Derek Walcott, *The Last Carnival*

Heathcote Williams, *Hancock's Last Half-Hour*

1971

Edward Bond, *Lear*

Marguerite Duras, *Suzanna Andler*

Simon Gray, *Butley*

Peter Handke, *The Ride across Lake Constance*

John Mortimer, *A Voyage Round My Father*

Heiner Müller, *Germania Death in Berlin*

Harold Pinter, *Old Times*
David Rabe, *Sticks and Bones*
Neil Simon, *The Prisoner of Second Avenue*
David Storey, *The Changing Room*
Michel Tremblay, *Forever Yours, Marie-Lou*

1972
John Arden and Margaretta d'Arcy, *The Island of the Mighty*
Alan Ayckbourn, *Absurd Person Singular*
Athol Fugard, John Kani and Winston Ntshona, *Sizwe Bansi is Dead*
Franz Xaver Kroetz, *Request Concert*
Franz Xaver Kroetz, *Staller Farm*
Sam Shepard, *The Tooth of Crime*
Tom Stoppard, *Jumpers*
Botho Strauss, *The Hypochondriacs*
C. P. Taylor, *The Black and White Minstrels*
Ted Whitehead, *Alpha Beta*
Charles Wood, *Veterans*

1973
Michael Abbensetts, *Sweet Talk*
Samuel Beckett, *Not I*
Alan Bennett, *Habeas Corpus*
Edward Bond, *The Sea*
Athol Fugard, John Kani and Winston Ntshona, *The Island*
Pam Gems, *Piaf*
Trevor Griffiths, *The Party*
Christopher Hampton, *Savages*
Hugh Leonard, *Da*
John McGrath, *The Cheviot, the Stag and the Black, Black Oil*
Peter Shaffer, *Equus*

1974
Alan Ayckbourn, *The Norman Conquests (Table Manners, Round and Round the Garden, Living Together)*
Edward Bond, *Bingo*
Howard Brenton, *The Churchill Play*

Barry Collins, *Judgement*
Dario Fo, *Can't Pay? Won't Pay!*
A. R. Gurney Jr, *Children*
Peter Hacks, *A Conversation in the House of Frau Stein*
Peter Handke, *They are Dying Out*
Rolf Hochhüth, *Judith*
Heiner Müller, *The Battle*
Ntozake Shange, *for colored girls who have considered suicide when the rainbow is enuf*
Tom Stoppard, *Travesties*

1975
Edward Albee, *Seascape*
John Arden and Margaretta d'Arcy, *The Non-Stop Connolly Show*
Alan Ayckbourn, *Absent Friends*
Steven Berkoff, *East*
Edward Bond, *The Fool*
Ed Bullins, *The Taking of Miss Janie*
Michael Frayn, *Alphabetical Order*
Athol Fugard, *Dimetos*
Pam Gems, *Dusa, Fish, Stas and Vi*
Simon Gray, *Otherwise Engaged*
Trevor Griffiths, *Comedians*
David Hare, *Fanshen*
Václav Havel, *The Vanek Plays (Audience, Private View, Protest)*
David Mamet, *American Buffalo*
Stewart Parker, *Spokesong*
Harold Pinter, *No Man's Land*
Stephen Poliakoff, *City Sugar*
Martin Sherman, *Cracks*
Wole Soyinka, *Death and the King's Horsemen*
Ted Whitehead, *Old Flames*

1976
Samuel Beckett, *Footfalls*
Thomas Bernhard, *Minetti*
Caryl Churchill, *Light Shining in Buckinghamshire*

David Edgar, *Destiny*
Michael Frayn, *Donkeys' Years*
Peter Gill, *Small Change*
David Mamet, *Sexual Perversity in Chicago*
Roger Planchon, *Gilles de Rais*
David Rabe, *Streamers*
David Rudkin, *The Sons of Light*
Botho Strauss, *Three Acts of Recognition*
Michel Tremblay, *Saint Carmen of the Main*
Derek Walcott, *O Babylon!*
Arnold Wesker, *The Merchant*
Heathcote Williams, *AC/DC*

1977
Alan Ayckbourn, *Bedroom Farce*
Howard Barker, *That Good Between Us*
Alan Bennett, *The Old Country*
Robert Bolt, *State of Revolution*
Howard Brenton, *Epsom Downs*
Maria Irene Fornes, *Fefu and Her Friends*
Tunde Ikoli, *Scrape off the Black*
Barrie Keefe, *A Mad World My Masters*
Bernard-Marie Koltés, *The Night Just Before the Forests*
Mike Leigh, *Abigail's Party*
Stephen Lowe, *Touched*
Tom McGrath and Jimmy Boyle, *The Hard Man*
Arthur Miller, *The Archbishop's Ceiling*
Heiner Müller, *Hamletmachine*
Peter Nichols, *Privates on Parade*
Mary O'Malley, *Once a Catholic*
Stephen Poliakoff, *Strawberry Fields*
Bernard Pomerance, *The Elephant Man*
Franca Rame, *The Mother*
James Saunders, *Bodies*
Martin Sherman, *Bent*
Derek Walcott, *Pantomime*
Derek Walcott, *Remembrance*

1978
Howard Barker, *The Love of a Good Man*
John Byrne, *The Slab Boys*
Brian Clark, *Whose Life is it Anyway?*
David Hare, *Plenty*
Arthur Kopit, *Wings*
Franz Xaver Kroetz, *Through the Leaves*
Hugh Leonard, *A Life*
Richard Nelson, *The Vienna Notes*
Harold Pinter, *Betrayal*
Sam Shepard, *Buried Child*
Tom Stoppard, *Night and Day*
Botho Strauss, *Great and Small*
Nigel Williams, *Class Enemy*
Lanford Wilson, *Fifth of July*
Charles Wood, *Has 'Washington' Legs?*
Nicholas Wright, *Treetops*

1979
Steven Berkoff, *Greek*
Thomas Bernhard, *Vor dem Ruhestand*
John Byrne, *Cuttin' a Rug*
Caryl Churchill, *Cloud Nine*
Sarah Daniels, *Neaptide*
David Edgar, *Mary Barnes*
Brian Friel, *Aristocrats*
Brian Friel, *Faith Healer*
Amlin Gray, *How I Got That Story*
Beth Henley, *Crimes of the Heart*
Bernard-Marie Koltés, *Battle of the Black and the Dogs*
Mike Leigh, *Ecstasy*
Caryl Phillips, *Strange Fruit*
Mustapha Matura, *Welcome Home Jacko*
Mark Medoff, *Children of a Lesser God*
Trevor Rhone, *Old Story Time*
Willy Russell, *Educating Rita*
Peter Shaffer, *Amadeus*

Sam Shepard, *Seduced*
Michel Vinaver, *A Smile on the End of the Line*
Michael Wilcox, *Rents*
David Williamson, *Travelling North*
Nicholas Wright, *The Gorky Brigade*

1980

Alan Ayckbourn, *Season's Greetings*
Howard Brenton, *The Romans in Britain*
Michael Frayn, *Make and Break*
Brian Friel, *Translations*
Athol Fugard, *A Lesson from Aloes*
Ronald Harwood, *The Dresser*
Ernst Jandl, *Aus der Fremde*
Tom Kempinski, *Duet for One*
Claire Luckham, *Trafford Tanzi*
Emily Mann, *Still Life*
Arthur Miller, *The American Clock*
Trevor Rhone, *Two Can Play*
Sam Shepard, *True West*

1981

Howard Barker, *No End of Blame*
Ingmar Bergman, *Scenes from a Marriage*
Steven Berkoff, *Decadence*
Alan Bleasdale, *Having a Ball*
Andrea Dunbar, *Rita Sue and Bob Too*
Nell Dunn, *Steaming*
Dario Fo, *Trumpets and Raspberries*
Charles Fuller, *A Soldier's Play*
Simon Gray, *Quartermaine's Terms*
Peter Handke, *The Long Way Round*
Wendy Kesselman, *My Sister in This House*
Franz Xaver Kroetz, *Neither Fish Nor Fowl*
Hanif Kureishi, *Borderline*
Julian Mitchell, *Another Country*
Peter Nichols, *Passion Play*
Manuel Puig, *Kiss of the Spider Woman*

Wallace Shawn (with André Gregory), *My Dinner with André*
C. P. Taylor, *Good*

1982
Karim Alrawi, *Migrations*
Samuel Beckett, *Rockaby*
John Byrne, *Still Life*
Caryl Churchill, *Top Girls*
Sarah Daniels, *Neaptide*
Harvey Feirstein, *Torch Song Trilogy*
Peter Flannery, *Our Friends in the North*
Michael Frayn, *Noises Off*
Athol Fugard, *'Master Harold' . . . and the Boys*
A. R. Gurney, Jr, *The Dining Room*
Christopher Hampton, *Tales from Hollywood*
Catherine Hayes, *Skirmishes*
Terry Johnson, *Insignificance*
Manfred Karge, *Man to Man*
Liz Lochhead, *Blood and Ice*
David Mamet, *Edmond*
Frank McGuinness, *The Factory Girls*
Heiner Müller, *Despoiled Shore Medeamaterial Landscape with
  Argonauts*
Louise Page, *Salonika*
Harold Pinter, *A Kind of Alaska*
Sam Shepard, *Fool for Love*
Tom Stoppard, *The Real Thing*

1983
Howard Barker, *Victory*
Steven Berkoff, *West*
Caryl Churchill, *Fen*
Sarah Daniels, *Masterpieces*
David Edgar, *Maydays*
Dario Fo and Franca Rame, *The Rape*
Noël Greig, *Poppies*
David Mamet, *Glengarry Glen Ross*
Tony Marchant, *Welcome Home*

David Pownall, *Master Class*
Neil Simon, *Brighton Beach Memoirs*
Edgar White, *The Nine Night*
Hugh Whitemore, *Pack of Lies*

1984

Thomas Bernhard, *Ritter, Dene, Voss*
Thomas Bernhard, *Der Theatermacher*
Howard Brenton, *Bloody Poetry*
Caryl Churchill, *Softcops*
Ray Cooney, *Run For Your Wife*
Marguerite Duras, *Savannah Bay*
Michael Frayn, *Benefactors*
Herb Gardner, *I'm Not Rappaport*
John Godber, *Up 'n' Under*
Simon Gray, *The Common Pursuit*
Richard Harris, *Stepping Out*
Michael Hastings, *Tom and Viv*
Václav Havel, *Largo Desolato*
Robert Holman, *Today*
Ron Hutchinson, *Rat in the Skull*
Franz Xaver Kroetz, *Fear and Hope in the German Federal Republic*
Doug Lucie, *Progress*
Sharman Macdonald, *When I Was a Girl I Used to Scream and Shout*
Louise Page, *Golden Girls*
Stephen Poliakoff, *Breaking the Silence*
David Rabe, *Hurlyburly*
Joshua Sobol, *Ghetto*
Botho Strauß, *The Park*
Michel Tremblay, *Albertine in Five Times*
Edgar White, *Redemption Song*
August Wilson, *Ma Rainey's Black Bottom*

1985

Alan Ayckbourn, *A Chorus of Disapproval*
Howard Barker, *The Castle*

Peter Barnes, *Red Noses*

Howard Brenton and David Hare, *Pravda*

Hélène Cixous, *The Terrible but Unfinished Story of Norodom Sihanouk, King of Cambodia*

John Clifford, *Losing Venice*

Ann Devlin, *Ourselves Alone*

Janusz Glowacki, *Hunting Cockroaches*

John Godber, *Bouncers*

Philip Kan Gotanda, *The Wash*

Václav Havel, *Temptation*

Lyle Kessler, *Orphans*

Thomas Kilroy, *Double Cross*

Larry Kramer, *The Normal Heart*

Frank McGuinness, Observe the Sons of Ulster Marching Towards the Somme

Daniel Mornin, *The Murderers*

Eric Overmyer, *On the Verge*

Wallace Shawn, *Aunt Dan and Lemon*

Botho Strauss, *Tourist Guide*

Timberlake Wertenbaker, *The Grace of Mary Traverse*

August Wilson, Fences

1986

Alan Bennett, *Kafka's Dick*

Jim Cartwright, *Road*

April De Angelis, *Breathless*

Nick Dear, *The Art of Success*

Robert Holman, *Making Noise Quietly*

Dusty Hughes, *Futurists*

Manfred Karge, *The Conquest of the South Pole*

David Lan, *Flight*

Terence McNally, *Frankie and Johnny in the Clair de Lune*

Anthony Minghella, *Made in Bangkok*

Richard Nelson, *Principia Scriptoriae*

Willy Russell, *Shirley Valentine*

Hugh Whitemore, *Breaking the Code*

August Wilson, *Joe Turner's Come and Gone*

George C. Wolfe, *The Colored Museum*

1987
Kay Adshead, *Thatcher's Women*
Stephen Bill, *Curtains*
Lee Blessing, *A Walk in the Woods*
Eric Bogosian, *Talk Radio*
Caryl Churchill, *Serious Money*
Lucy Gannon, *Keeping Tom Nice*
Peter Gill, *Mean Tears*
John Godber, *Teechers*
Iain Heggie, *A Wholly Healthy Glasgow*
Holly Hughes, *Dress Suits to Hire*
David Henry Hwang, *M. Butterfly*
Charlotte Keatley, *My Mother Said I Never Should*
Tom Kempinski, *Separation*
Bernard-Marie Koltés, *In the Solitude of the Cotton Fields*
Tony Marchant, *The Speculators*
Marlane Meyer, *Etta Jenks*
Winsome Pinnock, *Leave Taking*
Stephen Poliakoff, *Coming in to Land*
Christina Reid, *The Belle of the Belfast City*
Peter Shaffer, *Lettice and Lovage*
David Spencer, *Releevo*
Michel Tremblay, *The Real World?*
Alfred Uhry, *Driving Miss Daisy*
Nick Ward, *Apart from George*
August Wilson, *The Piano Lesson*
Lanford Wilson, *Burn This*

1988
Thomas Bernhard, *Heldenplatz*
Martin Crimp, *Dealing with Clair*
Claire Dowie, *Adult Child/Dead Child*
David Hare, *The Secret Rapture*
Tony Harrison, *The Trackers of Oxyrhynchus*
Len Jenkin, *American Notes*
Howard Korder, *Boy's Life*

David Mamet, *Speed-the-Plow*
Clare McIntyre, *Low Level Panic*
Percy Mtwa, Mbongeni Ngema and Barney Simon, *Woza Albert*
Billy Roche, *A Handful of Stars*
Botho Strauss, *Seven Doors*
Nick Ward, *The Strangeness of Others*
Wendy Wasserstein, *The Heidi Chronicles*
Timberlake Wertenbaker, *The Love of a Nightingale*
Timberlake Wertenbaker, *Our Country's Good*
Nicholas Wright, *Mrs Klein*

1989
Harwant Bains, *Blood*
Dermot Bolger, *The Lament for Arthur Cleary*
Jim Cartwright, *Bed*
Trish Cooke, *Back Street Mammy*
Peter Flannery, *Singer*
Aleksandr Gelman, *A Man with Connections*
Bernard-Marie Koltés, *Roberto Zucco*
Tony Kushner, *Angels in America, Part One (Perestroika)*
Ronald Harwood, *Another Time*
Stephen Jeffreys, *Valued Friends*
Gregory Motton, *Looking at You (Revived) Again*
Richard Nelson, *Some Americans Abroad*
Winsome Pinnock, *A Hero's Welcome*
Billy Roche, *Poor Beast in the Rain*
Michael Wall, *Amongst Barbarians*
Keith Waterhouse, *Jeffrey Bernard is Unwell*

1990
Sebastian Barry, *Prayers of Sherkin*
Caryl Churchill, *Mad Forest*
Brian Friel, *Dancing at Lughnasa*
Sarah Daniels, *Beside Herself*
Herb Gardner, *Conversations with My Father*
Simon Gray, *Hidden Laughter*
Trevor Griffiths, *Piano*

John Guare, *Six Degrees of Separation*
David Hare, *Racing Demon*
Manfred Karge, *Wallplays*
Howard Korder, *Search and Destroy*
David Lan, *Desire*
Bryony Lavery, *Kitchen Matters*
Anthony Neilson, *Normal*
Gillian Plowman, *Me and My Friend*
Michel Vinaver, *The Television Programme*
August Wilson, *Two Trains Running*

1991
Edward Albee, *Three Tall Women*
Martin Crimp, *Getting Attention*
Fred D'Aguiar, *A Jamaican Airman Foresees his Death*
Ariel Dorfman, *Death and the Maiden*
David Hare, *Murmuring Judges*
Tony Kushner, *Angels in America, Part Two (Millennium Approaches)*
Sharman Macdonald, *All Things Nice*
Philip Ridley, *The Pitchfork Disney*
Billy Roche, *Belfry*
Sam Shepard, *States of Shock*
Timberlake Wertenbaker, *Three Birds Alighting on a Field*

1992
Jim Cartwright, *The Rise and Fall of Little Voice*
Tony Harrison, *Square Rounds*
Ron Hutchinson, *Pygmies in the Ruins*
Elfriede Jelinek, *What Happened after Nora Left her Husband*
Doug Lucie, *Grace*
Deb Margolin, *Lesbians Who Kill*
Frank McGuinness, *Someone Who'll Watch Over Me*
Phyllis Nagy, *Weldon Rising*
Neil Simon, *Lost in Yonkers*
Anna Deveare Smith, *Fires in the Mirror*
Arthur Smith, *An Evening with Gary Lineker*
Derek Walcott, *The Odyssey*

1993

Alan Bennett, *The Madness of George III*
Richard Cameron, *Not Fade Away*
Martin Crimp, *The Treatment*
April De Angelis, *Playhouse Creatures*
Simon Donald, *The Life of Stuff*
Helen Edmundson, *The Clearing*
Brad Fraser, *Unidentified Human Remains and the True Nature of Love*
David Hare, *Absence of War*
Jonathan Harvey, *Beautiful Thing*
Kevin Hood, *Hammett's Apprentice*
Stephen Jeffreys, *The Libertine*
Terry Johnson, *Hysteria*
John B. Keane, *Big Maggie*
Tony Kushner, *Slavs!*
David Mamet, *Oleanna*
Arthur Miller, *The Last Yankee*
Anthony Neilson, *Penetrator*
Han Ong, *The L.A. Plays*
Philip Osment, *The Dearly Beloved*
Harold Pinter, *Moonlight*
Diane Samuels, *Kindertransport*
Tom Stoppard, *Arcadia*
Biyi Bandele Thomas, *Marching for Fausa*
Naomi Wallace, *The War Boys*
Peter Whelan, *The School of Night*

1994

Howard Barker, *Hated Nightfall*
Anne Devlin, *After Easter*
Kevin Elyot, *My Night with Reg*
Tim Firth, *Neville's Island*
Brian Friel, *Molly Sweeney*
Nick Grosso, *Peaches*
Terry Johnson, *Dead Funny*
David Mamet, *The Cryptogram*

Kay Mellor, *A Passionate Woman*
Arthur Miller, *Broken Glass*
Phyllis Nagy, *Butterfly Kiss*
Joe Penhall, *Some Voices*
David Pownall, *Elgar's Rondo*
Rebecca Prichard, *Essex Girls*
Philip Ridley, *Ghost from a Perfect Place*
Judy Upton, *Ashes and Sand*
Naomi Wallace, *In the Heart of America*
Wendy Wasserstein, *The Sisters Rosenweig*
Michael Wynne, *The Knocky*

1995

Sebastian Barry, *The Steward of Christendom*
Simon Block, *Not a Game for Boys*
Jez Butterworth, *Mojo*
David Edgar, *Pentecost*
David Eldrdge, *Serving It Up*
Sue Glover, *Bondagers*
David Hare, *Skylight*
David Harrower, *Knives in Hens*
Jonathan Harvey, *Rupert Street Lonely Hearts Club*
Ronald Harwood, *Taking Sides*
Sarah Kane, *Blasted*
Tracy Letts, *Killer Joe*
Sharman Macdonald, *The Winter Guest*
Patrick Marber, *Dealer's Choice*
Louis Mellis and David Scinto, *Gangster Number One*
Phyllis Nagy, *The Strip*
Joseph O'Connor, *Red Roses and Petrol*
Joe Penhall, *Pale Horse*
Sam Shepard, *Simpatico*
Tom Stoppard, *Indian Ink*
Judy Upton, *Bruises*
Nick Ward, *The Present*
Timberlake Wertenbaker, *The Break of Day*

1996
Marina Carr, *Portia Coghlan*
Jim Cartwright, *I Licked a Slag's Deodorant*
Nick Darke, *The King of Prussia*
Pam Gems, *Stanley*
Nick Grosso, *Sweetheart*
Sarah Kane, *Phaedra's Love*
Howard Korder, *The Lights*
Ayub Khan-Din, *East is East*
Mick Mahoney, *Swaggers*
Martin McDonagh, *The Beauty Queen of Leenane*
Clare McIntyre, *The Thickness of Skin*
Winsome Pinnock, *Mules*
Stephen Poliakoff, *Blinded by the Sun*
Mark Ravenhill, *Shopping and Fucking*
Yasmina Reza, *Art*
Shelagh Stephenson, *The Memory of Water*
Peter Whelan, *The Herbal Bed*

1997
Martin Crimp, *Attempts on her Life*
April De Angelis, *The Positive Hour*
Ben Elton, *Popcorn*
David Hare, *Amy's View*
Marie Jones, *Woman on the Verge of HRT*
Doug Lucie, *The Shallow End*
Patrick Marber, *Closer*
Martin McDonagh, *The Lonesome West*
Martin McDonagh, *A Skull in Connemara*
Frank McGuinness, *Mutabilitie*
Conor McPherson, *The Weir*
Anthony Neilson, *The Censor*
Tom Stoppard, *The Invention of Love*

1998
Sebastian Barry, *Our Lady of Sligo*
Kevin Elyot, *The Day I Stood Still*
Michael Frayn, *Copenhagen*

Nick Grosso, *Real Classy Affair*
Jonathan Harvey, *Guiding Star*
Sarah Kane, *Cleansed*
Sarah Kane, *Crave*
Liz Lochhead, *Perfect Days*
Mick Mahoney, *Sacred Heart*
David Mamet, *The Old Neighbourhood*
Gary Mitchell, *Trust*
Phyllis Nagy, *Never Land*
Stephen Poliakoff, *Talk of the City*
Rebecca Prichard, *Yard Gal*
Yasmina Reza, *The Unexpected Man*
Shelagh Stephenson, *An Experiment with an Air Pump*
Judith Thompson, *I Am Yours*
Paula Vogel, *How I Learned to Drive*
Che Walker, *Been So Long*

1999

Rebecca Gilman, *The Glory of Living*
Richard Greenberg, *Three Days of Rain*
David Greig, *Mainstream*
Lee Hall, *Cooking with Elvis*
Jonathan Harvey, *Hushabye Mountain*
Ronald Harwood, *Quartet*
Marie Jones, *Stones in His Pockets*
Sarah Kane, *4:48 Psychosis*
Ayub Khan-Din, *Last Dance at Dum Dum*
Hanif Kureishi, *Sleep With Me*
Frank McGuinness, *Dolly West's Kitchen*
Mark Ravenhill, *Some Explicit Polaroids*
Philip Ridley, *Sparkleshark*
Nick Stafford, *Battle Royal*
Nicholas Wright, *Cressida*
Richard Zajdlic, *Dogs Barking*